SELECTED POEMS OF

Solomon Ibn Gabirol

The Lockert Library of Poetry in Translation

Editorial Advisor: Richard Howard

◆

FOR OTHER TITLES

IN THE LOCKERT LIBRARY,

SEE PAGE 327

SELECTED POEMS OF
Solomon Ibn Gabirol

Translated from the Hebrew by

PETER COLE

PRINCETON UNIVERSITY PRESS

PRINCETON AND OXFORD

Copyright © 2001 by Princeton University Press
Published by Princeton University Press, 41 William Street,
Princeton, New Jersey 08540
In the United Kingdom: Princeton University Press, 3 Market Place,
Woodstock, Oxfordshire OX20 1SY
All Rights Reserved

Grateful acknowledgment is due to the National Endowment for
the Humanities for its support of this project. Some of these poems were first
published in *Parnassus* and the *Treasury of World Poetry* (Norton, 1998)

Grateful acknowledgment is made for permission to reprint the diagram
on page 34, Copyright © Raphael Loewe, from *Ibn Gabirol*,
by Raphael Loewe (Peter Halban, 1989). The original appears
in the Oxford Arabic manuscript, Huntington 382.

Library of Congress Cataloging-in-Publication Data

Ibn Gabirol, 11th cent.
[Poems. English. Selections]
Selected poems of Solomon Ibn Gabirol / translated from the Hebrew by Peter Cole.
p. cm. — (The Lockert library of poetry in translation)
Includes bibliographical references.
ISBN 0-691-07031-8 (alk. paper) — ISBN 0-691-07032-6 (pbk. : alk. paper)
1. Ibn Gabirol, 11th cent.—Translations into English.
I. Cole, Peter, 1957–   II. Title.   III. Series
PJ5050.I3 A23 2000
892.4'12—dc21   00-044124

This book has been composed in Dante

The paper used in this publication meets the minimum requirements of
ANSI/NISO Z39.48-1992 (R 1997) (*Permanence of Paper*)

www.pup.princeton.edu

Printed in the United States of America

1 3 5 7 9 10 8 6 4 2

3 5 7 9 10 8 6 4
(pbk.)

The Lockert Library of Poetry in Translation is supported by
a bequest from Charles Lacy Lockert (1888–1974)
ISBN-13: 978-0-691-07032-2

ISBN-10: 0-691-07032-6

For Gabriel Levin

✦

CONTENTS

✦

Solomon Ibn Gabirol: An Andalusian Alphabet   3

FROM THE DIWAN OF SOLOMON IBN GABIROL

CONTENTS

Poems of Devotion

CONTENTS

SELECTED POEMS OF
Solomon Ibn Gabirol

SOLOMON IBN GABIROL:
AN ANDALUSIAN ALPHABET

◆

His METAPHYSICS emerge from desire: his ethics evolve to a science of sense. What begins there in wisdom ends in anger: what was anger gives way to a grace. He a poet of poles and swells and reversals, of splits that propose a completion. He is the most modern of the Hebrew medievals, the most foreign to a modernist approach. In his verse what looks like a mirror is meant in fact to be passed through: transparency marks a divide. Hebrew is Arabic, Muslim Jewish, his resistance a form of embrace.

Abu Ayyub Sulaiman Ibn Yahya Ibn Jabirul

The reconstructed facts are few. He is born Shelomoh Ben Yehudah Ibn Gabirol, in either 1021 or 1022, in Malaga, to an undistinguished family that may have fled the collapsing capital of the Umayyad Caliphate, Córdoba, with the same wave of refugees that included Shmuel Ha-Nagid, who would go on to become the period's first great Hebrew poet. At some point his father moves the family north to Saragossa, and Ibn Gabirol—or, in Arab circles, Abu Ayyub Sulaiman Ibn Yahya Ibn Jabirul—is raised in that important center of Islamic and Jewish learning. Ibn Gabirol's father dies while the precocious son is still in his early teens, and the young man is looked after by a Jewish notable at the Saragossan court, Yequtiel Ibn Hasan al-Mutawakkil Ibn Qabrun. He is writing accomplished poems by age sixteen, important ones by nineteen, though he is ill, already afflicted with the disease that will leave him embittered and in constant pain, suffering from boils that scholars reason were caused by tuberculosis of the skin (the actual condition has never been precisely identified). We can also infer from his poems that he was short and ugly. In 1039 Yequtiel gets mixed up in court intrigue and is killed, and Ibn Gabirol loses his patron. He leaves Saragossa sometime after 1045, when his mother dies, and most scholars assume that he goes south, to Granada, in order to try his luck at the court of HaNagid, who is, at that point, governor (nagid) of the region's Jews, prime minister of that Muslim ta'ifa (party state) under its Berber king, and commander-in-chief

---

of the Granadan army. Things appear to work out for a time, but wires get crossed, or the young, upstart poet insults his elder poet-patron, and even this meager trail vanishes, with Ibn Gabirol still in his mid-twenties. He is known, says Moshe Ibn Ezra, author of the age's most important work of Hebrew literary criticism, *The Book of Discussion and Remembrance*, for his philosophical temperament, and for his "angry spirit which held sway over reason, and his demon within which he could not control."

He writes secular verse, often gnarled with ambition and anger, and it is probable that later in life he is supported by his writing for the synagogue, composing radical and, in comparison with his court-centered verse, remarkably self-deprecating *piyyutim*, or liturgical poems, for the weekday, Sabbath, and festival services. Apart from his diwan and his philosophical masterwork, *The Fountain of Life*, he produces a short but striking ethical treatise, *On the Improvement of the Moral Qualities*, and claims in one of his poems to have written some twenty books—now lost—on philosophical, linguistic, scientific, and religious topics. (*A Choice of Pearls*, a volume of proverbs, is often attributed to him, but it is a bland gathering, hardly in keeping with the rest of his extraordinary oeuvre; and while other medieval authorities quote his biblical commentary, no mention of a collection survives.)

"Arrogant, orphaned, itinerant," in Allen Mandelbaum's characterization, he dies, says Ibn Ezra, in Valencia, not yet forty. His religious poems now form part of the regular prayer service in Jewish communities throughout the world, and downtown Tel Aviv traffic jams take place on a street that bears his name.

BEZALEL

"Shelter me in your shadow," he writes, "be with my mouth and its word."

The vocabulary of Jewish *poesis*, or making, goes back to a crisis of refuge and interior design. It has always been cultic, just as its ethos has most often been abstract, at a certain remove from the figure. Where the much more talked-about and vatic abstraction derives from the ambiguous second commandment, itself an extension of the first, "I am the Lord thy God: Do not make idols or likenesses," the more modest if not maligned ornamental idiom comes from the scriptural role played by Bezalel Ben Uri, of the tribe of Judah, whose God-given task was to build and outfit the desert Sanctuary, "to adorn Him." He was to construct the Ark and the Tabernacle, to fashion the curtains and cast the candlesticks that the midrash tells us baffled the more pedantic Moses. Bezalel saw to the loops and the veils and the sockets—the altar, the court, and the laver. Even the priestly vestments. His name means "in the shadow of God, the son of my light (or 'fire')," and Exodus 31:2 says that he was "filled . . . with the spirit of God, in wisdom, in understanding, and in knowledge, in all manner of workmanship . . . of the craftsman, and of the skilful workman, and of the weaver in colors."

Like the Bezalel of Scripture and midrash, and like King Solomon his successor and the poet's namesake, who built the Temple and composed the most beautiful and wisest of biblical books, Ibn Gabirol would charge his ornament with complex value, bringing sublime vision to a space that artifice defined. Lacing his poems with allusions to the work of these forbears, he would devote his skill to the pursuit of wisdom and the evocation of magnitude.

CORRIDORS: CLUES

Scriptural figures apart, key precursors and contemporaries include:

the blind and reclusive Syrian ascetic poet Abu 'l-'Ala al-Ma'arri (974–1058), known for the dense patterning of his caustic poems, like Ibn Gabirol's, at once "boundless and self-contained." After beginning as a conventional poet working in the court modes, "milking the udders of time," in his *Luzumu ma la Yalzam* (The Necessity of What Isn't Necessary) Abu 'l-'Ala sets out against the grain of the poetry of his day and its neo-Aristotelian motto—the most pleasing poetry is the most feigning—and seeks "to speak the truth": "You stand there as the driven / wheels of heaven spin / and choose, / while the fates are laughing";

Abu al-Hakim al-Karmaani, a prominent scholar (born in Córdoba, d. 1066) who, after his travels in the East, introduced to Saragossa the doctrine of the tenth-century *Ikhwaan As-Safa'*, The Brethren of Purity. Their ecumenical, encyclopedic *Epistles* were read throughout the Muslim world and played an important role in the rise of Sufism. In the world of the *Epistles*, the pattern of the whole is always represented in the pattern of the parts: man is a microcosm, and correspondences exist between astronomical, ethical, and social planes. The sciences there are treated not as ends in themselves, so much as vehicles by which mankind gains awareness of the harmonies and beauty of the universe. When a new edition of the *Epistles* appears in the first half of the eleventh century, it makes its way to Andalusia where, within months, it is circulating among the Islamic scholars, and also reaches Ibn Gabirol;

Abu Muhammad 'Ali Ibn Hazm (994–1064), the harem-raised Córdoban theologian-poet, perhaps the most vigorous and representative Muslim thinker of the period. Ibn Hazm is best known for his *Ring of the Dove*, a psychologically astute treatise detailing the signs and stages of love, but he is also the author of a vast work on comparative religion and at least one qasida that recalls Ibn Gabirol's greatest poem, *Kingdom's Crown*. Also reminiscent of Ibn Gabirol is Ibn Hazm's moral essay, *A Philosophy of Character and Conduct*: "I am a man who has always been uneasy about the impermanency and constant instability of fortune. . . . In my investigations I have constantly tried to discover an end in human actions which all men unanimously hold as good and which they all seek. I have found only this: the one aim of escaping anxiety. . . . [A]s I investigated, I observed that all things tended to elude me, and I reached the conclusion that the only permanent reality possible consists in good works useful for another, immortal life" (trans. Kritzeck);

the unnamed poets mentioned by Moshe Ibn Ezra in *The Book of Discussion and Remembrance*: Ibn Gabirol's "way in the art of poetry was subtle," says Ibn Ezra, "like that of the later Muslim poets," referring perhaps to the major "modern" Arabic writers—poets of the "new," ornamental (*badii'a*) style, such as the ninth-century innovator Muslim Ibn Walid and the master mannerist Abu Tamaam, and perhaps to the metaphysical Saragossa circle as well.

ON the Hebrew side of the ledger, one counts among Ibn Gabirol's predecessors and peers the aforementioned Shmuel Ben Yosef Halevi HaNagid, the major Jewish cultural and political figure of his day. Ibn Gabirol contacts HaNagid when the former is sixteen years old and the latter at the height of his several powers. The young poet writes him at length, in verse, initially from Saragossa, singing the vizier's praises, and setting the stage for their somewhat mysterious confrontation and falling out several years later in Granada;

hovering in the background is the ongoing influence of several key figures: Sa'adiah Gaon, the great Eastern rabbi, leader of Babylonian Jewry in the first half of the tenth century, translator of the Bible into Arabic, redactor of the first standard prayer book, liturgical poet, compiler of the first rhyming dictionary in Hebrew and the first Hebrew–

Arabic lexicon, and author of *The Book of Beliefs and Opinions*, which includes modern-sounding, "scientific" chapters on money, children, eroticism, eating and drinking, and the satisfaction of the thirst for revenge. It was Sa'adiah's student Dunash Ben Labrat who introduced Arabic poetry's secular genres and quantitative meters into Hebrew in the middle of the tenth century and set off a debate that split the Jewish intellectual community: Dunash was accused of desecrating the holy tongue with his importation of an alien poetic, and his work was attacked. Things turned nasty, and Dunash's primary rival, an older and more experienced court-poet named Menahem Ibn Saruq, fell out of favor with the principal Jewish patron of the day, Hasdai Ibn Shaprut, and was thrown into prison. The new spirit of rationalism and innovation took hold in Hasdai's court, which, in turn, was modeled on the Córdoban court of the Caliph 'Abd ar-Rahman III, where Hasdai served as a senior physician, customs director, and personal envoy for the caliph.

In the small body of his work that has come down to us, however, where he seems to have handled the new forms awkwardly, Dunash was more innovator than master, and it turns out that credit for the qualitative lyric breakthrough rightfully belongs to his wife, whose name we do not know. In a marvelous 1984 discovery, scholar Ezra Fleischer identified a single extant work of hers in the papers of the Cairo Genizah; this short poem to her husband (who also appears to have quarreled with Hasdai) is, says Fleischer, the first realized personal poem in the post-biblical Hebrew canon:

> Will her love remember his graceful doe,
>> her only son in her arms as he parted?
> On her left hand he placed a ring from his right,
>> on his wrist she placed her bracelet.
>
> As a keepsake she took his mantle from him,
>> and he in turn took hers from her.
> He won't settle in the land of Spain,
>> though its prince give him half his kingdom.

Other echoing voices include the popular tenth-century liturgical poet and teacher Yitzhak Ibn Mar Sha'ul, of Lucena, who took up Dunash's prosodic innovations and reportedly was the first Hebrew poet to write of the "gazelle," the young, male love interest in so many of the erotic poems of the period; his central claim to fame lay in his penitential poetry, particularly his petition, "Lord, Do Not Judge Me for What I Have Done," which entered the liturgy in many communities and finds direct echoes in *Kingdom's Crown*;

the powerful, prolific, and somewhat reactionary liturgical poet Yosef Ibn Abitur (c. 950–after 1024), legendary for having "interpreted" the Talmud for the Andalusian Caliph al-Hakim II (whose Córdoban library of some 400,000 volumes was the largest collection of books in Europe at the time). His poems for the synagogue often dealt vividly with religious-nationalist themes, especially that of exile, and he was also famous for his mystical poems of angelology, which were to have a marked influence on Ibn Gabirol. Ibn Abitur's lone innovation was major: he was the first poet to develop the lyrical preludes, or *reshuyot*, to hitherto neglected parts of the Sabbath and festival morning liturgy. The genre would go on to figure prominently in the work of the great poets of the period, with Ibn Gabirol counted as the first master of this quintessentially Andalusian form;

Ibn Abitur's contemporary, the first exclusively "professional" and secular Hebrew poet of the period, Yitzhak Ibn Khalfon, who was born in North Africa and raised in Córdoba in the latter third of the tenth century. Ibn Khalfon eventually set out as an itinerant poet, writing eulogies and other poems for Jewish patrons in Spain, North Africa, and even far-off Damascus. The outstanding member of the second generation of the new Hebrew poetry, he greatly widened the tonal and prosodic range of that verse, above all adding a personal, graceful and often comic dimension to its rhetoric;

and, finally, Ibn Gabirol was surrounded and no doubt influenced by a contemporary Saragossan Who's Who of Jewish intellectuals that included the poet-linguist Yosef Ibn Hasdai, author of a single extant poem, known as the "Orphaned [unique] Qasida," an erotically charged, petitionary encomium dedicated to his lifelong friend, Shmuel HaNagid, and looked upon as a model of its kind by many of the Andalusian Hebrew poets; the sharp-tongued, learned, and promising satirical poet, Moshe Ibn al-Taqaana, killed in his twenties when a wall fell on him along the Toledo Road; and one of the leading linguists of the age, Yonah Ibn Janaah, author of the important *Book of Roots* and, along with Ibn al-Taqaana, an outspoken detractor of HaNagid.

"NEXT to Ibn Gabirol," however, proclaimed the thirteenth-century author Yehudah al-Harizi, with characteristic hyperbole and, it would seem, without full knowledge of HaNagid's output, the previous poets were "only wind and emptiness."

DEATHS, DIWANS, DETECTIVES

The better part of his social life seems to have been spent making enemies, and the payback wasn't long in coming. Ibn Ezra tells us that after Ibn Gabirol's death—scholars have established the correct date as 1054, 1058, or 1070, with the middle figure being most probable—after his death, or deaths, his reputation came under assault and his work was criticized "by pedants" for assorted flaws, much as happened with the work of HaNagid after he died in 1056. "The poet sings," wrote Jacob Glatstein in a Yiddish poem some nine hundred years later, "the Jewish coffin-birds snap."

The medieval snip, it would seem, was equal to its snap, for the secular poems of both Andalusian poets came to similar fates: seldom copied and, on the whole, forgotten for reasons personal and political (fundamentalist Muslim invasion from the south, Christian reconquest in the north, with subsequent expulsion of the Jews), they were relegated to that underground nexus through which strong marginal poetry is often passed on. In HaNagid's case only fragments circulated, and a sixteenth-century copy of his collected poems, or diwan, surfaced in a crate in early twentieth-century Syria, though it wasn't published in an edition the general reader might absorb for another thirty years. The case of Ibn Gabirol is more complex, and in some ways even more fabulous. While many of his liturgical poems were taken up by communities throughout the Jewish world and preserved in prayer books, the nonliturgical poems were harder to come by and clearly not in great demand. Nor, prior to the discovery of the Cairo Genizah and its scrap heap of Scripture, scrolls, shopping lists, recipes, letters, and assorted literary gems, was there any mention of a complete diwan of Ibn Gabirol's poems. When German scholars in the mid-nineteenth century sought to assemble a selection of the poet's work, the material had to be pieced together from manuscripts held in libraries in Oxford, Parma, Vienna, St. Petersburg, and elsewhere. The texts were sometimes in poor condition, and the overall picture was hard to construct.

Enter an Iraqi Jewish writer by the name of David Tzemah, who tells his story in a 1931 letter to David Yellin, a Jerusalem scholar who was preparing an edition of another of the Hebrew Spanish poets. Tzemah, it appears, was aware of a family legend about an important manuscript of medieval poetry that had once been belonged to a certain eminent forebear but had been lost during that relative's lifetime, toward the middle of the nineteenth century. His curiosity piqued, Tzemah-the-younger set out in search of the lost manuscript. He wrote to all his Iraqi relatives, traveled to remote villages, but came up empty-handed. Ten years passed, he says, with neither rest nor repose. Finally he decided to become an antiquarian bookseller, on the outside chance that in this way he might some day come across his treasure! He announced himself in synagogues and to other booksellers, stating his readiness to buy old manuscripts any time and any place, but nothing turned up, and Tzemah came to despair of ever finding the legendary manuscript. Either it had been destroyed, lay tattered in a genizah, or else, he reasoned, it was not in Iraq.

One day, he continues, he was walking on his way, headed for the celebration of a *brit milah*, a circumcision, where he himself was to do the honors—a group of children were singing behind him, as was done in that part of the world, he notes for Yellin—when a woman began calling out to him. She had heard that the good scholar bought old books, and she had some; perhaps the honorable gentleman would like to see them. Tzemah explained that he couldn't come now, as he was expected at the *brit*, but his servant would go with her and see where she lived, and then bring him by later on. And so, after the ceremony and the meal that followed, his servant brought him to the woman's house. Tzemah climbed up to the attic where the "old books" were stacked, but found only dusty Pentateuchs, Psalters, and prayer books. Nothing of interest to an antiquarian. "I came down from the attic," he wrote, in his precise, if somewhat odd and old-fashioned Hebrew, "I and my servant, to return to my house, when I saw the kitchen open before me. A big pot of water was set out for the laundry and beside it was a basket of papers, all of them what looked to be old scraps, to feed the fire and heat the pot. I asked her: What is *that?* And she said: Tomorrow is our day for the laundry and we'll get up early to prepare the fire. I said to her: When will you people be done with this awful practice? Perhaps there are sacred writings among them. She said: We have already checked them. They don't contain any print. Anyway, what can I do? I want to rent the attic and I need the space. The books are for sale; the papers—for the fire."

"I approached the basket to see what it held, and there among the papers was the manuscript I'd been searching for all these years! How can

I describe for you, good sir, that instant upon which I beheld both life and death at once, that moment which resembled the revelation at Mount Sinai! And here I was, the final redeemer among the sons of the sons of that righteous man! I could have taken the manuscript for nothing, but in my delight I gave her a proper reward."

In his hands Tzemah now held a seventeenth-century manuscript containing more than four thousand poems, nearly complete diwans of Ibn Gabirol, Moshe Ibn Ezra, Yehuda Halevi, Todros Abulafia, and selections from other minor but important poets from Spain, Provence, and the Near East—which is to say, a sizable share of medieval Hebrew poetry's greatest works, all of it literally snatched from the fire. Its lineage was spelled out within it as well: it had been copied in Egypt, then brought to Iraq, Bombay, and then back to Iraq. Tzemah's letter goes on in similar fashion, telling of his attempts to find a buyer for the manuscript who would issue the books in accessible editions, and of the eventual sale to a Viennese antiquarian whose partner came to Baghdad to see him. The partner lit his cigarette, Tzemah explained that he preferred the narghila ("Had not the gentlemen read his 'Song of the Narghila'?"), they hit it off, and the promise of publication was confirmed, though nothing had yet come of the pledge, Tzemah observes, as he closes: "But I must cut this letter short, for the postman is about to depart. . . . Here is the address of Benjamin the buyer and his partner in Vienna. And David sends blessings to David, [signed] David Ben Salmaan Tzemah."

EMBRACING EVASION: THE EXOTIC

Perhaps the primary obstacle facing the contemporary reader of medieval Hebrew poetry is the overstuffed critical baggage of its ornament, which the textbooks would have us drag about on our way from line to line and poem to poem. Again and again the poetry is described as decorative or ornamental, without our ever stopping to ask what that means. The tacit assumption of modern art-talk is that ornament is unnecessary or quaint (domesticating). Baroque theories of the fold notwithstanding, we think of it often as fluff, or a lie. "Arabesque," for Ezra Pound, was the ultimate put down, the representative figure of evasion and flight from the real. "The world is still deceived with ornament," we hear in the *Merchant of Venice*, at the heart of another age of embellishment. "Thus ornament is but the gilded shore to a most dangerous sea . . . the seeming truth which cunning times put on to entrap the wisest." Also prominent in the anti-ornament camp is Adolf Loos's equation of "Ornament and Crime," as the title of his 1908 essay on the subject has it, and his saying elsewhere that "the less civilized a people is, the more prodigal it will be with ornament and decoration. . . . The Red Indian within us," he urges, "must be overcome."

There are, however, less mechanical or reductive ways to think about ornament. The apocryphal book of Ben Sira says: "To a sensible man education is like a golden ornament, and like a bracelet worn on the right arm," a reasonably familiar sentiment. But then it says: "A mind settled on an intelligent thought is like the stucco decoration on the wall of a colonnade" (22:17), already a much more interesting notion.

For the phenomenon *is* cosmetic, though in saying so we unwittingly arrive at the root and truth of the matter, the complex of definitions that accrue around the Greek word for the verbal form of the term, *kosmein*, that is, to order, and, secondarily, to ornament. It is from this cluster of meanings that we get our "ordered world," "a cosmos," as in the pseudepigraphic *Prayer of Manasseh*: "He who made the heaven and the earth with all their embellishment [*kosmo*]. . . ." Which returns us to Bezalel and the sanctuary designed to "adorn Him."

Several modern writers who look at ornament in the visual arts and without condescension bring us closer still to the heart of the matter. The art historian A. K. Coomaraswamy traces the development of the word in Sanskrit, Greek, and English, from cult to court and on to the swamp of pretension and the dismissal of "arts and crafts." At the outset, he notes, ornament was "that which makes a thing itself"; and *ornamentum* in Ecclesiastical law didn't convey superfluous decoration, but the *equipment* of the sacred service. Discussing the various words used in traditional art-theory to express the phenomenon he says: "Most of these words, which imply for us the notion of something adventitious and luxurious, . . . originally implied a completion or fulfillment of the artifact or other object in question [. . . with a view to proper operation] . . . until . . . the art by which the thing itself had been made whole began to mean only a sort of millinery or upholstery that covered over a body that had not been made by 'art' but rather by 'labor'."

And Oleg Grabar states in *The Mediation of Ornament*: "Ornament is, to coin a word . . . calliphoric: it carries beauty with it." Echoing Coomaraswamy he observes that the words used to express the act involved in ornamentation imply "the successful completion of an act, of an object, or even of a state of mind or soul." He notes the daemonic, intermediary nature of ornament, and its extraordinary capacity as part of the work of art to shape our lives and thought, to question meaning with the pleasure it channels, or to use that pleasure to cultivate meaning and intensify relation to value.

All of this might be summed up in the artist-craftsman Eric Gill's saying that "a pendant on the neck is useful and possibly more so than a trouser button."

The issue's relevance comes into focus when we look at one of the most conspicuous ornaments in medieval Hebrew literature, the kind of biblical allusion that has come to be known as *shibbutz*, which means "setting" or "inlay," whereby elements of the biblical text are woven through the "fabric" of the verse. In that nineteenth-century term, a parallel to the German for "mosaic style," we have a classic case of distortion in East–West transmission, a failure of sympathy. For the term itself, *shibbutz*, implies an effect that is static while the use of biblical phrasing was brought over, in part, from Arabic literature, where it was based on the Quran and was known as *iqtibas*, "the lighting of one flame from another." It implied a source and transfer of energy. Far from constituting a rote application to an otherwise useful but plain poetic surface, biblical quotation and the other ornaments of this poetry act like tiny turbines to the current of the verse, thousands of finely constructed stations-of-power set out along its flow.

Apart from quotation, what do we mean here by ornament? Nearly everything that contributes to the unparaphrasable weave of the writing—alliteration, assonance, irony, metaphor, rhetorical and rhythmic effects, manipulations of tone—the ceremonial equipment of the verse that makes it a poem and not a theme: "The little weddings between the words," as Israeli novelist Dan Tsalka has put it. All that's exotic to reduction's impulse.

THE FOUNTAIN

Diwans weren't the only thing that vanished in the course of the Ibn Gabirol saga, and Tzemah not the only detective involved. At one point the poet's name turned up missing as well. . . .

In 1846 the French scholar Solomon Munk discovered among the Hebrew manuscripts at the Bibliothèque Nationale in Paris excerpts of a philosophical work by Ibn Gabirol that had been translated by the thirteenth-century Jewish writer Shem Tob Falaqera. The work bore a suspicious resemblance to sections of *Fons Vitae* (The Fountain of Life), a Latin text by the philosopher known variously as Avicebrol, Avincebrol, Avicebron, and Albenzubron—believed to have been a Muslim or a Christian—which Munk knew from quotations in Albertus Magnus's *De causis et processu universitatis*. (As it turned out, he would soon find the entire Latin manuscript of Avicebron's work in the same library.) Studying and comparing the two manuscripts, Munk was able to determine that the Falaqera was made up of excerpts from a (still) lost Arabic original, of which Avicebron's Latin was a complete translation. Munk then put the remaining pieces of the puzzle together, and on 12 November of the same year he announced that the great Christian/Muslim philosopher Avicebron was none other than the Jewish poet Solomon Ibn Gabirol, his name having undergone the Latinizing mutation that turned Ibn Sinna into Avicenna and Ibn Rushd into Averroes.

Written in the universalist spirit of the times, and, scholars speculate, very late in the poet's life, Ibn Gabirol's work had, a century after his death, been rendered into Latin by a team of two working in Archbishop Raymond's Toledo translation center. Sitting at a table in a room with other translators, as was the common practice, the Jewish convert Ibn Daud, whose Christian name was Johannes Hispanus, read from the Arabic and translated orally into Spanish, and then Dominicus Gundissalinus, the Archdeacon of Segovia, translated from Hispanus's spoken Spanish into a written Latin. The volume that came of that project was to play a key role in European intellectual history, and one important French scholar has gone so far as to say that a knowledge of thirteenth-century European philosophy is impossible without an understanding of *Fons Vitae* and its influence. Guillaume d'Auvergne, the mid-thirteenth-century Bishop of Paris, declared that the author of *Fons Vitae* was the "most exalted of all the philosophers." Something in the work obviously held a strong appeal for these Christian thinkers, much as it appealed later on to the work's leading champion, the Franciscan scholastic Duns Scotus, "of reality the rarest-veined unraveller," as Gerard Manley Hopkins has it.

But the very elements that appealed to Duns Scotus and other Neoplatonist Christians may have doomed it within the Jewish community, where interests and methods grew less "universal" as social circumstances changed in Spain and the Christian reconquest gathered strength. With the exception of its title, which is drawn from Psalms 36:10, "For with Thee is the fountain [source] of life (*meqor hayyim*); In Thy light do we see light," the book contains not a single reference to Hebrew Scripture or tradition, and Plato is the only philosopher mentioned there by name. Perhaps the key mediating force in *Fons Vitae*, the Divine Will, was too close for Jewish comfort to the Christian Logos. Scholars have suggested that this, in combination with its total independence from Jewish dogma, prompted the Jewish neglect over time. ("The odor of heresy ... clung to its author," says one commentator.) In any event, whatever influence it may have had was soon dispersed by the less threatening and much more conservative Aristotelian philosophy of Maimonides.

The following miniature anthology from *The Fountain of Life* might serve as an aperitif to the whole of Ibn Gabirol's philosophical system:

> If you raise yourself up to the Primary Universal Matter and take shelter in its shadow, you will see wonders more sublime than all. Desire, therefore, for this and seek, for this is the purpose for which the human soul was formed and this is the most tremendous pleasure and the greatest of all forms of happiness (III:57);

✦

> Matter has no reality apart from its form, for the real derives from form, and therefore matter moves toward the reception of form, in other words, to be released from the sorrow of absence to the pleasure of existence (V:29);

✦

> *Student:* What is the proof that the motion of matter and the other substances is desire and love? *Master:* Because it is apparent that desire and love are nothing but an effort to join the beloved and be united with it, and matter makes an effort to join form; it follows that its movement comes from love and desire for form (V:32);

✦

> The creation of all things by the Creator, that is, the emanation of form from the first source, which is to say, the will, and its overflowing across matter resembles the upwelling of water flowing from a fountain and descending ... except that this flow is unceasing and entirely outside of motion and time ... And the imprinting of form in matter, when it reaches it from the will, is like the return of the form of one *who is gazing into a mirror* (V:41);

✦

One can compare creation to a word, which man utters with his mouth. In man's expression of the word, its form and meaning are registered upon the hearing of the listener and in his mind. Along the same lines it is said that the exalted and holy creator expresses his word, and its meaning is registered in the substantiality of matter, and matter preserves that meaning, in other words, that created form is imprinted in matter and registered upon it (V:43);

◆

Master: The purpose for which all that exists exists [is] the knowledge of the world of the divine.... *Student:* And what is the fruit that we will achieve with this study? *Master:* "Release from death and adherence to the fountain and source of life (V:43).

GENTILITY, THE GOOD, THE GOOD LIFE

The second obstacle to the successful transmission of the Hebrew medievals' art: the widely held genteel picture of the court society in which these poems took shape. The textbook version of it comes down to us in Joseph Weiss's 1947 essay, which for fifty years has told students that

the court of the patron serves as a school of advanced studies for the development of superior taste. Its members know no other ideal apart from fineness of form, no finer deed than the exercise of aesthetic tact. Wherever a 'court' exists, there you will find 'style'—nobility, refinement, and linguistic elegance. The pleasures of society, such as play, laughter, music, literature and of course the bonds of love and friendship, all pass through the crucible of subtle stylization until the social life of the court becomes entirely a game of art ... poetry, song, entertaining rhymes and riddles, laughter, and light, cultured conversation.

Coming to this description directly from a reading of the poems one rubs one's eyes in disbelief: Is *this* the cultural setting that produced the Jewish courtier/poet/Talmudist/prime minister/general Shmuel Ha-Nagid? Where in this scenario is there room for the vigor, wisdom, sublimity, irony, sensuality, and range of emotion and thought in his work? Or for the high stakes and backstabbing intrigue that have characterized court cultures in medieval China, Arabia, and Elizabethan England, and that played a central role in upper-crust Spanish Jewish society as well? Can we truly believe that the Andalusian medieval best and brightest, men of staggering talent and learning, devoted themselves to the world presented in this museum-diorama-like tableau? Weiss, it should be granted, acknowledges HaNagid—who is usually regarded as the courtier-rabbi par excellence—as something of an exception, as his military and civic roles balanced the otherwise "illusory" and one-dimensional world of the politically powerless Jewish court; and the general cultural cheer, he adds, is tempered by the poets' awareness of the cruel hand of fate, *zeman*, or Time, which undermines their sense of security. But the interaction of these two conventional aspects of existence is, in Weiss's view, "atomistic": it results in the atrophy of the poets' individual personalities.

And we are back where we started: Is *this* the culture that produced Solomon Ibn Gabirol, famous for his early mastery of the lesser literary court conventions and a later reconfiguration of these same conventions that gave us some of the most powerful, personal, mythic, and even antisocial hybrid poetry postbiblical Hebrew has known—to say nothing of his major liturgical verse and his philosophical *Fountain of Life*? (At this point we are already three generations into the period's poetry, halfway through its Golden Age.)

Clearly something is wrong with this picture. Something recognizably human, something essential to the distinctive, not the typical, poetry of the period is missing in this reconstruction of the social context. The problem is, in fact, more tonal than anything else, a blurring of terms and associations (one shudders to imagine how twentieth-century poetry would look through the telescope of thirtieth-century thumbnail sociology, let alone sociology that focused on a "representative" rather than exceptional poet). For Weiss and others are not wrong to direct the would-be reader of Hebrew-Andalusian verse to the court of the patron, and its poetry does in fact involve a discrete world with its own highly stylized modes of social and poetic behavior. This world is in several respects strange to modern sensibilities and, its lightest verse aside, play was a major part of it—though judging from the poems and prose works of the period, that play seems to have involved less diversion and frippery than an examination of the dynamics of rhetoric and human creation, or re-creation—what T. S. Eliot meant when he said that poetry is "serious amusement," implying an extra-utile and gratuitous act, which also happens to be the Welsh modernist poet David Jones's definition of art, or at least of the valid signs, the made things that comprise it.

It is true, as well, that our medieval poets sought the support of a patron and all the perks that entailed, and that numerous poems were written for the reasons often spelled out: to make sure one's bread got buttered, to please a friend, to exercise one's gift, to get out a message, to bask in the limelight, and so on. The poets' highest ideal, however, their notion of the good, and by extension, the good life, hardly led to a literary country club of witty conversation, croquet, and afternoon couplets and tea; it was an *otium* opposed to *negotium*, at the heart of which lay the artist's perennial question of leisure, of freedom *from* the business of earning a living, and freedom *for* a "relaxation" of mind into a critical, nourishing entanglement of words and the world. It involved formidable learning, a considerable range of affective and intellectual experience, and a highly demanding, self-conscious, complex art. And it was, for the most part, permeated with a sense of the divine and its textual extension through history.

A strong reading of the poetry that emerged in that environment, then, requires both a more nuanced understanding of the court and its literary conventions, and the abandonment of what pop-cultural critic Gilbert Seldes once called, in another context entirely, "the lorgnettes of prejudice provided by fashion and gentility."

HEINRICH HEINE OR THE HISTORY OF TRANSMISSION

Heine was dealing with a similar sort of interference some one hundred and fifty years ago. Working from his Parisian "mattress grave" at the same time as the jigsaw editions of Ibn Gabirol's poems were being assembled and, in part, translated in Germany, and very likely under their spell—also, one can assume, in dialogue with Goethe's *East–West Diwan*—the German Jewish-Protestant poet is in the middle of a longish poem called "Judah Ben Halevy," which would become part of "Hebrew Melodies" (in *Romancero*, a book that was floated on an enormous publicity campaign and sold 15,000 copies in four printings when it was released in 1851, with the first illustrated book jacket in publishing history). He sketches a kind of biography in verse, full of flowery detail about the fourth major Andalusian-Hebrew poet's troubadourlike love songs for Jerusalem and his legendary death there at the hands of a Saracen on horseback. Along the way he inserts a labyrinthine version of Plutarch's story about the fancy box of jewels that Alexander the Great took in his victory over Darius III, a box in which Alexander then put his beloved

Homer's poems. Part IV of Heine's poem begins as he breaks off to tell us that his wife wasn't happy with the previous section, because she disapproved of Alexander's behavior (he should have sold the box and bought his wife a cashmere sweater) and, anyway, she'd never heard of this Judah Halevy, whose poems her husband says he would have placed in Darius's box were he given the chance. Keep the box if you must, she implies, but why waste it on an obscure poet's poems? In her view, says Heine, Halevy's work "would have been honored quite enough by being kept in any pretty box of cardboard with some very swanky Chinese arabesques to decorate it, like a bonbon box from Marquis." She and the other students of "the boarding schools of Paris" know about mummies and pharaohs and porcelain pagoda princes, Heine says, "all of this is crammed into them"—but

> If you ask them for great figures
> In the golden age of glory
> Of the Arabic Hispanic
> Jewish school of poetry—
>
> If you ask about the trio
> Of Jehuda Ben Halevy
> And of Solomon Gabirol
> And of Moses Ibn Ezra
>
> If you ask about such figures
> Then the children stare back at you
> With their goggling eyes wide open
> Like the cows along a hillside.
>
> (trans. Hal Draper)

The poem continues with Heine telling her to go learn Hebrew—a language he himself barely knew.

I, IDEAL

The hyperextension of the particular, the "I," at times, from on high, speaking down to us from the idealized, or up through us toward it, and the hybrid first person of his liturgical poetry, braiding us into the poet's verse, in his turning, like the Psalmist. Often the first person of the poetry takes its place in that ideal landscape, within its palaces and walled gardens. But through almost all of it, or the best of it, a specific individual is speaking, toadlike within these imaginary gardens, where hyperbole yields to an intimacy, and the real to an experienced ideal, or vice versa, in a balance proposed (through language) between the elements, the season, the sexes, and the senses—between the beyond and what's under one's feet. So Ibn Gabirol's poems are cut and set like the jewels that line them—faceted to reflect, include, and raise, even as they coolly dazzle and deny.

The poet, too, becomes both less and more than he is, emptying himself, in part, as he takes on the conventions and typologies of the verse. His Arabic honorific, for example, Abu Ayyub, "Father of Job," is purely formal, the standard *kuniyah* (agnomen) for anyone whose name is Sulaiman. Yet his life and writing charge it with valence. He, too, is plagued by "friends," fate, a debilitating disease of the skin. He, too, turns sarcastic in his pursuit of understanding and wisdom. He, like Job, is inclined to flip Scripture on its head for ironic effect as his speech mounts to a cosmic perspective. Both that most sophisticated of biblical books and his poems are coiled by swift transformations of mood. Light for both is central, standing for all that's alive and of worth: "Wherefore is light given to him that is in misery, and life unto him that is bitter in soul" (Job 3:20). Ibn Gabirol:

> It was night and the sky was clear,
> and the moon was pure at its center
> as it led me along discernment's sphere,
> teaching me by its light and direction—
>
> though as my heart went out to that light,
> I feared extended misfortune.

And we have already seen what Solomon the Small does with Solomon of Scripture—possessor of creation's secrets and an ongoing echo in the poems.

JERK

That said: The stench of his boasting and sense of self-worth, his truculence and misanthropy, his inability to sustain friendships or stay in one place for any length of time, even his essential sense of the world and time and fate as hostile—all the evidence points to his having been, as Berryman said of Rilke, a jerk.

KINGDOM'S CROWN

But a jerk who rang the cosmic gong.

Keter Malkhut, his most well-known poem, has been translated into English at least seven times over the past two hundred years, first in 1794 by David Levi, a London hatter with rabbinical training. Versions of the poem exist in German, French, Italian, Dutch, Yiddish, Latin, Persian, and Arabic (the latter was found in David Tzemah's manuscript), and the poem appears in prayer books of Jewish communities throughout the world, where it is read on Yom Kippur, the Day of Atonement.

It has come a long way. While the poem is framed by its magnificent hymn to the Creator and the magisterial concluding confession, the bulk of the work consists of a cosmography based on the Ptolemaic universe, a mapping of "what there is"—lower limit world, upper limit Lord. The ascent from earth's four elements to the Throne of Glory takes one up through the spheres and the planets, and contains a good many astronomical, and some astrological, considerations, which, in combination with the poet's philosophical tendencies, ruffled the feathers of the local, and formidable, religious establishment of the time. This, it seems, was an ongoing problem for Ibn Gabirol, whom scholars suggest may have been forced to leave Saragossa because of his particular mix of philosophy, mysticism, religion, and science. Isolated and ostracized by his fellow Jewish intellectuals, he had found himself surrounded there by people who

> . . . quarrel with all my teachings and talk,
> as though I were speaking Greek.
> "Speak," they carp, "as the people speak,
> and we'll know what you have to say"—
> and now I'll break them like dirt or like straw,
> my tongue's pitchfork thrust into their hay.

As he grew older, his hybrid philosophical inquiry only intensified.

We have nothing in the way of first-hand evidence of response to the poem, but we find a contemporary such as Ibn Janaah calling in his *Sefer HaRiqmah* for the avoidance of "books . . . that deal with the origin and foundation of things . . . the nature of the creation of the upper and lower world, for this is something whose truth cannot be determined, and whose end is attained often at the expense of the Law and faith, and with endless weariness to the soul. It brings no pleasure." And Ibn Ezra writes in his book of poetics that, generally speaking, the intrusion of scientific and astronomical matters into the liturgy was more of a burden than pure Hebrew could bear, and what began as petition and prayer often evolved into heated discussion and argument. He cautioned moderation.

An approach much closer in spirit to Ibn Gabirol's is found in the Muslim *Epistles of the Brethren of Purity*:

> When the educated man of understanding considers the study of astronomy, and thinks of the tremendous dimensions of the spheres and the swiftness of their movement, his soul longs to ascend to those spheres and to see them with his very own eyes. This, however, it cannot do, on account of the weight of the body. But when the soul separates itself from the body, and is not held back by its wicked doings, its harmful attributes, and its great ignorance, it arrives there in an instant, with the blink of an eye.

The prosody of the poem is worth pausing over, as it has important implications for understanding and translation. Written in the medium of *saj'a*, which is most often if inadequately translated as "rhymed, rhythmic prose," *Kingdom's Crown* is a symphonic work whose primary poetic virtues are musical. It might be regarded as a reprise of the poet's entire diwan, and Ibn Gabirol makes it clear that he considered it the summit of his work. Although there are important Hebrew precursors (to begin with, Sa'adiah Gaon's two poems of petition, where both the rhyme and theme resemble those of Ibn Gabirol's poem), insight with regard to poetic practice once again comes from Arabic literature, where the *saj'a* was used in the Quran. The Arabic term for the form derives from the verb meaning "to coo," or, as the lexicographer E. W. Lane illustrates it: "A pigeon continuing its cry uninterruptedly in one uniform way or manner . . . cooing and prolonging its voice"—a definition that recalls lines by the poet Mina Loy, from "Property of Pigeons": "Pigeons make an irritant, alluring / music; / quelled solfeggios / of shrill wings winnowing / their rejoicing, cooing / fanaticism for wooing . . ."; or García Lorca's free translation of the medieval Arabic of Sirj al-Warak: "The turtledove that with her complaints keeps me from sleep, has a breast that burns like mine, alive with fire" (trans. Christopher Maurer). The circle comes almost round with the thirteenth-century traveler Ibn Khatib's describing the daybreak call of Granada's muezzins, and observing that they "vied with one another with melodies like [those of] turtle doves." While in early eleventh-century Hebrew the form was most often reserved for epistolary writing, the effect of the *saj'a* in *Kingdom's Crown* is in practice much closer to that of certain kinds of incantatory free verse—*Leaves of Grass*, say, or Robert Duncan's *Opening of the Field*. The poem should be taken in, or offered up, quite literally as a music of the spheres.

LOST AND FOUND IN TRANSLATION

The finest Hebrew poetry of the period is the product of an age of translation. But translation, particularly in an age of translation, is not only what hired or inspired workers have rendered into another language; it is also what writers who read in multiple languages translate in thought alone—the force of which is brought to bear on the written language they use. This, granted, is simply influence; in this instance, however, it is influence born of a steady passage across linguistic and regional borders.

Often this passage followed the trade routes. Just as in the nineteenth century the new (albeit lesser) literature and cultural attitudes of the European *Haskalah*, or Enlightenment, were disseminated along with agricultural and other goods and ideas at the Leipzig trade fair each year, when Jewish businessmen from Polish Galicia and Germany would meet, so too in the Judeo-Arabic middle ages immigrants, information, and artistic practices followed the money (read: ships, silks, spices, and scents). Some scholars suggest that the influence of Arabic Andalusian verse made its way along these routes into France, where it was taken in by the troubadours. In the twentieth century this is how one of the most gifted of the freelance pioneers in the study of medieval Hebrew poetry, Sha'ul Abdullah Yosef, found himself in Hong Kong, having relocated for business purposes from Baghdad to Bombay before settling at the far-eastern end of these routes, where he worked daily after hours on a commentary to the poems of Yehudah Halevi.

All of this "translation" from East to West and back again—this removal of people, goods, armies, and art forms—from one context (or soil) to another took place during an Arab literary and scientific renaissance that over time became the critical link in the transmission of Greek thinking to the West. Historian Richard Walzer points out the difference between the Arabs in Europe, who maintained their language and religion as they adopted the learning native to the conquered territory, and the

Germanic tribes that invaded Italy, who gave up both their language and religion for that of the local culture but remained closed to the intellectual heritage that the latter had to offer. (And Dante, we remember, placed Muhammad in the ninth pouch of the eighth circle of Hell, which is reserved for the "sowers of scandal and schism.") Al-Andalus was, then, an extension of a culture that thrived on the news from abroad. Between the eighth and ninth centuries CE, the major Eastern schools of translation gathered manuscripts from across the Arab and Byzantine world, and in either literal, literary, or summary form virtually the entire Greek curriculum of study was translated into Arabic, often through Syriac intermediary texts, with much of the work being done by Christian translators. Thus Muslim and Jewish thinkers in Baghdad and Spain had at their disposal, in addition to a large body of original Arabic and Hebrew compositions, versions of over a hundred works by Galen, most of Aristotle, key books of Plato, Neoplatonic pseudo-Aristotelian texts, pseudo-Empedocles, Indian stories, Persian musical treatises, scientific collections of a diverse nature, mathematical studies of conics, spherics, and pneumatics, medical textbooks, and more.

The "dictionally pure," Scripture-based Jewish poets of Córdoba, Granada, and Saragossa opened their lives to the entire expanse of that learning, and, in the process, carried out an act of profound if paradoxical cultural redemption: in translating both the essence of their Greco-Arabic learning and the effects of Arabic poetry into an innovative Hebrew verse, in risking loss of linguistic and religious self to immersion in the foreign, the Hebrew poets of Spain found, or founded, the most powerful language of Jewish expression post-biblical literature has known.

METAPHYSICS, OR THE MECHANICALS

It's through thinking Gabirol sparkles,
and it's thinkers that he pleases . . .

—Heine

Discussions of the problem (but never the pleasure) of translation of medieval Hebrew poetry into English almost always turn for guidance to either the English Metaphysical poets or the neoclassical school of Pope, and with good reason. There are obvious parallels to both. Like the Hebrew Andalusian poets, the poets labeled metaphysical by Dryden and

Samuel Johnson (for convenience's sake and then as a pejorative), and poets of the English Renaissance in general (and it is *always* in general that the comparison is made), produced a body of work that is often ornamental, conventional, and centered on a situation of court, church, or garden. Their poems, too, are characterized by a fascination with artifice and creation, with transcendentalism and the obscurity that can entail. They, as well, share a worldview marked by imports and correspondence, by heightened awareness of detail, pattern, and form.

There are numerous passages of uncanny similarity: Henry Vaughan's "I saw eternity the other night, / Like a great *Ring* of pure and endless light, / All clear, as it was bright, / And round beneath it, Time in hours, days, years, / Driven by the spheres / Like a vast shadow moved . . ." seems a none-too-distant if more mild-mannered descendant of the moonstruck Ibn Gabirol quoted above: "It was night and the sky was clear . . ." Donne's verse sometimes bears a striking resemblance to Ibn Gabirol: "And don't be astonished by a man whose flesh / has longed for wisdom and prevailed; / He's soul encircling physique, / and a sphere in which all is held" summons "Good Friday, 1613. Riding Westward," by the MP turned deacon and priest: "Let man's soul be a sphere, and then, in this, / The intelligence that moves, devotion is." The much celebrated metaphysical conceit recalls the figures of the Hebrew and Arabic poets of our period; and of course the poems of Herbert's *Temple* have their partners in the realm of *piyyut* and contemplative nonliturgical verse alike.

And yet . . . compelling and even classroom-correct as these parallels are, and worth pursuing in much greater depth and along historical lines, they seem always, at root, somehow misleading. For behind the analogy, from which the most problematic versions of this poetry usually emerge, there is an implicit assumption that Christian England is in some fundamental respect equivalent to Judeo-Muslim Spain and, by extension, that our hearing "reconstructed" sixteenth- or seventeenth-century verse in Chicago today is parallel to eleventh-century Arabic-speaking Jews hearing masterful eleventh-century Hebrew verse in Berber Granada. They aren't, it isn't, and what we get in translation from the comparison too often sounds less like the major poetry of an age than like Snug, Snout, Starveling, and friends—Shakespeare's Mechanicals performing their *Most Lamentable Comedy and Most Cruel Death of Pyramus and Thisby* in *A Midsummer Night's Dream*: "O grim-looked night, O night with hue so black! O night, which ever art when day is not! / O night, O night; alack, alack, alack."

A welcome voice-over again intrudes from the visual plane, this time from the French scholar Louis Massignon, who is comparing the idea of the Arab and European garden, both of which emerge within a neo-classical cultural frame:

> In our classical garden, which began with the Roman Empire and continued with the Medicis and Louis XIV, the intent is to control the world from a central point of view, with long perspective lines leading to the horizon and great water basins reflecting the distances, all framed by relentlessly pruned trees, leading the eye, little by little, to a sense of conquest of the whole surrounding land.
>
> By contrast, the Muslim garden's first and foremost idea is to be enclosed and isolated from the outside world; instead of having its focus of attention on the periphery, it is placed in the center. The garden is created by taking a piece of land, "vivifying" a square section of the desert, into which water is brought. Inside a very high enclosing wall, one finds a staggered arrangement of trees and flowers growing close to one another as one moves from the periphery to the center, and in the center, next to a spraying fountain, is a kiosk. This garden, contrary to the Western garden . . . enables thought to unfold in an atmosphere of relaxation.

The parallel to the verbal arts is not exact, but its basic thrust seems more instructive than the comparison across centuries within the medium. (To move onto somewhat more stable ground, consider Alexander Pope's "grottofied" landscape at Twickenham, which was "expressive of his deepest values as a man and a poet . . . an actual metaphor and emblem of the poet's trade," in the words of his best biographer.) Massignon continues, describing another important locus of the culture, the mosque, noting that the *types* of materials, ornaments, and subjects employed in its construction "are a reminder . . . that faces and forms do not exist in themselves but are unceasingly recreated by God. We find thus intertwining polygons, circling arcs of varying radii, the so-called arabesque, which is essentially a kind of indefinite negation of closed geometrical forms." Extending this analysis to all aspects of "the decorative side of Muslim life," including carpets, mosaics, greetings, and clothes, even the way that foods are seasoned and served, Massignon observes that in each the mind is taken through structurally similar cycles of concentration and release.

In short, we are, in the referential field of the medieval Judeo-Muslim aesthetic, compositional light years away from the feel of the eighteenth-century English couplet. And while the poems of Ibn Gabirol *are* metaphysical, and share numerous formal and thematic concerns with the verse of the English renaissance, the specific tones of his metaphysic, and the vector of his thought, point—in as much as translation is concerned—away from, not toward, the diction of Herbert and Donne.

NATURE'S NEOPLATONISM: A METAPOETICS

"The microcosm is the model of the macrocosm," he says in the third book of *The Fountain of Life* (III:2), taking up the Greek and common medieval notion, "As above, so below." "If you would picture the composition of the All . . . look at the form of the human body" (III:58). In a complicated adjustment of pure Neoplatonic doctrine (derived through summary intermediate texts brought to Spain in Arabic translation—*The Theology of Aristotle*, for example), the human form is linked by the Divine Will to the larger world beyond us, though these links do not add up to a pantheism. In fact more than one writer has characterized the purpose of Ibn Gabirol's philosophical project, evident in his poetry as well, as an attempt to rescue his Jewish Neoplatonic monotheism from pantheism. Nevertheless, some of the poet's contemporaries and successors remained unconvinced, and the historical record shows (and his poems imply) that he was sometimes accused of a heretical tendency toward pantheistic thinking, or at least of drawing dangerously near it.

The key terms in Ibn Gabirol's philosophical scheme, especially, for a reading of the poetry, are "form" and "matter." The First Essence (God) creates Universal Matter and Form through the enactment or emanation of his Will. The conjunction of this Universal Form and Matter gives rise to the simple substances, including intellect, soul, and nature, and the chain of emanation extends down into the corporeal world and all its parts. This emanation of divine energy Ibn Gabirol likens to light from the sun—but not to the sun itself; or to intelligence acting in the limbs of the body—but not the soul itself taking action; or, as we have seen, to a fountain whose flow transcends all temporal and spatial dimension. In this way the process of creation is continuous and ongoing at all levels at all times in a universal chain of transformation reaching from that pure source to the lowest point of the cosmos and back up to its unknowable origin. "Help the celestial bodies grow with your souls," Ibn Gabirol quotes the Arabic *Epistles,* in his ethical treatise, "even as tilling and irrigating help the seed to grow."

Throughout this talk, the terms of the discussion are identical to those used in describing the period's poetry: matter takes on form as a body takes on clothing—a vocabulary that has given rise in discussion of the literature to the absolute separation of poetic form and content. But as Ibn Gabirol again and again makes clear in *The Fountain of Life,* "it is impossible for matter to have any reality without form, for it does not take on existence unless it is dressed in form. The existence of a thing comes into being only within its form" (V:8).

Which is the point that Jaroslav Stetkevych makes in his *Zephyrs of Najd* when he says that "instead of looking for signs of dichotomy of form and content, one could, with equal ease, reverse the lens and see in Arabic poetry the closest possible—or the will to the closest possible—marriage between form and content, precisely because that poetry is so highly 'formalistic'. . . . [P]oetic content not only survives [there] but flourishes, albeit in unaccustomed ways, and extracts out of its predicament a strange power and solidity of imaginative impact."

As above, so with Ibn Gabirol:

> But I'll tell you something I've heard
> and let you dwell on its strangeness:
> sages have said that the secret
> of being owes all
> to the all who has all in his hand:
> He longs to give form to the formless,
> as a lover longs for his friend. . . .

ORIENTALISM

Regardless of how one enters this poetry, no matter what angle of approach one adopts, at some point the route to understanding runs through a Near Eastern world that, for many of us, is at best a mystery, at worst a demonized entity. We're familiar with some of its mystical literature, often in translations with a New Age veneer, and we have *A Thousand and One Nights,* Disney's *Aladdin,* Lean's *Lawrence of Arabia,* and, from the Persian, Edward FitzGerald's best-selling Victorian fantasia, *The Ruba'iyat;* but, as anyone who tries to absorb it in translation knows, the gist (let alone the bulk) of Arabic and Persian poetry lies on a still very dark side of the literary moon. The same situation holds for the Hebrew.

The third great obstacle, then, to successful transmission: our relation as Western readers to the largely unknown world of Sephardic and Arab culture. For the vast majority of speakers of English, and even for those with a Jewish education, the literary culture of medieval Spain is by and large a rumor, perhaps a likeness paused before on a crowded vacation itinerary. (For native Israelis it is the memory of an exasperating, murky unit of high-school literature class, required for matriculation.) Debates rage in the Hebrew papers about the relative "universal" worth of other expressions of Sephardic cultures, and attitudes evident in that public controversy inevitably derive from, or trickle down to, scholarly and artistic treatments of even this most Western of Eastern poetries.

So, for example, critics raised on the post-Romantic notion of the self have often sought to explain the mentality behind the "atomized" nature of Arabic, Persian and, by extension, Hebrew medieval poetry—each of which, in various ways, has been called artificial, cloying, fantastic, and decorative or mannered. In part the blame is laid at the feet of the elitist courtly environment and its restrictive system of patronage. But as Julie Meisami points out in *Medieval Persian Court Poetry*, a more lethal source of trouble derives from Orientalist projections and misreadings of the work, which charge that the poetry of the East "is unaware of the correct relationship between the poetical ego and the world, mankind and itself." According to this line of thinking the literature of the East lacks a constituent element of what we recognize as great poetry, and it is therefore best treated as part of a taxonomical study of the mentality it represents. The gist of the problem, Meisami says, is that in an effort to find the symbolic (metaphorical) import of things, readers have often failed to perceive the actual (analogical) dynamic at work in the verse itself. If the former is based on likeness of qualities and uses this likeness to bridge the gap between man and the universe, the latter presupposes what she calls "an elaborate network of correspondences" between nature and humanity, a continuity. Once these cosmological differences are understood, the esthetic preferences of "Eastern" poetry (relating to hyperbole, embellishment, and type, for starters, but extending to sensibility and notions of unity in the poem) can be read in a far more sympathetic light. Lacking that background of understanding, the road to the work is a critical minefield. Even as partisan a reader as Haim Nahman Bialik, the great Hebrew modernist poet who devoted many of his best years to the project he called the "ingathering of our Spanish poetry," confessed that early in his career he was put off by the "broken glass" and alien poetics of the adopted Arabic poetry, the latter of which he saw as shackles around the feet of the medieval Hebrew poets, artificial fetters that kept them from a natural approach to the world and their language.

Biases of this sort infect translation as well, and readers have come to equate a lush *Ruba'iyat*-like diction and haze as authentically "Eastern"—this despite the fact the Omar Khayyam's eleventh-century *Ruba'iyat* were direct, hard, sometimes harsh, and above all unsentimental. This is not to say that some of Ibn Gabirol's (or HaNagid's) poems aren't sensuous in a way that meets Orientalist expectations, only that to read the poetry well, to derive from it the clear, full sort of pleasure it was intended to give, one might do better to come at it without the residue of Victorian dreams of the East. Instead, one might start with the testimony of the age itself, with, say, the assumption given voice in Ibn Ezra's *Book of Discussion* and al-Harizi's *Takhkemoni*, and in countless poems from the period, that we are dealing with a major literature that spoke with tremendous force and range to the educated people of its day. For without a deep and somehow physical sympathy with the poem as a link between the reader and the real, or *a* real, without our keeping our eye on the prize these poems describe, this poetry *as poetry* will elude us.

Mystique and mistrust, then—the whirlpool and six-headed dragon of these waters.

Pus

"Sometimes pus, sometimes a poem," Yehuda Amichai writes, in a poem called "Ibn Gabirol."

Qabbalah: Facts, Quacks, and Quibbles

Qabbalists from the thirteenth century on have looked to him as a stellar figure in their lineage, much in the way that André Breton and the surrealists reached back into the past to claim Poe and Sade as surrealists before their time. Breton, of course, was establishing a constellation of affinity; the case of the Qabbalists is trickier, as the argument has from time to time been put forth that Ibn Gabirol was either a secret early Qabbalist (who fashioned a lady golem and engaged in various forms of magical activity), a Jewish Sufi, or—and here a kind of wonder-dust is released into the air, as if by the syllables themselves—"a mystic."

Bracketing the problem of locating Ibn Gabirol with any precision in the history of Qabbalah—an issue that is still unresolved, though it has been dealt with in exemplary fashion by scholars such as Gershom Scholem, Shlomo Pines, Moshe Idel, and Yehuda Liebes—one is struck by the recurrence in the poet's liturgical work of elements drawn from esoteric Jewish doctrine, including *Merkavah* (Chariot) literature, *Sefer Yetzirah* (The Book of Creation), and the apocalyptic *Pirke Rabbi Eliezer*, all of which in turn have roots in the hard-to-unravel, heretical, but not un-Hebraic tradition of Greek Gnosticism. One finds related elements in so-called secular poems such as "I Love You," and even—though this is more controversial—in what on the face of it appear to be straightforward court panegyrics such as "The Palace Garden." In short, whether one defines the term Qabbalah in a strict historical fashion, as the scholars must, or reads ahistorically, as the Qabbalists proper (and poets) often do, it is clear that Ibn Gabirol and the later Qabbalists draw in places on common sources. For a reading of the poetry one need only observe that we are dealing here with a poetic consciousness as visionary as that of Yeats.

READING RELIGIOUS POETRY, OR REACTION

Religion is at its etymological root a "binding back." It arouses antipathy wherever it goes, and it goes almost everywhere. The religious instinct is, Henry Adams reminds us, the second most powerful of *emotions*.

It doesn't necessarily make for great poetry, however, any more than the first on Adams's list—the sexual—guarantees great cinema. The roster of demurrers is distinguished, from Samuel Johnson's warning that "metrical devotion . . . supplies nothing to the mind" to Auden's cautioning discretion with regard to the baring of soul in verse.

Throughout the contemplative, satirical, erotic, devotional, elegiac, and encomiastic poems of Ibn Gabirol, religious elements exert a constant pressure. There is of course the raw material of the verse itself—scriptural Hebrew. But there is also the nature of the surrounding society and its most ordinary of assumptions. On the one hand we have our own modern literary expectations of invention and concretion, and on the other we're presented with a medieval Semitic culture whose every occurrence, even whose science, is understood in a wholly religious framework: the "empty" abstraction offends the aesthete, and a patriarchal monotheism and a chauvinistic Judaism put off not only the politically correct. Culture clash is inevitable. Belief and disbelief alike, therefore, must be suspended.

For the motion of the mind in this work is not merely a binding back as in a restriction, but a profound reorientation of attention, a stretching of thought and sensibility, however quietly, to perception's extremity, to the moment's relation to first things and last, to an existential bottom-line. With their subtle blending of the personal and communal "I," the poems bear witness to an extension of range, not an abdication of interest or involvement. And there is in Ibn Gabirol's work, above all in its ornamental poetics and liturgical forms, an Eastern (some would say Indian or even Chinese) sense of connectedness—from the body's humors up through nature, the spheres, to the Throne of Glory or the seat of the soul. His is a religion of knowing, a gnosticism. It involves a vital mythic configuration, alive with sound, movement, and spirit at every turn.

SPAINS

When tourists, students, scholars, rabbis, writers, and even politicians talk about medieval Spain, chances are good that they are talking about different things:

There is the Golden Age of Jewish poetry, the period of unrivaled Hebraic literary achievement, with the occasional story of political success: the Spain of Jewish pride, which emerged with miraculous suddenness in the late tenth century, one of the abiding mysteries of Jewish history;

—there is the Spain of the Jewish "neo-lachrymose historians," in which all paths lead to expulsion or worse;

—there is the elegiac Palestinian equivalent, in which Andalusia equals the abandoned campsite of the beloved in the pre-Islamic qasida, equals Palestine and the lost paradise of Islamic power, splendor, and culture;

—and there is the Andalusian rainbow coalition, the Spain of *convivencia* and "inter-faith utopia," where Arabs, Berbers, Iberians, Slavs, and Jews lived—or seemed to live—in relative comfort side by side;

—there is the enchanted Spain of romantic engravings and Washington Irving's *Tales of the Alhambra*;

—there is a melodramatic Spain of the Arab-menace and sensual delight, the bodice-ripper Spain of concoctions like Colin de Silva's airport-paperback *Alhambra*, which picks up where Yehosef HaNagid's head falls off, and presents us with the young Prince Ahmed, whom we overhear reciting pantheistic doggerel to a blossoming magnolia until . . . "From the holy ecstasy of his adoration of beauty, the sight, the sound, the scent enshrined in pure air, from the sweet joy of beauty's clean spirit symbolized by the tree, holy lust emerged. He rose . . .";

—and there is the Spain-of-the-past as imagined literary future, the Andalusia of poets such as Mahmoud Darwish, the eminent Palestinian writer who, in a 1996 interview with a Hebrew literary journal, spoke of an "Andalus that might be here or there, or anywhere . . . a meeting place of strangers in the project of building human culture. . . . It is not only that there was a Jewish–Muslim co-existence," he says, "but that the fates of the two peoples were similar. . . . Al-Andalus for me is the realization of the dream of the poem."

Tiqqun Middot HaNefesh: The Poet in Training

Far-fetched and fanciful in much of its argument, Ibn Gabirol's ethical treatise *Tiqqun Middot HaNefesh* (The Improvement of the Moral Qualities) is nonetheless of real interest to readers of the poetry. Written in Arabic when the poet was twenty-four, and modeled on Arab ethical handbooks such as Abu Bakhr al-Raazi's ninth-century *Book of the Treatment of the Soul*, it graphs an undissociated sensibility in which the physical and psychological endowments, or impulses, of a person are correlated to ethical conduct. Qualities of the soul, in this not always decipherable scheme, are manifest in the senses, which consist of four humors: blood, yellow gall, black gall, and white gall, which in turn correspond to the four elements, air, fire, earth, and water. The senses (impulses) can be mixed and matched so that the soul's tendencies might be trained for wisdom. Knowledge of the soul is a prerequisite for its development (its ascent) and the soul can be known solely in a descent into physical detail:

> If a man be wise, he will employ [the senses] in the right place and restrain them from everything in connection with which he ought not to use them. Let him rather be like a skilful physician, who prepares prescriptions, taking of every medicine a definite quantity . . .

Ibn Gabirol's somewhat eccentric approach yields the Rimbaud-like association of the senses and the qualities of the soul, as follows:

SIGHT	HEARING	SMELL
Pride	Love	Wrath
Meekness	Hate	Goodwill
Pudency	Mercy	Jealousy
Impudence	Hard-heartedness	Wide-awakeness
	(Cruelty)	

TASTE	TOUCH
Joy (Cheerfulness)	Liberality
Grief (Apprehensiveness)	Stinginess
Tranquillity	Valor
Penitence (Remorse)	Cowardice

This he derives from a typically medieval mandala-like map of possibilities, where conflicting elements and traits are held in complex balance:

ETHICS

alike in respect of heat

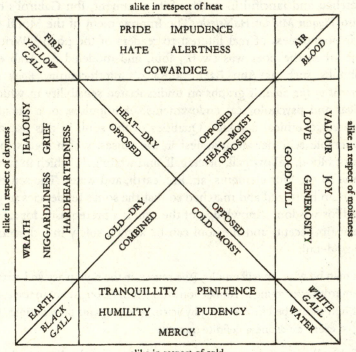

alike in respect of cold

Chapter by chapter, impulse by impulse, *Tiqqun Middot HaNefesh* treats all of the above, quoting Arabic poems and a variety of philosophers, including Socrates, "the God-like Plato," Aristotle, Galen, Origen, The Book of Kuti, Saʿadiah, Alexander the Great, and Ardeshir, the founder of the new Persian dynasty in 222. All chapters begin with the characterization of the quality under discussion, which is then located in a scriptural anatomy. For instance, Grief (Apprehensiveness), which is aligned on our chart with taste:

> This quality usually succeeds in establishing itself in the soul when wishes fail of realization, and then the soul is brought to such a point as almost to be killed when it loses the objects of its love. . . . Thus it was said, "Apprehensiveness is living death." . . . The constitution of apprehensiveness is cold and dry, like the black gall (humor). No man can absolutely escape it. In some it attains immense proportions, so that they thereby become afflicted with psychical ailments. Thus it is said (Proverbs xii:25), "Gloom in the heart of man maketh it stoop, but a good word maketh it glad."

Ethical implications and exhortations follow. Early in the book the author apologizes for the gaps in his argument, which he attributes to difficult times and the fact that "human power is but slight, especially in the case of a man like me, who is always greatly troubled and who does but scantily realize his hopes."

UNDERTOW

The risks of involvement, the threat presented by the force and hidden currents of the work, to writer, reader, translator:

Tracing the arc of Andalusian Arabic poetry, from its tenth- and eleventh-century heyday to the fourteenth-century calligraphed verse of Granada's court poet turned chief vizier, Ibn Zamrak, which one can still see on a visit to the Alhambra, the Spanish scholar Emilio García Gómez lamented the expressive thinness of the later work and suggested that it was the price paid for its decorative brilliance, an inevitable outgrowth of the aesthetic of the Andalusian poetic art: "It had to die really like that," he says, "on the walls."

By the same token the biblical quotation in the Hebrew verse can overpower by sheer strength or deception, and one must be alert to the particular spin of the implant, which—its loaded provenance notwithstanding—was used neutrally much of the time, though also for conscious allusive effect, and sometimes in an ironic manner. Shelomoh Delmedigo, a seventeenth-century Italian-Hebrew author, regrets the misguided use of the biblical allusion by the Hebrew poets of his day, saying that it has devolved from an ornament of power and purity to the treacly stuff of a baroque, mannered game—allusion for allusion's sake alone.

And stock phrases lurk—the line between revivification and strain is shifting, and often in the ear of the listener alone, who himself becomes a kind of transmitter. So that problems of reception abound, and spill into the English equation: convention that was once effective turns stale; the link between poet and public weakens; communal and private seem hopelessly split. Translators are tempted to sidestep these obstacles, reducing the verse to prose or a limited imagism, or, in an effort perhaps to overcome these difficulties en masse, inflating their lines with an artificial diction, to account for the non-vernacular nature of the Hebrew (the language of education, encountered from age three on). Slackness here, inadvertent stiffness or comedy there . . . as the poem is swept out to sea.

VOICE

Homogenization: they all look alike to me.

Ibn Gabirol lived during HaNagid's lifetime, yet the poetic distance between the two, despite all they share, is the distance between Whitman and Dickinson. Ibn Gabirol's experience of the language overlapped with his mentor's; his experience of the body was worlds away.

Some eighty-five years separated HaNagid's death from Yehudah Halevi's: Spenser, say, to Dryden. Or Emerson to Robert Lowell.

WHY, WHY NOW

Given the various obstacles to successful translation of the work, the tradition of failure, the cultural disparity, the (real) psychological risks, the stretches of time, the tiny audience—the translator would have to be something of a fool not to ask, at one point or another: Why bother?

Because "the poem must move from reader to reader, reading to reading, to stay alive," as Eliot Weinberger has written. "The poem dies when it has no place to go. Poetry is that which is worth translating," he concludes, correcting Frost's isolationist aphorism. And little in the Hebrew of the last two millennia can approach Ibn Gabirol line by line, for "worth."

And because there is in the poetry of Ibn Gabirol and his peers a rich and pertinent (even postmodern) suspension of time and text; a compelling tension binding the past and present, the personal and that which transcends it; a stunning fusion of nature and the reality of what artifice posits; and an improbable union of the Hebraic and Islamic at root . . . just when it seemed that poetry had lost much of its power to matter—to instruct, delight, nourish, and transport.

X-Ray

An X-ray of the work on the student's table, then, would show its biblical skeleton and its rabbinic ligatures, the influence of Arabic and its cultural graft. An X-ray of these elements of the poem *in motion* would yield only a blur; it would reflect but not reveal the secret sources of the verse, its turning in will and desire, which we can only intuit.

Yhwh

As though the nature of the unpronounceable Name ran through the poem like an underground stream, now a promise, now a ripeness, giving the language constellation, and surfacing when topography allowed.

Sometimes echoed, but never directly heard.

Zygote

Above all, as reader of the Hebrew or English, as translator, scholar, one is trying to keep it fresh—to make it new, a phrase Pound lifted from an Emperor's washbasin, circa 1760 BCE, where (during a drought) it referred not to a Robert Hughesian shock, but to the wheat crop, the annual source of his people's food: to prayer for rain, fertilization, and sustenance.

Wherever one looks in Ibn Gabirol's work and his culture of verse, hybrid creations are taking shape. Forms are giving birth to an infinite variety of similar forms, boundless and self-contained, at once sensuous and stark, not necessarily symbolic, suggestive of something beyond themselves, and meaningful in relation alone. This *is* a poetry of flight, from one version of the real to another. But it is also a war for expression, waged by a man who was "tried seven times in the furnace of fate" and lived only for the truth of his poem.

FROM

THE DIWAN OF
SOLOMON IBN GABIROL

TRUTH SEEKERS TURN

✦

Truth seekers, turn to my poems,
    and you who are ignorant, learn:

they'll teach you hidden wisdom
    and instruct you in all that's arcane.

Don't fall for words that are empty and vain,
    but hold to these poems and you'll hold to faith.

For the weak poem kills the soul of its author—
    while he's still alive, it dies;

where the excellent in memory endures,
    like the new moon, month by month in its rise.

Personal Poems
and Poems of Court

I'M PRINCE TO THE POEM

✦

I'm prince to the poem my slave,
    I'm harp to the court musicians,
my song is a turban for viziers' heads,
    a crown for kings in their kingdoms:

and here I've lived just sixteen years,
    and my heart is like eighty within them.

My words are driven by worry,
   my joy in sighing's put out—
when I see others laughing my heart splits
   for my life as it slips away from me.

"Should a boy of sixteen be sighing, my friend,   5
   and mourning the day of his death,
when he could be strong in his youth,
   with his cheek like a rose in the sun?"

From boyhood my heart has judged me
   and so my soul has been bowed,   10
and it placed understanding and learning across it
   and cut my soul along wrath.

"What good does anxiousness do you?
   Be patient, your wound will heal.
You moan inside your trouble in vain: 15
   What help could you bring with your tears?"

But why should I wait, and how long can I hope
   when the day is full, and the end is far,
and no one in Gilead knows of balm
   for the pain of a plague-stricken man.   20

✦

"Forget about 'if' and 'maybe'
    and listen instead to me;
and don't go reaching for hope,
    and know that time is stingy"
—thus the world rebukes me,   5
    envying me and my song,
carping and seeking to show me
    the future for which my enemies long.
I've always laughed in fate's face,
    though now its laughter's facing me;   10
but why should I fear what it brings
    when it offers me verses daily?
For I'm, indeed, a soul
    that moves man in creation,
and I'm a sphere as well, it's true,   15
    the planets circle through me;
and the world is like my chariot,
    my train fills it completely.
Evil will never enter my heart,
    never cross its threshold.   20

And so I won't complain—
    and yet if I do complain
know that I'll weep and moan
    for wisdom's distance alone.
And so I won't rejoice—   25
    but if I do rejoice
the cause of my joy will be
    only an excellent friend.
A fire burns within me,
    it glows as though in my heart,   30
to offer him, I swear—
    let God here be my witness—

---

my soul's portion and honor,
   and not begrudge his success;
and to see my enemy trampled   35
   like dust beneath my feet;
to place him before me as though
   beneath my sole and heel,
to make him a mark for my mouth's arrows
   and fuel for my fire's meal.   40

✦

A poem of glory and power I'll offer my Maker
  who set the heavens on high with his span,
because he created the language and mouth of man
  and gave them the crown of honor and splendor,
causing their growth in knowledge of wonder the Lord   5
  works in the world and the world-to-come.
Declared the Spaniard Solomon Ben Judah the Small,
  who culled for his people the holy tongue:
Examining the Lord's congregation with all my soul,
  I saw the exiled remnant escaped,   ·   10
found among them the sacred speech destroyed,
  almost wholly in ruins or erased,
given over to languages distant from Hebrew
  and utterly strange to the lips of the Jews,
half of whom speak in the manner of Edom,   15
  and half with the darkening tongue of Qedar,
in their hopelessness drowning, engulfed by the deepening whirl,
  in their ignorance sinking within it like stone—
joining pain for my people to pain through my bones,
  trapped like a fire burning inside me.   20
Knowing the foolish were lost in their groaning, I moaned
  in my heart like a harp or the harp-like sea.
Lacking all vision, living far from their Law,
  they couldn't fathom the simplest inscription.
My Lord, who could save the blind in their drowning?   25
  Who could bring their ship into port?
"Now that your eyes are clear," my heart spoke out,
  "you see that your people are lost . . .
Only you can guide them— give voice to mouths
  gone mute. Surely the Lord will reward you."   30

_____

Pushed, I cowered, seeing that I was still young
    and easily given to anger and fury:
Reason in youth is dismissed categorically;
    what can a boy of nineteen really do?
So said my heart, when a dream like a secret came through me,   35
    and I heard a voice from the city call me—
taunting my spirit—during the night as it told me:
    The hand of the Lord will surely strengthen you
under your burden; your youth doesn't excuse you.
    It isn't the elders who hold up the kingdom.   40
Viewing this image my confidence grew; and I knew
    very well in my heart what the Lord
wanted, and set my mind to make of this treatise a

    xyst as fine as my hand was able,
yearning to forge through this book of our grammar a   45
    zone of repair for the language of Cain . . .

MY CONDITION WORSENED

✦

My condition worsened and worsened my grief,
    and in its wake my strength waned—
but then your letter arrived with its call
    and its pleasures eased my pain.

So I'm writing you not with news of my illness,
    but to ask instead a friend's forgiveness
because I haven't been able to visit.
    I swear, I'll come if I have to crawl:

for I know that the minute I see your face
    I'll be healed, as my grief withdraws.

ALL MY DESIRE

✦

All my desire and hope is with you:
  I long just for your company.
My stomach churns and I moan for you,
  who drives my sleep away from me,

as though you alone could cure me,
  if, in my illness, you'd visit;
if ever my heart thought to betray you
  my anger would rise up against it.

If only my heart-in-its-chest were glass—
  you'd see my love within it.

✦

Take, my lord, this sweetness in hand,
    and forget about all of your longing—
it's blushing like a bride on both sides as her breasts
    are first caressed by her husband.
She's an orphan, and has neither father nor sister,
    and she's far from her home and kin.
Her friends envied her going the day she was stripped
    from her branch and cried: "Bring
greetings to Isaac, your lord . . . Bless you—
    soon you'll be kissing his lips. . . ."

THE ROSE

✦

With the rose blush of your cheeks like shields,
    you're like a hero or soldier,
and with your arrows and spear which pierce me,
    in pain all night I wander.

What would atone for your servant's transgression:
    Could I offer a bull, or slaughter a lamb?

SEE THE SUN

✦

See the sun gone red toward evening
as though it were wearing a crimson dress,
   stripping the edges of north and south
and, in violet, lining the wind from the west:

and the earth—left in its nakedness—
takes refuge in the shadow of night, and rests,
   and then the skies go black, as though
covered in sackcloth, for Yequtiel's death.

THEY ASKED ME AS THOUGH
THEY WERE MYSTIFIED

◆

They asked me as though they were mystified:
Is it true your friend's hands are like clouds?
And I told them: They were tied for being too open,
and for goodness of heart of hunger he died.

ON LEAVING SARAGOSSA

✦

My tongue cleaves to the roof of my mouth,
  my throat is parched with pleading,
my heart is loud, my mind confused
  with pain and continual grieving.
My sorrow swells and will not bear   5
  sleep's gift to my eyes:
How long will this rage and yearning
  like fire inside me burn?

Who could I turn to for help,
  who could I tell of my plight?   10
If only someone would offer me comfort,
  someone have mercy, take hold of my hand,
I'd pour out my heart before him
  and manage to reach but the edge of my grief—
though maybe in putting my sorrow to words   15
  my heart's rushing would find release.

You who seek my peace, come near—
  and hear the roar of my heart like the sea.
If your heart has grown hard it will soften,
  faced with the hate that faces me.   20
How could you call me alive,
  when you know of my distress;
is it nothing to live among people
  who can't tell their right hand from left?

I'm buried, but not in a graveyard,   25
  in the coffin of my own home.
I suffer with neither father nor mother,
  indigent, young, and alone—
on my own without even a brother,
  not a friend apart from my mind: 30

I mix my blood with my tears,
   and my tears into my wine.

I'll be consumed in my thirst
   before my thirst for friendship is quenched,
as though the sky and its hosts were arrayed   35
   between me and all that I crave.
I'm treated here as a stranger, despised—
   as though I were living with ostriches,
caught between crooks and the fools
   who think their hearts have grown wise.   40

One hands you venom to drink,
   another strokes you with words
and lies in wait in his heart,
   addressing you: "Please, my lord . . ."
—people whose fathers were not fit   45
   to be dogs to my flock of sheep—
their faces have never known blushing,
   unless they were painted with crimson cheeks.

They're giants in their own eyes,
   grasshoppers here in mine.   50
They quarrel with all my teachings and talk,
   as though I were speaking Greek.
"Speak," they carp, "as the people speak,
   and we'll know what you have to say"—
and now I'll break them like dirt or like straw,   55
   my tongue's pitchfork thrust into their hay.

If your ears aren't able to hear me,
   what good could my harmonies do?
Your necks aren't worthy of wearing
   my golden crescents and jewels.   60
If these boors would only open their mouths
   to the rain that descends from my clouds,
my essence would soon come through them
   with its cinnamon scent and myrrh.

Have compassion for wisdom, compassion for me,   65
   surrounded by neighbors like these—

---

people for whom the knowledge of God
  is a matter of spirits and ghosts.
Therefore I mourn and wail,
  and make my bed in ashes,   70
and bow my head like a reed and fast
  on Monday and Thursday and Monday.

Why should I wait any longer
  with nothing like hope in sight?
Let my eyes in the world wander,   75
  they'll never glimpse what I want:
Death grows daily sweeter to me,
  the world's gossip means less and less;
if my heart returns to that path,
  thinking its intrigue might offer success,   80

whatever I do will come round,
  my scheming against me revolve.
So my soul refuses its glory,
  for its glory brings only disgrace.
I'll never rejoice again in the world,   85
  my pride will find there no pleasure,
though the stars of Orion call me to come
  and take up my station among them.

For the world has always been
  like a yoke around my neck—   90
and what good does it do me to linger
  by blindness and grief beset?
My soul in my death will delight
  if it leads to the Lord and his rest—
I'd put an end to my life,   95
  an end to this dwelling in flesh.

My delight's in the day of my downfall,
  my downfall the day of my greatest delight,
and I long for heart's understanding—
  the exhaustion of sinew and strength.   100
For a sigh settles into repose,
  and my leanness leads to my meat,

---

and as long as I live I'll seek out in search
    of all that the elder Solomon preached:

perhaps the revealer of depths, the Lord,
    will show me where wisdom lurks—
for it alone is my reward,
    my portion and the worth of my work.

THE MOON WAS CUT

✦

The moon was cut in the heavens' heights
    like beryl embedded in amethyst,
and a star in its spell was fixed and hovered
    like ellipses begun in parenthesis—

and the hair was raised on the flesh of the wise
    who saw there the name of the Lord . . .

MY HEART THINKS
AS THE SUN COMES UP

✦

My heart thinks as the sun comes up
  that what it does is wise:
   as earth borrows its light,
    as pledge it takes the stars.

✦

Come, my friend, and friend to the spheres,
    come, we'll rest by fields as we go—
for winter has passed, and again we hear
    the call of swifts and doves.
We'll lie in the shadow of the apple and palm,   5
    pomegranate trees and citrus.
We'll walk in the shade of the grapevine's trellis,
    longing for sight of illustrious faces
high on the hill over town in the palace
    with massive foundations and towering walls.   10
Around them galleries run looking out,
    while rose-filled courtyards open within:
the rooms there are lavishly made
    and lined with carved arabesques and screens.

Onyx and marble cover the floors   15
    and gateways too many to count can be seen.
The doors are like those of an ivory mansion,
    reddened like cedar in the Temple's halls,
and panes of glass are inlaid above them,
    windows where the planets and sunlight can pass.   20
There's a dome like Solomon's palanquin there
    within which jeweled mosaics are hung,
and they seem to spin and like crystal revolve,
    like sapphire, ruby, and mother-of-pearl—
this by day—and at dusk it recalls   25
    the panoplied sky with its stars in array:
the hearts of all who enter are raised,
    the sorrows of the bitter and poor fade away.

My troubles vanished when it came into view,
    and my heart in its straits took comfort—   30

I was nearly lifted away with joy,
    as though on the wings of an eagle.
There was also a basin like Solomon's sea,
   · though it wasn't set upon oxen:
lions were posted as spouts instead,   35
    as though they were roaring for prey,
dispersing the spring they held within them
    as rivers ran from their mouths.
And deer lined the channels nearby—
    hollow where the stream flowed through—   40
to moisten the ground in the flowering beds
    and bring fresh water to where the reeds grew:

and they carried their water to the bed of myrtles,
    whose branches blossomed in freshness—
their scent was the scent of choice perfume,   45
    as though they'd been scented with myrrh.
And birds sang from the uppermost boughs,
    looking out over the palms,
and the fine shoots of the budding lilies,
    and those of the camphor and nard,   50
one overcoming the other in boasting—
    all in excellence before our eyes—
and it seemed as though the camphor was saying:
    "Our whiteness outshines the sun and moon,"
while the doves moaned and cooing explained: 55
    "We rule with the rings around our necks,

we lure others' hearts with their spell—
    —for they're more precious than crystal. . . ."
And virgins came, and the marvelous deer
    covered their splendor with splendor,   60
and over the others they lorded their glory
    for they're like young gazelles.
When the sun started rising across them I said:
    Be still, don't go any further!
Admit there's a lord who darkens your light   65
    with a glow that cancels the heavens',
before whom kings in their majesty bow,
    reducing their viziers' honor.

Through him all kings derive their power,
    all the princes consult him—   70

they look to him as their leader in counsel,
    like a lion surrounded by oxen.
Among them he reigns like an angel of god
    when word from the Lord isn't heard;
he guides his sheep to quiet pastures,   75
    and nothing lacks from his flock;
a priceless soul, a gem to the sky,
    he fulfills his pledges without any vows;
he's a man whose eye with giving's not dimmed,
    whose rain is never withheld,   80
whose words to his work and deeds are bound
    as crowns are bound to the heads of kings.
As rivers in time are drawn to the sea,
    to him all the princes come:

he's been set as though over the earth   85
    —and against the many he's one.

WINTER WITH ITS INK

◆

Winter with its ink of showers and rain,
with its pen of lightning and palm of clouds,
   wrote a letter of purple and blue
     over the beds of the garden.

No artist in his cunning could measure
   his work beside it—and so,
     when earth longed for the sky
it embroidered the spread of its furrows like stars.

THE GARDEN

✦

Its beads of dew hardened still,
    he sends his word to melt them;
      they trickle down the grapevine's stem
        and its wine seeps into my blood.

The beds blossom, and open before us   5
    clasps of their whitening buds,
      sending a fragrance up to our faces,
        as we wander out to the myrtles.

As you go, each flower lends you a petal—
    a wing so you won't crush it;   10
      and the sun's face glows like a bride
        whose jewels shine in her glow.

Through its circuit, daily, she glides,
    though no one at all pursues her—
      and so we think it a king's chariot   15
        drawn by galloping horses.

As it passes over the garden you notice
    the beds now coated in silver,
      and then when the day declines it lines
        their border with a shimmering gold.   20

In its sinking, soon, you find yourself thinking
    it's bowing, before its Maker;
      as it swiftly sets it seems to be veiled
        in darkening red by the Lord.

THE FIELD

✦

The storm-clouds lowed above us like bulls.
Autumn was angry, and its face darkened
and put them to chase like wisps of wool,
   like a ship's captain blasting its horn.

The heavens went black in a thickening mist,
as the morning stars and their light were absorbed,
then the sun with its wing whisked them across
   the earth until they split and it burst.

The wind beat at the sheets of rain,
and the clouds were cut into threads reaching down
into the world below—drenching
   ridges, preparing the furrows for sowing.

On the hills, hidden grasses emerged
like secrets a man had long withheld:
all winter the clouds wept until suddenly
   life again swept through the trees of the field.

THE BEE

✦

Hear, O Israel the Lord is one . . .
that ye remember and do all my commandments.

Take, little bee, your time with your song,
    in your flight intoning the prayer called "Hear"—
declaring and stretching "the Lord is *one*,"
    raising on high the hum of *remember*
to he who put honey under your tongue
    and gave you the gall to drive out foes.
It's true, in your eyes you're small—
    but your being transcends *the things that swarm,*
and the choicest words are yours. Your merit
    refines you: you're pure as the birds of the air.

ISN'T THE SKY

✦

My friend, isn't the sky
   above like a garden,
its stars like lilies budding,
and the moon like a chalice on high?

THE LILY

◆

I

Haven't you seen the lily
　　whose body resembles its dress—
before every eye it withdraws
　　like a bride by her wedding-night bed,

　　or like a young girl dancing,
　　　　her hands clasped over her head.

II

　　Haven't you seen the lily
　　　　whose body resembles its dress—
　　before every eye it withdraws
　　　　like a bride by her wedding-night bed,

　　　　or like a young girl wailing,
　　　　　　her hands clasped over her head.

NOW THE THRUSHES

✦

Now the thrushes have gathered
   to sing on the sprigs without thinking;
  how could you hear their song in the trees
and not be glad with all you've got and start drinking?

   What could be better than branches renewed
    by time, with buds peeking
  into the garden? When a wind comes on
they nod to each other, it seems, as though they were speaking.

THE APPLE: II

✦

Take a bite from that
    shimmering figure,
like emerald here,
    and there like beryl,
or ruby-like now,   5
    and now like crystal,
its aspect changing—
    as though it were ill
at first with a flush
    and then with a pallor,   10
as though it were really
    a scroll of silver
encased in gold,
    a virgin who'd never
known a lover,   15
    and yet whose breasts
were ready to suckle.
    When men arrive
with their swords and desire
    to strike at its cord,   20
it falls to the grass
    and lands at their feet:
they bend to a knee
    and take it in hand,
then raise it   25
    to their lips and eat.

THE LIGHTNING

✦

Let lightning the color of crystal
    send on a nursemaid to the garden of myrtles
and visit the beds of spices and hold
    the clouds close by so they won't drift off:

Let it strike soon above the small trees,   5
    bent in despair beneath the skies,
whose clouds long to hover until
    they've quenched the thirsty soil's soul.

I witnessed the wonders of God when my eyes
    saw the clouds shedding their tears   10
as the garden began to sparkle. They scattered
    their drops like blood being dashed at the altar,

inking designs on the blossoms' skin
    in settings of crimson and linen-like whiteness.
Then the beds of herbs offered a scent   15
    like myrrh before the clouds that had burst.

✦

When they saw the flowers in bloom they said:
"They're covered with the colors of an illness but well."

✦

If only, my friends, you had seen your servant,
    moaning in the shadows of the grove alone.   20
If I die bearing my grief before you,
    bury my heart beneath the best vine.

"Don't bother us with your precious troubles
    just because love has hold of your soul.
You're stricken with the look of a fine gazelle—   25
    if she spoke it would probably kill you!"

Don't mention or stir up desire, my friends:
    young love sears, and tortures like fire.

THE LIP OF THE CUP

✦

The lip of the cup kissing mine
   in my friend's hand was like the sun;
      a fire burned in the vine's water,
         devouring me but not my gown.

No eye had ever seen a finer   5
   mirror making a man in my image:
      whose sweetness said to me, silently: "Stop,
         before you're struck by my splendor.

How could you liken my light to the sun,
   whose might I surpass by far—   10
      when its body is naked and bare,
         and mine is covered with gems?

How could you ever compare
   my flow to a man who steals my desire?"
      We drank it and lightning flashed and drove   15
         the darkness out of my dwelling

and replaced it with crystal and onyx,
   dispersing my sleep through its rooms.
      It gloried in gold above a cloud   20
         which gathered golden chains in my home,

and the rains were cold as the snow of Senir
   or Samuel the Levite's poems.

I'D GIVE UP MY SOUL ITSELF

✦

I'd give up my soul itself for one
    whose light is like the sun:
He softly entreated me, saying: "Drink,
    and banish your grief and longing—"
the wine poured from the beaker's spout
    a viper in the mouth of a griffon.

And I answered him: "Could one contain the sun
    within a jar that's broken?"
But my heart didn't yet know of its power
    to utterly crush its burden—
which was lying safe and secure inside it,
    like the king on his bed in Bashan.

✦

Tell the boy whose cheeks are gently
    held by the curl of his hair:
How can the gold of noon enfold
    the first blush of morning?

Don't hold it against Agur for saying
    that charm is false and beauty vapor.
Your cheeks are ample proof of the truth
    that the Lord's ways are inscrutable.

BE SMART WITH YOUR LOVE

✦

"Be smart with your love," my friend chided,
"find solid ground for the circle it clears."
And while I was probing love's wisdom,
Adina beside me was poised as a queen,
saying: "How long do you think you can hide

your love, refusing to let it be seen—
when you know the harvest is gathered with hatchets,
by putting the sickle and scythe to the corn
. . . and Jesse's David, at love's extreme,
cried out and sent for Avigal while she mourned."

ALL IN RED

✦

All in red, and come from Edom,
   settle down and be still:
By god, I love you well—
   but not like the men of Sodom.

SHARDS

✦

I

in love astray
a single truth among thousands
        your friends
        your secret to her
the people of Jacob

II

and the doves moan

III

who will raise me up from the well of her mouth and who

IV

A fawn grazing

V

they begged me to remove

VI

I asked him who he was moaning for

VII

Try the ships of the deep and their whirl.
You'll find what you reap unbearable

THE APPLE: III

✦

Is there anything like it on earth,
  gold without and silver within?
When we looked, its flesh went pale,
  as though we'd filled it with sin—

like a girl fleeing a circle of men
  as a blush came over her skin.

YOU'VE STOLEN MY WORDS

✦

You've stolen my words and denied it—
   lied and broken down walls.
Did you think you could soar with my songs
   or use them to hide your flaws?

Could a man scale the heavens
   and eclipse the light of the world?
It's all, as I see it, quite simple:
   can the Nile be drained with a pail?

THE ALTAR OF SONG

✦

Your answer betrays your transgression,
your words are empty, your verse is weak—
you've stolen a few of my rhymes,
    but your spirit failed: you're meek.

Try taking on wisdom's discipline,
instead of poetry's altar and pose:
for as soon as you start your ascent,
    your most private parts are exposed.

✦

Tell the prince who has risen in power,
of whom glorious things have been said in the world:
   "In you my heart put its trust in vain,
and where it had hoped, and longed, was shamed
like the Song's daughter opening to her lover
   who'd slipped away and was gone."

WHAT'S TROUBLING YOU,
MY SOUL

✦

What's troubling you, my soul,
    silent as a captured king—
that you've drawn in the wings of your hymns
    and drag them around in your suffering?
How long will your heart be in mourning?   5
    When will your weeping give way?
One who clings so long to his grieving
    within it wears out a grave.
Be still, my soul, before the Lord—
    be still, but don't despair: 10

Hold on until he gazes
    down from his throne in heaven;
close your doors behind you and hide
    until your anger has faded.
Whether you thirst or go hungry   15
    hardly merits attention:
the rewards to come will be greater—
    you'll count them all soon as a blessing.
Distance yourself from the world's concern,
    don't waste away in its prison . . .   20

And you, earth, in your fickleness,
    why all the pomp and procession?
My soul is sick of your pageantry,
    you parade before me in vain.
Hold on to your gifts, for tomorrow   25
    you'll take back whatever you've given.
Return, my soul, return to the Lord,
    restore your heart to its place:

---

pour out your tears like water,
    before him plead your cause—   30

perhaps he'll see to release you
    from the dungeon where you brood
with boors you've come to abhor,
    who can't understand what you've written,
or determine what's worth preserving   35
    and what would be better erased—
who can't hear what you're saying,
    or know if it's true or mistaken.
Rejoice in the day you leave them
    and offer your thanks on an altar.   40

Others elsewhere will know
    the worth of the person you are.
Rise, my troubled soul,
    rise up and take yourself there,
rise up and live where people   45
    will hold you in proper regard.
Leave your father and mother,
    and save your love for the Lord.
Rise up and race in pursuit of that place,
    be swift as an eagle or deer.   50

When trouble and anguish confront you,
    don't let panic consume you.
Whether you'll need to take on
    mountain, gorge, or wave,
put Andalusia behind you,   55
    and do it without delay—
until you've set foot near the Nile,
    the Euphrates or the Land of the Jordan,
where you'll walk in the power of pride,
    be lifted and held in awe.   60

Why, my troubled soul,
    why languish there in your longing?
Is it leaving your people or household
    that holds you back in your grief?

Keep them in mind as you go   65
    and your sorrow will find relief,
for the Lord's shadow is with you,
    whether you leave or stay—
and I'll be considered a stranger,
    until my bones are worn away.   70

Remember the fathers in exile,
    keep them always in mind:
Abram and tent-dwelling Jacob,
    and Moses who fled in haste:
each in distance took refuge   75
    in the Lord who rides the sky.
Let the land of my rivals behind me
    be stricken with Deborah's curse—
with brimstone and fire and salt—
    let its yield be consumed in the mire.   80

Woe to the land of my enemies,
    woe unto you when I'm gone.
I have no portion among you,
    whether you're kind or hard.
My heart's desire is distance;   85
    how far will we manage to go—
here we're trapped among beasts
    and I sigh for the state I've come to,
I sigh for these men in their smugness,
    numb to my designs;   90

sigh for the time I've spent with them
    and all my reliance upon them.
Sigh for instransigent time,
    whose stubbornness I can't fathom;
sigh for this world and its smallness   95
    which can't contain my longing.
Until I make my way out
    I'm in it on my own—
bitterness drives my poem
    and God knows where I'm going.   100

THE PEN

✦

Naked without either cover or dress,
utterly soulless, and hollow—
from its mouth come wisdom and prudence,
and in ambush it kills like an arrow.

WHAT'S WITH YOU

✦

What's with you
    in your secret network,
riddled with worms like a gourd?

With great delight
    you badmouth the beggar
you didn't know was a priest to the Lord.

GOD-FEARING MEN

✦

God-fearing men are like
     magnificent mountains
  even when
they've been wounded and beaten down.

But liars are small, like nothing
    at all, my friends,
    though they be legion
and like illness's lesions abound.

YOUR SOUL STRAINS
AND YOU SIGH

✦

"Your soul strains and you sigh—
   how long will you keep at your notions?
You moan hoping like fire to rise,
   whose smoke is most of its offering and motion.

Do you think you're a heavenly sphere   5
   over the earth and its hordes?
Is your mind like the depths of the sea
   where the world's foundations are moored?

How could you reach what your heart desires
   when you scorn even the stars on high?   10
Once you've found your knowledge you'll find
   the world's elect are last in its line—

so turn your heart from wisdom's course
   and your way here on earth will be fine."

✦

My soul, friends—grieve for this,   15
   and offer me comfort as well in that grief—
my soul thirsts for a man of discernment
   where thirst can't possibly find relief.

Search among thousands of men,
   perhaps one's heard of wisdom's trace—   20
if the world has been unjust to your friend,
   in his heart he'll spit in its face.

If it can't see the light that I offer,
   let it grope about in its darkness—
if tomorrow it wants to appease me,   25
   in turn I'll forgive its injustice.

Sphere of Fortune—turn and keep
   the hand of time from the head of the wise;
you've brought about injustice enough,
   reducing our cedars to gourds. 30

Weaken the feeble who weigh on me more
   than all the stones of the world;
cut off the line of those who mock me
   asking where wisdom's faithful have gone.

If the world were to judge them with justice, 35
   time wouldn't leave them a bone:
they've been busy with rest and sloth and have reached
   its delights by chance alone.

They've lured away the sun's daughters
   and given birth to folly. 40
Why contend against my mind,
   you thistles and nettles around me?

If wisdom is small in your eyes,
   in hers you're nothing at all;
she's obscure and distant to you because 45
   your hearts have long been enclosed in their cauls.

Here—I'll open her arks:
   let's see what treasures they hold . . .
How could I ever abandon wisdom
   when the Lord between us has formed a pact? 50

Or how could it ever neglect me when
   it's been all along like the mother I've lacked,
and I've been like a bracelet around her wrist,
   a bead strung on her necklace?

How could you tell me to strip off these charms, 55
   or deny her throat these jewels?
My heart is glad in her alone,
   for all her pleasures are pure.

It isn't good for my soul to be
    like the sun darkened by darkening clouds,
so as long as I live I'll lift that soul
    up toward its dwelling beyond their mist—

for I've vowed that I will not rest—
    until I've known her lord.

DON'T LOOK BACK

✦

Don't, my son, look back,
   or bother with right and left;
and don't say: "Tomorrow I'll die
so why should I walk around bereft?"

Remember the day to come
   when your flesh will be eaten and gone,
when over your head the plows will plow
as the farmers make their furrows long.

You sinned well enough in your youth.
   Don't drag its legacy on.

✦

If this life's joy only ends in mourning
and its respite gives way to failure and pain,
and a person's existence is a passing shadow
suddenly shattered and crushed like an urn,

what can we hope for apart from the Lord?
All that we do without him is vain.

WHEN YOU FIND YOURSELF ANGRY

✦

When you find yourself angry
remember the Lord Almighty who holds
    your spirit and strength in His hand:

then turn from your wrath
and know that the God of heaven drives
    the arrogant out of his land.

I AM THE MAN

◆

I am the man who harnessed his spirit
and will not rest with his promise unkept:
    a man whose mind has been split by his mind,
whose soul has sickened of its dwelling in flesh.

From earliest youth he held to wisdom   5
though tried seven times in the furnace of fate,
    which razed all that he built
        and uprooted all that he planted,

as it broke through all his defenses.
As misfortune burned he'd approach it—   10
    even as destiny hemmed him in—
seeking the limits of wisdom and discipline,

wanting the source of knowledge's treasure:
    know, however, that no one will ever
        discover the mystery's secrets   15
    until his flesh begins to give way.

I'd gained a grain of discernment,
when time came on and exacted its price—
    and now for as long as I live I'll ride
        out in search of wisdom,   20

even as the day won't saddle my mount;
my heart, I vow, won't weaken with time,
    or break its vows, it will follow them out.
And know, my friends, I've feared what was coming,

    and nothing comes that fear doesn't bring. . . .   25

It was night and the sky was clear,
    and the moon was pure at its center
        as it led me along discernment's sphere,
teaching me by its light and direction—

---

though as my heart went out to that light   30
    I feared extended misfortune,
like a father's feeling for his firstborn son.
And the wind sent a cover of clouds across it,

wrapping its face in a mask—
as though craving the currents inside them,   35
    it leaned on the clouds till they ran.
        And the sky was clothed in darkness,

and it seemed that the moon had died
    —its grave a vapor . . .
Then the thickened heavens wept for it,   40
    like the nation of Aram weeping

    for its prophet Bilaam,
and the night put on its mail of gloom
and the thunder stabbed it with lightning,
    which flew out toward the horizon   45

as though it were laughing,
    obeying the thunder's commands:
    it spread its wings like a bat,
and the ravens of darkness fled when they saw it.

Then the Lord closed in on my thoughts   50
blocking my heart's desire inside it,
    holding my heart in cords of darkness,
like the man besieged who stirred and broke free.

I no longer hope for the moon, my friend,
which thickest dark has replaced,   55
as though the clouds had envied my soul,
    and taken its light away from me—

but when its face appears I'll rejoice
    like a servant recalled by his lord.

◆

As a soldier in battle has his sword destroyed   60
    and falters as he runs, then stumbles,
so is man who is hounded by struggle,
    though Venus be home to his shrine.

AND DON'T BE ASTONISHED

✦

And don't be astonished by a man whose flesh
  has longed for wisdom and prevailed;
he's soul encircling the physique,
  and a sphere in which all is held.

THE TREE

✦

As the roots of a tree give length to its branches,
   a man's understanding yields virtue in speech,
and a person's discernment dictates his grief
   in his seeing the terror his future moves toward.
Anxiousness pitched its tent in my heart,   5
   my thoughts, stretched taut and staked, are its cords—
and it swore wherever that heart would travel,
   it would always pursue on the path it explored.

The world placed grief like a cup in my hand
   and forced me to drink down to the dregs,   10
and time through my spirit opened its wounds
   for I'm like a soul to its bodies' flesh.
My head has met with cloudfuls of trouble
   and torrents of rain across me have swept,
and the asp of the world bit at my heels   15
   while I, in my youth, played by its den.

It ordained for me days of quarrel and strife,
   and though I've had them, it isn't yet through,
for as I've risen over wisdom's heights
   I've seen the eagles fail as they flew,   20
and I've been like an eagle that climbed in flight,
   its wings breaking apart as it rose—
and still in knowledge's sea I'd swim
   to gather its crystals, its onyx and gold.

Knowledge's depths for me are sufficient;   25
   I'd happily live alone in its straits,
like a craftsman hard at work at his art,
   or a writer bent over his books in search.
How could a man disobey his heart
   listening to friends who chide him, saying: 30

"As his wisdom wanders, heart's terror draws near,
    and all from around his home disappear,

he's wasting away his life and his mind,
    exhausted from struggling in chains.
He sees what's wrong with the people around him—   35
    to the flaws of his own he's blind. . . ."
But how could someone put knowledge aside
    when he's already turned his back on the world,
and long delivered his flesh to his spirit
    and driven his heart to rule over time.   40

He sheds these people like a viper its skin,
    caught in a foul summer wind—
his soul has closed the breaches of heaven,
    through the stars of the Bear soon he'll spring.
His discourse is wondrous to mind and he reaches   45
    the sun's chambers, where he sets his shrine—
across the leaves of his twenty books
    with ease he tramples the stars of Orion.

With a heart encircling the sphere of earth
    he fills the space of the six directions,   50
it extends to his mind's most distant ambition,
    keeping his vows on his mission and quest—
if it asked for so much as a moment's relief
    I'd tear it to pieces and burn each shred.
Tell me if I haven't been strict with instruction,   55
    if fire within my heart doesn't rage,

and I'll ask it: Is that the end of your learning?
    is that the limit of your powerful will?
Tread the waves of wisdom's sea,
    and split the fields to its slopes of mind,   60
and know that in your ascent of that height
    I'll ask you to weigh out its dust by the grain,
and I will not rest on that mountain of wisdom
    until I've hunted and slaughtered its lions.

For I have an eye that ranges the world   65
    and sees the secrets of other men's hearts,

and my heart's gates have always been open
  and my poems' blades are sevenfold sharp;
and my hand is always bound to time—
  I bind the light of its days and its darkness,
and I've made the robe of night my mantle
  and sewn its edge to the edge of dawn.

From my heart's eyes I strip the blinds
  when dusk's bands of darkness are hung,
and the sun sinks and night rises
  to cover the earth with its bulk like a dragon,
and the moon puts on its breastplate of gold,
  its brilliance and splendor absorbed from the sun,
and across its face it stretches a cloud
  like a mask as though it feared my glow.

At the door to its tent it's set like a prince
  amassing his troops and ready for war,
and the moon is poised like a king while around him
  like fires to warm him his men are deployed.
He scatters his stars about like a shepherd
  sending his flock across a field,
and they flee when they see the day's chariot
  —one by one to dawn they yield;

and night anoints its head with dew
  for its hair has all been shaven clean,
and the morning star unfurls its light
  like a weaver stretching his cloth on a beam.
And because I'm always in search of knowledge
  my nights are joined to my days without seam.
It's true I once hoped to find many friends,
  for friends in life can be like a cure,

but I returned from friendship's arms
  like a reaper from fields of his wind-blasted corn.
One who'd make friends among my peers
  sets his money on the antlers of deer:
"Choose peace," they say, "over war, and rest,
  even *if* your forces are strong"—

70

75

80

85

90

95

100

but no one alive is saved from distress
    like one who's been tried seven times by the world,

so broken by evil and in poverty bound   105
    that even his bitterness quenches his thirst.
How could a man compel his heart
    to bow before this hay and its thistles,
and why should I choose to dwell among fools
    when wisdom has drawn me into its chambers.   110
How could I weary of seeking admission
    when its gates have been opened already by words?

The Lord created this people mindless
    and fashioned its bulls without any horns,
and every boor now puffs himself up   115
    as though by right of just having-been-born:
they set their hearts after wealth alone,
    and worship gold in place of the Lord,
but my God has a day when the stubborn and false
    will be like stubble within a great storm—   120

and the honest before him will exult and prevail
    while the insolent wither and fail.

IF YOU'D LIVE AMONG MEN

◆

If you'd live among men on earth forever,
   if your soul's afraid of the steel fires of hell,
despise what the world rushes to honor
   and don't be swayed by fame, family, or wealth.

Let neither shame nor poverty distract you.
   Die childless, like Seled, Judah's kin.
And know your soul within you as well as you can:
   it alone will last of your sinew and skin.

WHY ARE YOU FRIGHTENED

✦

Why are you troubled and frightened, my soul?
Be still and dwell where you are.
Since the world to you is small as a hand,
    you won't, my storm, get far.

Better than pitching from court to court
is sitting before the throne of your Lord;
if you distance yourself from others you'll flourish
    and surely see your reward.

If your desire is like a fortified city,
a siege will bring it down in time:
You have no portion here in this world—
    so wake for the world to come.

A KITE

✦

My pain is severe and my wounds won't heal,
   my strength wanes and my vigor gives way.
I know of no refuge, nowhere I might flee—
   no place to find any rest for my soul.

Three things converge to consume
   my failing frame, my spirit, and being:
continual sorrow, estrangement, and sin,
   and who could stand before them alone?

Am I, my Lord, a monster or sea?
   Are my bones made of iron, or my flesh of brass,
that trouble and intrigue should come without end
   as though it were all that fate had bequeathed?

Would you ask after only *my* carelessness,
   as though on others you'd placed no demands?
See the affliction and work of your servant
   whose soul is like a kite in a snare—

and I'll live as your slave forever and ever,
   and seek no freedom beyond your command.

AND HEART'S HOLLOW

◆

And heart's hollow
  and wisdom is blocked;
  the body apparent
    but soul obscured:
those who wake in the world
  for gain come to corruption.
On earth a man rejoices in nothing. . . .

The servant, soon, will slaughter his master,
the handmaidens turn on their mistress and queen;
a daughter will rise—against her own mother,
  a son—against his father's name.
  My eye in the world dismisses
    what others most love,
  and all is labor, a plowing for worms.
    Slime—to slime returns.
    Soul—ascends to soul.

I LOVE YOU

✦

I love you with the love a man
  has for his only son—
with his heart and his soul and his might;
and I take great pleasure in your mind
    as you take the mystery on   5
  of the Lord's act in creation—
though the issue is distant and deep,
and who could approach its foundation?

But I'll tell you something I've heard
and let you dwell on its strangeness: 10
  sages have said that the secret
    of being owes all
to the all who has all in his hand:
He longs to give form to the formless
  as a lover longs for his friend.   15
And this is, maybe, what the prophets
meant when they said that he worked
  all for his own exaltation.

I've offered you these words—
now show me how you'll raise them.   20

Poems of Devotion

BEFORE MY BEING

✦

Before my being your mercy came through me,
   bringing existence to nothing to shape me.
Who is it conceived of my form—and who
   cast it then in a kiln to create me?
Who breathed soul inside me—and who
   opened the belly of hell and withdrew me?
Who through youth brought me this far?
   Who with wisdom and wonder endowed me?
I'm clay cupped in your hands, it's true;
   it's you, I know, not I who made me.
I'll confess my sin and will not say
   the serpent's ways, or evil seduced me.
How could I hide my error from you when
   before my being your mercy came through me?

THREE THINGS

✦

Three things meet in my eyes
    and keep the thought of you always before me:
the skies, which make me think of your Name,
    as they bear faithful witness for me;

the place where I stand, which brings my mind
    back to the hand that set it beneath me;
and bless, my soul, my Lord at all times
    for heart's reflection within me.

I LOOK FOR YOU

✦

I look for you early,
my rock and my refuge,
offering you worship
morning and night;
before your vastness
I come confused
and afraid for you see
the thoughts of my heart.

What could the heart
and tongue compose,
or spirit's strength
within me to suit you?
But song soothes you
and so I'll give praise
to your being as long
as your breath-in-me moves.

✦

Forget your grief
  and longing, my soul:
    Why go in fear
of earth's sorrows?
    Your body tomorrow   5
    will lie in Sheol,
forgotten as though
    it never was. . . .
    Learn and be wise—
tremble before   10
    the promise of death.
    Trust in his ways—
you may just save
    your self in return
      to your God and maker,   15
your master and Lord—
    whose account of your action
    will shape your reward.

Why, why be
  distraught and appalled,   20
    abject in a world
the spirit leaves
    as the body gives way?
    When you return
to the dust of your birth,   25
    you'll take with you none
      of your honor and wealth,
which will drive you on
    like a bird to its nest,
      on to your Lord,   30
whose account of your action
    will shape your reward.

Why conceal your
    self on a road
        where majesty turns   35
to utter abasement?
    The promise it holds
        is a bow that's drawn—
its treasure a lie—
    its refinement loss.   40
        It will simply dissolve
like a wound in pus
    you leave to others.
        What good could your riches
do for your Lord,   45
    whose account of your action
        will shape your reward?

Life's vine
    is tended by death,
        whose watch extends   50
over the vineyard's
    length and breadth.
        Return, my soul,
and seek your creator—
    the day is short   55
        and his court far off—
and bread is enough
    for you in transgression.
        Lie in sorrow
and dwell on the grave,   60
    and fear the day
        of judgment to follow
before your Lord—
    whose account of your action
        will shape your reward.   65

Wretched and poor,
    cower like a pigeon—
        but always remember

the rest to come,
   and know the eternal
     place of the Lord.
Weep and plead
   always before him—
     obtain his favor.
And then his chamber
   angels will bring you
     into your garden
at last with the Lord,
   whose account of your action
     will shape your reward.

THE HOUR OF SONG

✦

I've set my shelter
   with you in my awe and fear
     and in despair
established your name as a fortress;
   I looked to the right
and left and no one was near—
    and into your hands
I committed my loneness. . . .

I give you my portion
   of the world's worth,
    of all my labor
you're my desire and cause.
   And here out of love
in you my mind is immersed:
    in song's hour
the work of my worship is yours.

TWO THINGS MEET IN ME

✦

Two things meet in me,
    alike in kind,
and in me now stand
    guard in my mind:
my tongue which would hasten   5
    to speak of your glory
and my heart which knows
    and beholds the sublime.
But your servants have failed
    to unravel the story   10
of your greatness, so how
    could man in his shame?
As you were offered
    lean and fattened
pigeons and bulls,   15
    by hearts that were full
of right intention—   ·
    so I bring my
prayer for your pleasure,
    like an offering brought   20
through vision or labor.
    My spirit and soul
in your praise are entwined:

two things meet in me,
    alike in kind . . .   25

SMALL IN MY AWE

✦

Small in my awe
 and fear
in my own
 eyes like an inchworm . . .

OPEN THE GATE

✦

Open the gate my beloved—
    arise, and open the gate:
my spirit is shaken and I'm afraid.
My mother's maid has been mocking me
    and her heart is raised against me,
so the Lord would hear her child's cry.
From the middle of midnight's blackness,
    a wild ass pursues me,
as the forest boar has crushed me;
and the end which has long been sealed
    only deepens my wound,
and no one guides me—and I am blind.

MY THOUGHTS ASKED ME

✦

My thoughts asked me in wonder:
    where are you rushing
        like the heavenly spheres?

To the god of my life,
    my desire's desire,
        whom my soul and flesh
        long to be near.

My joy is all in my portion and Maker,
    the thought of whom brings me
        disquiet's reward:

How could song please
    my soul till it praises
        the Name of the
            Lord of Lords?

ANGELS AMASSING

✦

Holy, holy, holy is the Lord of hosts,
the whole earth is full of his glory.
                                    Isaiah 6:3

Angels amassing like sparks in flames,
their brightness like burnished brass in their casings,
before the exalted throne in a throng
   one to another in vision turn
   to laud their Lord the Creator in longing—   5
O sons of strength, give glory and strength to the Lord.

Sublime creatures beneath the throne,
charged carriers encased in light,
in four quarters acknowledge your glory
   and glow in entreaty and word and awe—   10
   on guard over day, keepers of night—
O sons of strength, give glory and strength to the Lord.

Leading the camps of your hordes they look on,
with Michael your eminent prince at the front—
a myriad chariots set to your right—   15
   they gather together to seek out your palace
   and bow before your partition in service—
O sons of strength, give glory and strength to the Lord.

The hosts of the second camp stand on the left,
and Gabriel over its army looks out   20
over thousands of seraphs, a tremendous force,
   together surrounding your holy throne—
   of-and-through fire on fire they roam—
O sons of strength, give glory and strength to the Lord.

From the third camp's ranks there rises song   25
with the Lord's prince Nuriel a turret before them,
at the sound of their rushing the heavens tremble,

---

in their seeking the place of I-am the Creator,
the reward of a vision of glory and splendor—
O sons of strength, give glory and strength to the Lord.   30

The fourth bears witness in majestic array,
with Raphael chanting your psalms and a prayer,
they wreathe the bud and crown of power
  and the four lift in perfect accord
    hymns you inspired to stave off despair—   35
O sons of strength, give glory and strength to the Lord.

In trembling and fear the assembled sparks
cry out as one with their will set strong,
they plead for your faithful, a people pursued,
  and send a thunderous noise to the void,   40
    three times invoking your station apart—
O sons of strength, give glory and strength to the Lord.

ALL THE CREATURES OF
EARTH AND HEAVEN

✦

All the creatures of earth and heaven
   together as one bear witness in saying:
      the Lord is One and One is his name.

Your path has thirty-two courses
and all who fathom your mystery see them,   5
and know in the mystery that all is yours—
   that you alone, O Lord, are king.
     All the creatures of earth and heaven
       together as one bear witness in saying:
         the Lord is One and One is his name.   10

Hearts find, observing creation,
all-being-but-you knows variation—
in number and weight is all calibration
   and all from a single shepherd derive.
     All the creatures of earth and heaven   15
       together as one bear witness in saying:
         the Lord is One and One is his name.

From limit to limit your signs exist—
north through south, east into west—
earth and sky for you bear witness,   20
   each in a way of its own—
     but all the creatures of earth and heaven
       together as one bear witness in saying:
         the Lord is One and One is his name.

All flows from you in extension;   25
you endure through others' exhaustion;
therefore all being honors your splendor

from beginning to end, there's one father alone,
and all the creatures of earth and heaven
together as one bear witness in saying:
the Lord is One and One is his name.

HE DWELLS FOREVER

✦

Thy kingdom is a kingdom for all ages.

He dwells forever, exalted, alone,
and no one comes near him
      whose kingdom is One—
from the light of his garment he fashioned his world
  within three words that are sealed.   5

He yearned, longing for the teacher's counsel;
thought to reveal the ten spheres and their circles;
and against them inscribed
      ten without end—
and five against five now depend.   10

Who fathoms the mystery is shaken with fear.
From this he discerns who's beyond all compare.
Prior to "One"—what does one number?
      He's prime to all primes—
and to all that's exalted he's higher.   15

For the ten are as-
      if caught in a siege.
Who dwells upon them knows and sees:
He's the Creator and within them rules.
  His witnesses' claims are made clear.   20

And so by means of the twenty-two letters,
he stretched out fire at the uppermost border;
    at the lower extension he gathered water;
and he sent out between them the wind of measure,
  and set the twelve constellations aloft.   25

It's he who brought forth Being from Nothing,
    and then from Chaos substance was formed;
he set up huge pillars beyond comprehension,

---

established an azure and inlaid circumference—
   the abysmal waters flow forth from its stones.   30

He fixed six-directions sealed with his Name:
From water hurled fire with heavenly strength;
he established within them
     his host and his throne
   for signs and seasons and days.   35

His Name which is raised and borne over all
   he placed in all with desire and labor;
the earth he hung like grapes in a cluster;
from his lofty place he's the place of all:
   The Lord is a Rock everlasting.   40

On the upper spirit he established his throne,
where his kingdom's glory is eternally home;
there his dominion
     over all is defined:
   for the spirit of God is Life beyond time.   45

High above all, and of all the strongest,
he sees the cosmos, and over all watches;
above all holds sway,
     surrounds all there is;
   by means of his Name all creatures exist.   50

He fashioned all with a blemishless word;
he alone leads, he's instantly heard;
the Lord carries all
     without growing weary—
   within their own wisdom he captures the wise.   55

He gives revolution to the belt of the skies;
it's he who suspends earth's lands where they lie.
He says: Let there be . . .
     and it is by his might:
   All that's hidden he brings to light.   60

It's he who parts and he who gathers;
he who enriches then brings on disaster;
he who crushes

and he who congeals—
he who gives form to matter revealed. 65

Know that it's he who brings light and shadow;
he who exalts
    then he who brings low;
he who swells and he who collapses
    the greatest of mountains and hills; 70

he who brings
    subsistence to men;
he who ripples their fields with grain;
he who gives them water to drink;
    it's he who brings down the rain; 75

and he who gives life to men of the world;
he who gives strength
    to the frame of a child;
he who over our sinew sends skin;
    he who lengthens our bones within; 80

he who breathes through the body his breath;
he who keeps it upright in health;
he who deep
    into earth returns it;
    and he who will wake us from sleep. 85

AND SO IT CAME TO NOTHING

✦

And so it came
    to nothing—all
that had been
    so fine to behold:
no chambers of stone,   5
    no palace or dwelling;
no shambles, no suet,
    no Temple or offering;
no wheels, no immersion,
    no flesh for transgression;   10
no altar, no wine,
    no loaves in a row;
no blood, no veil,
    no incense or coal;
no smoke, no ashes   15
    no splendor, no robes;
no priest, no wilderness,
    no appointment by lot;
no scapegoat, no cliff,
    no country cut-off.   20

HAVEN'T I HIDDEN YOUR NAME

✦

I seek you every evening and dawn,
    my face and palms turned up to you;
with a thirsty spirit for you I moan,
    like a beggar come to my door.

The heavens can't contain you,
    and yet my thoughts somehow do:
haven't I hidden your name in my heart
    until my love for you crossed my lips?

Therefore I'll praise the name of the Lord
    so long as his breath in me lives.

LORD WHO LISTENS

♦

Lord who listens and attends to the poor,
how long will you distance yourself from my soul and hide?
   I'm weary from calling all night with a faithful heart,
grateful always for your gracious mercy, which abides.

For you I hope, my king; in you I trust—
like a dreamer trusting a reader with a dream that's obscure.
   This is my prayer, hear my petition:
I ask of you nothing less, and nothing more.

I'VE MADE YOU MY REFUGE

✦

I've made you my refuge and hope—
   who's made me rich and then poor.
Your oneness I sought at the door to the poem
   so grace your servant, my Lord,
with the good that you've long laid in store.
   Extend your mercy across me
and my way with these words will be sure.

How could my failings distract you so—
   who fashioned the world in a void—
that the daughters of song
   should be humbled and stilled.
See now my dread, my Lord,
   I stand here before you exposed
[...............................]

LIPS FOR BULLOCKS

✦

The mountain of Sion is barren
because of our fathers' transgressions,
   neither priest nor temple exists
      to offer atonement for us;
in place of flesh we render words,   5
an offering of lips for bullocks.

The place of my dwelling's a ruin,
the house of my glory laid waste,
   the cloud of incense dispersed,
      the altar no longer there;   10
nothing remains apart from my prayer:
Bear my gall and shame
   as though on the scapegoat's skull.
Return your compassion and subdue my care.

Let a people troubled and fouled   15
see the good and forgiving Lord;
   and let their cry cross over
      like incense perfectly mixed.
Let a great ransom be sent
for every impure transgression,   20
   that our sin soon be forgiven
as though on the horns of the beast once rent.
Answer us when you will—
   do not abhor our impoverishment.

I TAKE GREAT PLEASURE

✦

I take great pleasure in you who dwell on high,
  and when I recall you my sorrow fades.
Mercy is yours and thanksgiving is due—
  though I've nothing to offer apart from my words.

The heavens cannot contain your power;
  how might my thought give it shape or form?
Grant me discernment, and honesty's grace—
  and my will, soon, will bend to yours.

Accept this praise in place of slaughter,
  and let this meal of remembrance serve you.
Your sight is pure, see how I suffer—
  and send your light, my blindness's cure.

Guard the greatness of your compassion for me
  that one day it might stand against what I am.
As your name like a pledge is kept within me,
  may my spirit be set in your hand.

SEND YOUR SPIRIT

✦

Send your spirit
   to revive our corpses,
and ripple the longed-for
   land again.

The crops come from you;
   you're good to all—
and always return
   to restore what has been.

YOU LIE IN MY PALACE ON
COUCHES OF GOLD

✦

You lie in my palace on couches of gold:
   Lord, when will you ready my bed
for the one with the beautiful eyes you've foretold?
     Why, my fine gazelle,
   why do you sleep while the dawn rises
      like a flag over the hills?
Ignore the mules and asses,
   and see to your guileless doe:
I'm here for one like you—and you for one like me.
    Who enters my chambers
   finds my treasure: my pomegranate, my myrrh—
    my cinnamon, my nectar.

Kingdom's Crown

Through my prayer a man might profit
        from the study of truth and merit,

and in its lines I've concisely told
        of the wonders of the living God:

over all of my hymns it deserves renown—
        and I call it the kingdom's crown.

PART ONE

✦

I

✦

Your works are wondrous and I know it acutely:

Yours, Lord, is the greatness and the power and the glory,
    the splendor and the majesty.
Yours, Lord, is the kingdom exalted over all.
    Yours is all wealth and all honor;
all beings above and below you bear witness
that they will perish, while you endure.

Yours is the strength within whose mystery
    our minds eventually fail;

your force exceeds their intensity.
Yours is the hidden chamber of power—

    of form's secret and matter;

yours the Name that eludes the wise,
and the might to bear the world in its void,
and the craft to bring what's hidden to light.

Yours is the kindness that infuses creation,
    and the goodness veiled
    for those who hold you in awe.

Yours is the secret no notion contains,
and life that destruction will not bring down,
and the throne raised higher than height's idea,
    and the hidden hall in the heavenly mansion;

yours is the real which becomes existence
　　in light's reflection
and in whose shadow we live;　　　　　　　　　　　　　25

yours the two worlds and the border between them,
　　one for action and one for reward . . .

yours the reward
reserved for the righteous in spirit
　　　　for whom it was hidden:　　　　　　　　　30

You saw it was good and concealed it . . .

II

✦

You are One,
prior to all computation
   and ground to all figuration.

You are One,
and your oneness's mystery amazes the wise,   5
   who've never known what it was.

You are One,
      and in your oneness
know neither loss nor addition,
neither lack nor magnification.   10

You are One,
but not as one that's counted or formed,
for neither enhancement nor change pertains to you,

   neither description nor name.

You are One,   15
and my speech can't establish your boundary or line,
therefore I said I would guard my ways,

   so as not to sin with my tongue.

And you are One,
sublime and exalted above all that might fall—   20

   that One might fall is impossible . . .

You abide
beyond the range of the ear in its hearing
    and the eye in its seeing,
ungoverned by how and where and when.

You abide
in a being unto its own,
    and not for another to come.

You abide
and before the beginning of time were there:
    the placeless place of the world.

You abide,
and your form's obscure and beyond detection

    and deeper than all revelation . . .

IV

✦

You are alive,
though not established in time,
   and not of a time that's known.

You are alive,
though not in spirit and soul:
   for you're soul to spirit's soul.

You are alive,
but not like breath in a man—
   whose end is the moth and the worm.

You are alive,
and those who reach your secret discover
   delight in the world,

   and eat and live forever . . .

V

✦

You are vast
and against your vastness all vastness gives in
and every virtue's a failing.

You are vaster than thought

and lifted beyond any chariot.

You are vaster than all dimension,

and exalted above all blessing and praise . . .

VI

✦

You are strong,
and nothing in all your work and creation
 can bring about what you've wrought
 in your strength and your action.

You are strong
through a strength that's total,
 and knows neither change nor reversal.

You are strong
and show in your majesty mercy
 in your anger,
 and for sinners suppress your wrath.

You are strong,
and your mercies are readied for all of creation—

 and this is strength everlasting . . .

VII

✦

You are the light of the upper regions,
and the eye of every soul that's pure
   will take you in—

and the clouds of sin
in the sinner's soul will obscure you.

Your invisible light in the world
will be seen in the world to come
   on the mountain of God:

You are the light everlasting the eye
   of the mind longs to behold
and may yet glimpse in extremity—

but the whole of will not see . . .

VIII

✦

You are the God of gods
   and the Lord of lords,
the ruler of all that's above and below.

You are Lord
as all of creation bears witness,   5
   and the Name in whose honor
all men are obliged in worship to serve.

You are Lord,
and every creature serves you as slave
   and nothing detracts from your glory,   10
not those who worship without you—
for the drive of all is to reach you—

although they resemble men who are blind,
walking along the way of the king
   and going astray,   15

sinking in the pit of destruction,

slipping in the trap of deception—

certain they'll reach their haven,
as each one labors in vain.

But your servants are wiser   20
and walk in their own integrity,
turning neither
            to the right or left,
and coming to the court of the king:

You are Lord,   25

all creation relies on your godliness;
all creatures feast on your oneness.

You are Lord,

and there is no distinction between
    your being divine and one;   30
between your past and the real,

between what you were and will be.

All is a single mystery:

though its name might alter in aspects,
all toward a single place move on . . .   35

You are wise,
and wisdom is a fountain and source
   of life welling up from within you,

and men are too coarse to know you.

You are wise,   5
and prime to all that's primeval,
   as though you were wisdom's tutor.

You are wise,
but your wisdom wasn't acquired
   and didn't derive from another.   10

You are wise,
and your wisdom gave rise to an endless desire
   in the world as within an artist or worker—

to bring out the stream of existence from Nothing,
   like light flowing from sight's extension—   15

drawing from the source of that light without vessel,
giving it shape without tools,
      hewing and carving,
      refining and making it pure:

He called to Nothing—which split;   20
      to existence—pitched like a tent;
      to the world—as it spread beneath sky.

With desire's span he established the heavens,
as his hand coupled the tent of the planets
         with loops of skill,   25
      weaving creation's pavilion,

---

the links of his will
reaching the lowest
    rung of creation—

the curtain
at the outermost edge of the spheres . . .

PART TWO

◆

X

◆

Who could put words to your power,
splitting the globe of earth in your making
    half of it land, and the other water?

The wheel of the wind you established
over the sea, which it circles in circuits,
    as the wheel of it rests in that circling,

and over the wind
    you established the sphere of fire.

These foundations are four,
though sharing a single foundation,
    source and font,
from which they emerge renewed

and then through a fourfold font diverge.

✦

Who could speak of your wonders,
   surrounding the sphere of fire
      with a sphere of sky where the moon
draws from the shine of the sun and glows?

Along its path of circumference
   it orbits in twenty-nine days and a half,
      its secrets profound and simple,
its mass a mere thirty-ninth of the earth's;

and yet in the world it ushers in action,
   month by month in its annals,
      in its phases of grace and misfortune,
with the will of the Lord who formed it to signal

   the world of his glory and splendor.

✦

Who could evoke your merit
   in making the moon
    the measure of months and seasons,
of the feasts and divisions of days and years?

By night it rules in the sky   5
till the time for its fading has come
   and its glow begins to darken,
    covered in a coat of blackness.
   For its light derives from the sun,

and two weeks into its cycle,   10
   if the two of them stand in conjunction,
in the line of the dragon with earth in between,
   the sun's light can't be cast
   and the moon's lamp soon goes dim—

so all of the creatures on earth might know   15
that heaven's creatures, though powerful,
   are governed in their rise and decline,
    though after its fall the moon lives on,
    lit in the wake of its darkness.

And then, again, in its cleaving   20
at the end of the month to the sun,
if the dragon's mouth is between them
   and there be a line along them,

   then the moon as well will pass,
   dark before the sun like a cloud,   25
   blocking its light from our eyes

so all who see them will know the kingdom
is not of the heavens' host and its legions—

that a Lord exists above them
to darken the light they're given.   30

From height upon height and higher he watches
and those who think of the sun as their Lord
    will surely be brought to shame,
    as their words will soon be tested;
and they'll know what his hand has done: 35
    that the sun has no dominion,
    and that he who lessens its light
        rules on his own.

In return for all of its kindness,
    he sends it a slave of its slaves   40
        who cancels its light—
to destroy her abominable image
and remove her as queen from her throne.

XIII

✦

And who could tell of your righteousness
    in surrounding the lunar heavens
    with a second sphere, perfectly sealed,
            within which is fixed
        the star that we call Mercury,
    one one-thousandth of earth in proportion
    and brisk in its ten-day journey.

It brings about strife and contention;
    bitter complaint and enmity;
    it lends one's weakness strength
    to accumulate riches and power,
        to amass great wealth and fortune—
in the Lord's appointing it over his being
    like a slave to watch over his master.

This is the star of wisdom and brightness—

    endowing the simple with prudence,
    and the young with discernment and mind.

✦

Who could fathom your mysteries
　　in surrounding the second sphere
　　with the glowing circle of Venus,
like a queen overlooking her armies,
like a bride adorned with her jewels?

In eleven month's time she traces her compass,
one thirty-seventh of earth in its mass
　　as its mysteries' initiates know;

with the Lord's will in the world she renews
　　quiet and all tranquility,
　　gladness and winning gaiety,
　　　song and wordless melody—
　　and the wedding canopy's joy and spell.

She ripens the fruit of the land and its wheat:

the choice fruit made sweet by the sun
and the fruit brought forth by the moon.

XV

✦

Who could explain your secret
in surrounding the circle of Venus
    with a fourth sphere of the sun
which runs its course in exactly a year,
surpassing the earth in volume   5
    by seventeen-thousand hundreds
    as scholars have made quite clear?

It lends light to the firmament's stars
as it sends out salvation, majesty, and fear,
    with wonder renewing the world,   10
with peace on occasion and often with war,
    in its bringing great kingdoms down
    and raising up others on ruins—
its power establishing rise and decline,
    endowed by the Lord,   15
    who formed it in Perfect Mind.

    Day by day it worships its king,
    along its paths at the crossroads, it stands:
        it lifts its head with morning,
        then westward burns to dusk—   20

with night it departs and at dawn, again, it returns . . .

✦

Who could contain your magnitude
   in your setting it up as a sign
   to measure the days and the years,
     and the seasons' appointed times—

in sending its light to grow fruit-bearing trees   5
   which blossom beneath the Pleiades,
   and under Orion grow heavy
     with seed that ripening swells?

For six months it moves to the North,
   warming the air and water,   10
   the trees and soil and stones;
     and then it approaches its border

and the light lingers, and the season slows,
   and it reaches the place where a day
   expands to the full six months of the cycle,   15
     according to faithful accounts;

and then it moves on to the South
   in a given series of circles,
   reaching the place of night's extension
     to six months' dark—as the proofs   20

of astronomers show; and so
   the creator is known in his aspects,
   a small part of his power is shown,
     a fraction of his strength and wondrous effect—

for the servant's greatness mirrors his master's   25
   to those discerning in knowledge—
   as the worker defines his castle's honor,
     for he holds the worth of his lord in his hand.

✦

Who could acknowledge your signals
 in granting power to the sun to send
 light to the stars above and below
  and the moon in her brightness—
while that spot of whiteness beneath it glows?   5

As the moon moves out from her source,
 she draws more strength from his luster;
 exposed to the sun in her orbit
  she takes his light in waxing,
 until she stands in her fullness,   10
 giving out light against him.

And as she passes the mid-month mark
 and approaches again from the side,
 and advances into her cycle—
  her power is taken from her—   15
 and only her rim remains
 when the month's circuit is done.

And then she cleaves to the sun and is hidden
 in a phase that's called obscure,
 for twenty-four hours and moments more—   20
  before she emerges renewed,
like a bridegroom coming forth from his chamber.

✦

Who really knows of your wondrous acts
in surrounding the sphere of the sun
with a fifth sphere where reddish Mars
   rests like a king in his palace,
its orbit in eighteen months being drawn,
  its mass like earth's but larger
by one and a half and half of one-quarter?

It resembles the fiercest warrior,
the shield of its powerful soldiers made red;
it brings about battle and loss and slaughter
and men leveled by fire and blade—
   their lifeblood soon dried out,
   their fat given over to flames;
through years of scorching heat and drought,
     and thunder and stone-sized hail;

those run through with swords and their slayers—
   who race alone toward evil
   and hurry to shed men's blood.

✦

Who could decipher the awe you inspire
in surrounding the sphere of Mars
   with a sixth of tremendous size
   within which Jupiter hovers,
     greater than earth
   by five and seventy times?

In twelve years it travels its circle,
the star of will and desire,
   arousing fear of The Name,
   uprightness, and also repentance,
     and traits of excellent temper.
It yields the harvest of fields—
brings war and contention and strife to an end:

under its aspect all breaches are sealed
and the world is judged by the Lord.

✦

Who could expound your greatness
   in surrounding Jupiter's path
   with the seventh sphere of Saturn,
   which moves along in its circuit,
     more massive than earth
by ninety-nine times in its volume?

In thirty years it orbits its course
   provoking battles and pillage,
   exile, capture, and hunger—
     for this is its nature;
   it ravages lands and uproots kingdoms,

all with the will of the one who appoints it,
to accomplish his action, strange as it is.

✦

Who could draw near your majesty
   in surrounding the circle of Saturn
   with an eighth sphere and its circuit?

It bears the twelve constellations
on the line of a band, skillfully woven—
   all of the stars of the upper heavens
     cast at the time of its casting—

their pitch so high they circle
   each thirty-six-thousand years;
their circumference such that their mass
is one hundred and seven times larger than earth's.

From the force of these stars the force
of every creature below them derives,
   with the will of the one who formed them
     and set them in patterns above us;

    he created each in its fashion,
      and all of them called by name—

appointing each to its burden and charge.

✦

Who understands your manner
in establishing chambers for the seven planets
   in the twelve signs of fortune?

The Ram and the Bull you aligned with your power
and Twins, the third, like brothers you joined—   5
   their faces drawn like a man—

and the fourth sign, the Crab,
and the Lion as well received your honor,
   and beside it the Virgin, its sister—

and likewise the Scales and Scorpion,   10
installed across from each other;

and the ninth sign was formed in the figure
of a man stretching taut his bow—
   like he who became the Archer—
   his strength will never fail.   15

And the Goat and also the Pail
were fashioned with incomparable power;
   and the twelfth sign was set on its own,
   an enormous fish the Lord had appointed.

   These are the firmament's signs,   20
      sublime in station:
         the twelve princes
      revolving over their nations.

✦

Who could expose the things you've hidden,
encasing the circle of signs
   with a ninth sphere in order
to surround creation's circuits and creatures
and close them within its border?

It drives the stars of the sky in its might
into their westerly motion;
   each day at dusk
it bows in the west
to its king and his rule of the kingdom.

All the creatures of the world are in it
like a mustard seed in the sea—
   such is its measure,
its greatness in truth is nothing
to the greatness of its king and creator.

Its proportion and vast dimension
beside him are Nothing and Void.

✦

Who could make sense of creation's secrets,
of your raising up over the ninth sphere
    the circle of mind,
the sphere of the innermost chamber?

The tenth to the Lord is always sacred.

  This is the highest ring,
transcending all elevation
    and beyond all ideation.

This is the place of the hidden
for your glory above in the palanquin . . .

You formed its frame from the silver of truth;
from the gold of mind you created its matter;
on pillars of justice you established its throne:
  its reality derives from your power;

  its longing is from you and for you,
and toward you ascends its desire.

✦

Who comprehends your thinking
in transforming the radiance of intellect's sphere
    into a glow
of souls and spirits on high?

These are your kingdom's soldiers,   5
messengers serving your will with their forces,
holding the flaming sword that revolves
    every which way—

as they work in all manner,
wherever the spirit moves them: 10

all are glass-like forms,
all are transcendent creatures,
guarding without and within,
    watching over your presence.

From a sacred place they descend,   15
from the source of light they extend,
    splitting into their ranks,
    each with its standard's signs,
engraved with the pen of a ready writer—

among them princes and servants,   20
and armies that depart and return
    with neither fatigue nor pause
    —seeing yet not-to-be-seen.

Some are hewn from flame;

others are wind in air;   25

some are fire and water paired;

some are seraphs, some electrum;

some are lightning, others a flare;

each rank bows down before the One
who rides the heavens and stands

in the heights before His hosts;

by watches they issue out—
at first by day, and then by night,
    sending up song and praise

to the One who's wrapped in power.

All in awe and trembling,
bow and kneel before you, saying:

We offer up thanks to you,
our Lord, who is God,
that we are able to serve you;
that you are the sole Creator
    and we alone bear witness;

that you it was
who gave us form—
        not we on our own—

that we are the work of your hand.

✦

Who could approach the place of your dwelling,
in your raising up over the sphere of mind
    the Throne of Glory
in the fields of concealment and splendor,
at the source of the secret and matter,
where the mind reaches and yields?

On high you were raised and rose
       to the Throne of your Power—
and beside you no man might ascend.

XXVII

✦

Who could accomplish what you've accomplished
in establishing under the Throne of Glory
    a level for all who were righteous in spirit?

This is the range of pure soul
raveled in the bond of all that's vital.   5
For those who've worked to exhaustion—
this is the place of their strength's renewal,
where the weary will find repose;
    these are the children of calm,

of pleasure that knows no bound in the mind: 10

    this is the World to Come,

a place of position and vision for souls
      that gaze
into the mirrors of the palace's servants,
    before the Lord to see and be seen.   15

They dwell in the halls of the king,

    and stand alongside his table,
      taking delight
in the sweetness of intellect's fruit
    which offers them majesty's savor.   20

This is the rest and inheritance
that knows no bounds in its goodness and beauty,
      flowing with milk and honey;
    this is its fruit and deliverance.

✦

Who could uncover the things you've concealed
in fashioning chambers on high and their treasures,
   some too tremendous to speak of
    and others matters of valor—

stores of life among them   5
for those who lived in innocence;

and also stores of salvation
for those given over to penitence;

and stores of sulfur and rivers of fire
for those who break their covenant;   10

and burning stores of gorge-like pits
   whose flames will never be smothered—
where those abhorred of the Lord will descend;

and stores of whirlwind and storm,
of heavy clouds and blackness;   15

of hail and ice, of drought and snow;
of heat and flooding waters;

of smoke and rime and fog;
and gloom and thickened darkness.

All you prepare in its time   20
and employ for judgment or mercy—

for correction in a world you designed.

✦

Who could grasp your intensity

in forming the radiance of purity
   from the glow of your glory,

      from a rock the Rock has hewn,
from the hollow of a clearness withdrawn?

You sent the spirit of wisdom along it
and gave it the name of soul,
   and formed it out of the fire
     of intellect's ardor
whose spirit burned on inside it;

and you sent it out through the body
    to serve it and guard it—

and you watch as it acts like a flame within it,
   though the body isn't consumed

which was formed from the spark of soul
and was brought into being from nothing

when the Lord came across it in fire.

XXX

✦

Who could approach your wisdom
in endowing the soul with the power of knowing
   you planted deep inside it?
   Its glory is knowledge
destruction will not bring down;

it exists in accord with its source's existence
and this is its secret and substance:
   and the wise soul will not see death,
   but souls in transgression
will suffer a fate more bitter by far . . .

✦

If it's pure it will find its favor
and laugh when the end has come;
if not it will wander in anger,
   in endless complaint and wrath—

an exile within its uncleanness,
touching no hallowed thing,
not drawing near to the temple until
   its purity's phase has been filled.

XXXI

✦

Who could return your goodness
in sending breath through the body
  to invest it with life,

in revealing a way of life to guide it
and save it from evil's contrivance:

Out of the ground you formed it,
  and into the blood breathed soul—
and you sent the spirit of wisdom along it,
  which sets us apart from swine,
  and allows for ascent on high . . .

You've shut us inside your world,
while you look in from beyond and observe;

  and all that we try to conceal

  within or without you reveal.

✦

Who could know your creation's key
   in devising the body's senses for action
   and granting it eyes to decipher your signs
   and ears to hear of your wonders,
   and a mind to grasp but the edge of your mystery,   5
   and a mouth to tell of your praises,
   and a tongue to declare your powers
      to all who'd come
as I today, your servant, the son of your servant,
   within the limits of his gift declaring   10
   a fraction alone of your grandeur;
   and these are only the borders
   of your ways which are greater by far in sum
     and life to those who find them:

All might find you who hear of them   15
   without having seen your glory—
   though how would they know your divinity
   without having heard of your splendor?

How could your truth in their hearts take hold
   and guide their thought to serve you?   20

Therefore your servant has taken heart
   to recall before his God
   a portion of his finest praises—
through these might a part of his sin be absolved.

   For how could a man reconcile himself   25
   with his Lord,
     if not with his finest?

XXXII

--- ◆ ---

PART THREE

XXXIII

◆

I'm ashamed, my God,
and abashed to be standing before you,
for I know that as great as your might has been,
   such is my utter weakness and failing;

as exalted as your power has been and will be,   5
   such is the depth of my poverty;
as perfect as your wholeness is,
   so is my knowledge flawed.

For you are one and alive;
almighty, abiding, strong and wise;   10

You are the Lord my God—
   and I am a clod of dirt and a worm;
dust of the ground and a vessel of shame;

   a speechless stone;

a passing shadow;   15

a wind blown-by that won't return;

a spider's poison;

a lying heart uncut for his Lord;

a man of rages;

a craftsman of scheming, and haughty,   20
   corrupt and impatient in speech,
perverse in his ways and impetuous.

What am I or my life?
What is my might and my righteousness?
Throughout the days of my being I'm nothing   25
  and what then after I die?

I came from nothing and nothing pursue;

against instruction I come here before you
with insolence and impure notion—

and impulse that strays to its idols   30

and greed as it calls—

and a soul that hasn't been cleansed—
and a heart that's lost and alone—

and a body afflicted with swarms of desire
  ceaseless within their resistance.   30

XXXIV

◆

My God, I know my transgressions have swelled
    and my sins are beyond calibration;
but I bring them to mind, like a drop in the sea—
    confessing and hoping
to quiet the noise of the waves   5
    and the breakers against their reefs,
that you in the heavens will hear and forgive me.

For I've gone against your teaching,
    and held your commandments in scorn;
my mouth has come to detest them,   10
and too often I've uttered blasphemy—
    and been perverse and lawless;
    fractious and full of violence;
I've lied and counseled evil—deceived, scoffed and
                                          rebelled;   15

been scornful, perverse and intransigent,
    stubborn, harsh and senseless;
I've cut off your reproach and been cruel.
I've committed abominable acts
    and wandered far from my path;   20
I've strayed from your way and instruction,
    and denied the truth you instilled.

✦

XXXV

My face fell when I thought, my God,
  of the ways I've made you angry—

for all the good you accord me
I offer you only transgression.

You didn't need to create me—   5
  it was only Magnanimity—

not an act of Necessity—
  but an act of Love and Will.

Before my being you established your Mercy
and gave me life with your Spirit-sent-through-me;   10
  and after I entered the air of the world
    you did not leave me:

with a father's compassion you raised me;
like a child in its nursery you taught me;
  on my mother's breast in me you put trust,   15
and from your pleasure I learned to be pleased.

When I stood in my place you gave me courage,
in your arms you took me and taught me to walk;

and you gave me instruction and wisdom;
from distress and trouble you saved me,   20
and when anger came on you concealed me
  behind the shadow of your right hand.

How much trouble my eyes
have overlooked as you helped me;
and before it came on you'd prepared   25
  a healing and did not strike me down.

When my vigilance failed you watched over me.
When I came to the mouth of the lion and entered,
  you broke its jaws and withdrew me.

I was ill with continual sickness—
   and you healed me.

When your harsh judgment came into the world,
from the path of the sword you removed me;
   from plague you spared me;
   in famine you fed me;
and I flourished in all that I did . . .

When I made you angry,
as a man rebukes his son you rebuked me,
   and in my sorrow I called:

If my life in your eyes is of value,
   do not turn me empty away.

Above all this you've done more,
in giving me perfect faith
   to believe that you are the God of truth—
that your way is the truth and your prophets are real.

And you kept me away from your enemies,
as they blasphemed mocking your book of the law,
and pursuing those who serve you;
   denying the prophets who speak of you.

They feign innocence, and cultivate guile;
pretend to be pure as they hide their corruption—
   like a vessel full of shame and confusion,

scrubbed without with the water of falseness,
   while all that's within is defiled.

XXXVI

✦

Lord, I am not worthy of the truth and the mercy
you've shown your servant,
    though I thank you:

for within me you've placed a soul of distinction—
although I've stained it with all that I've done,   5
    and profaned it with evil in thought,
        and across it brought disgust.

I've known that in my transgression
    the harm was all to my soul—

that temptation stands, an obstruction, beside me,   10
and keeps me from measured breath and repose.

And so with a double bridle I've sought it
    and year after year rowed to return it
    from desire's sea to the shore—

and again and again it escaped me—   15
blocking my thought and breaking my word.

My notions are simple beside its duplicity:
    I've been for peace, and it for war
as it turned me into its footstool—
and the blood of battle in peace was spilled.   20

I've gone out to fight it over and over,
and gathered a camp in my work and repentance

and held the camp of your mercies before me
    for help in your saying:

If evil comes to the one to strike it,   25
the other will flee to safety.

And all I'd envisioned occurred.

———————

It overcame me and scattered my soldiers,
and nothing remained but the host of your mercies.

With them now I'll attack
as they help me before my enemy,

and maybe I'll bring it down,

and cast it out of the land.

✦

XXXVII

Let it be, my God, your will
to bridle my fell inclination
and hide your face from my sin and transgression

   and not to take me away
   in the midst of my days   5

until I've prepared my provision
for the way,
   and my repentance
   for the day of my passing;

for if I depart from the world as I entered,   10
and naked and empty return as I came,
   why was I made—
or called to bear witness to struggle and pain?

I'd be better not having been born,
rather than adding to guilt and transgression.   15

Judge me, Lord, by the standard of mercy,
   and not in your anger,
unless you'd bring me to nothing.

For what is man that you'd judge him,
but haunted vanity and breath pursued.   20

How could you measure that in a balance?

You'd put it onto the scales
and the pan would neither rise nor fall;

what good would it do you to weigh out the wind?

From the day of his birth he's tortured and shamed,   25

afflicted and stricken by God and plagued.

He begins like chaff in a storm,
   and ends like driven straw;

   while he lives he's blighted grass—

and the fleeting moment is found by the Lord.   30

From the time he emerges from his mother's womb
his nights are grief and his days a sigh;
   if he's lifted one day in fortune—
   his fortune's worms are bred by dawn.

He's driven by chaff—   35
and stubble will bring him down.

Content he seeks out trouble,
and hungry he'd sin for bread.

His feet are light for wealth's pursuit;
he forgets the death that shadows him.   40

He prays in sorrow and multiplies words,
slickens his talk and piles up vows:

into the clear he breaks them all

and strengthens the bars on his doors,
   while death in his room is lurking.   45

He increases the number of guards about him;
   but the ambush will come from within—

his fence won't stop the wolves
   come for their lamb . . .

He'll swell with pride and not know why;   50
be glad and not know what for;

go to his death and not know when.

In his boyhood his heart is stubborn.
When the spirit of lust begins to move him
he wakens to gain's pursuit and leaves home   55

to sail the seas and quest across deserts,
and try his soul in the lion's den
   and walk about among beasts.

Just when he thinks his glory is great—
    that his hand has gotten much—
the destroyer in peace comes at him,
and he opens his eyes and is poor.

He's continually put through trial,
vexation at every turn,
    moment by moment through harm,
    day by day through terror.

If he's given a minute of respite,
    calamity suddenly comes—
either through war and the sword that slays
and the brass bow that brings him down,

or grief that overwhelms him,

or seething waters in flood,

or continual illness and plague;

until he becomes his greatest obstruction
and his honey turns in his mouth to gall.

As his pain worsens, his honor grows thin,
and the neighborhood children begin to taunt him,
    and the young men wear him down;

he becomes a burden to daughter and son
and his family and friends disown him;
and the time comes to leave his court
    and enter the court of earth,

to exchange the shadows of home
for the endless shadow of death.

He removes his robe of embroidered crimson
and puts on maggots and worms;
lies in the dust and to dust returns,
    as he was on the day he was formed.

How could a man who faces all this
find time for what's pure and repentance?

The day is short and the work is great
and the owners are all impatient—
   and anxious and full of contempt;

and time plays trick after trick;

and the landlord has started to knock.   95

Therefore, my Lord,
remember the whole of the struggle
   through which a man is put.

And if I've often ignored what's right,
look after my soul in the end,   100

and do not account for me sin by sin—

a man whose transgressions are endless,
who leaves this life without joy . . .

XXXVIII

If my sin, my God,
   is too great to bear,
what of your name and its majesty—

If I cannot hope for your mercy,
   who but you could protect me?
Therefore, though you would slay me,
   I hope and trust,

and were you to see my impiety,
I would flee from you to Thee:

I would hide from your wrath in your shadow.

I'll hold to the edge of your mercy
   until you have mercy—
and not allow you to go away,
not until you've blessed me.

Remember you made me of clay
and proved me within these trials.

Therefore I ask of you:
Don't hold me to all that I've done,
don't feed me the fruit of my action.

Defer, for me, your anger;
don't bring my time any nearer
until I've prepared my repentance,
prepared it for my place to come;

and do not rush to send me
out of the land with alarm—
   the kneading troughs
of guilt bound to my shoulder.

When you put what I've done on the scales,
set my trials in the opposite pan;
in recalling my defiance and evil,
    remember my wormwood and gall—   30

and gauge the one by the other.

And, Lord, remember
how long in my wandering you've thrown me about,
    and tried me in exile's furnace,   35
    as you tried to refine me of sin.

I've known it was all for the better,
    that faith is a kind of torture;
so as to sweeten the end
you brought me through tribulation.   40

Therefore, waken your mercies, my Lord,
    and do not pour out your wrath;
do not repay me for all that I've done,
but say *enough* to your leveling angel.

What merit or worth do I have   45
    when you begin with my sin?
Have you arranged a watch for me
to trap me in a net like a bull?

Most of my days are passed,
and those that are left   50
    will waste away with iniquity;
    . . . If I stand before you today,
you'll look tomorrow and I will not be.

Is it right, just now, that I die,
and that great fire consume me?   55

Cast, my God,
your eyes for good across me
    for the days that remain me,

and do not strike
those who are left like refugees   60
and that which remains in the wake
    of the hail of all my confusion;

---

do not devour the swarm of my sins,
for I am your own creation,
    and what would you gain
if I were turned into food for worms:

should they feed on the work of your hands?

✦

Let it be, my God, your will,
to respond to me with your mercy—
   to bring me back
with perfect repentance before you.

Focus my heart on its supplication—   5
and listen with all your attention.

Open my heart to your Law;
plant awe for you in my thinking.

Decree beneficent rulings for me;
annul for me harmful decrees,   10

and do not lead me through temptation
or into the power of scorn.

Protect me from all calamity
until misfortune has passed.

Shelter me in your shadow;   15

be with my mouth and my word;

and watch over my ways
so I will not sin again with my tongue.

Think of me
when you think of my people   20
and the restoration-
   to-come of your temple,

and grant me the power to see
the good of your chosen,
   the purity   25
to enter your desolate shrine—

to take delight
and pleasure in its dust and stones,

in its heaps of dirt and rubble,

as you rebuild in its ruins.   30

✦

I've known, my God, that those who implore you
have excellent action to speak for their fate,
or virtue they've helped in creating,

while I have nothing—

am hollow and shaken out—   5

a ravaged vine,

and in me is neither
honor or what seems right;

affection or candor of heart;

not prayer and not supplication;   10

not purity, faith, or simplicity;

not fairness or honest measure;

neither repentance nor service.

Let it therefore be your merciful will,

my God and the God of our fathers,   15
Sovereign Lord of all worlds—

to be near and have mercy upon me;

to remember me in the call of your will;

to lift the light of your face across me,
and conceive for me your graciousness—   20

and not repay me for all I've done
and make me an object of scorn for the base,

or take me away in the midst of my days,

or obscure your face before me;

to cleanse me of all transgression— 25
not to cast me away from your presence;

to quicken my being with dignity,
and lead me into honor.

And then, when you withdraw me
from the life of the world we know, 30
    bring me to peace
in the life of the world-to-come,

and call me to rise;

place me among the righteous,
with men who among the living were summoned 35
    to life everafter;

and cleanse me
with the light of your countenance;
return me to life from the earth's depths

and on that day, as today, I'll say: Lord, 40

I am grateful that you were angry
and turned away your wrath to assuage me.

Loving-kindness is yours
in all the good you've done me,

and until I die will do. . . . 45

For all this I'm bound to thank you,
to glorify, laud, and extol you:

May you be praised in the mouth of creation
and be hallowed by words of sanctification;
be known as One by those 50
    who seek to know you in oneness;
be extolled by those who extol you
and lifted by those
    who would lift you up in song;

and may you be raised in the mouth of those who pray— 55

---

for among the gods nothing is like you,
and nothing, my Lord,
   compares with what you have done.

May the words of my mouth and my heart's meditation
   before you be pleasing—

   my rock—

      and my redemption.

NOTES

✦

THESE NOTES are designed to allow for greater absorption of a given poem's detail, structure, and background—elements of which may at times seem strange to readers unacquainted with the conventions of medieval Hebrew and Arabic poetry. I have tried to make the commentary useful for general and specialized audiences alike; the poems can and should, however, be read on their own as well. For more on the principles of translation and the historical context of the poetry, the reader should consult the introduction, chronology, and preface to the notes in my *Selected Poems of Shmuel HaNagid* (Princeton, 1996) and the bibliography to this book.

A word is called for perhaps about the proliferation of scriptural citations here. While familiarity with the biblical text certainly intensifies and in some cases transforms the pleasure obtained from reading medieval Hebrew verse, experience has shown that the poems register with considerable power even without a developed knowledge of the biblical background. I employ a maximalist approach to citation below not because I feel that readers need to trace the link between each citation and a given passage in the poetry, but in the hope that the quotations will provide a better sense of the layered and sometimes collaged nature of the work. Along the same lines, these notes contain references to the several other traditions (rabbinic Hebrew, Greek, and Arabic) that quietly contribute to the resonance of the poetry and the society within which that poetry evolved. Scriptural citations throughout are drawn from the Jewish Publication Society 1917 version—itself based on the King James version—unless otherwise noted. Passages are quoted in full when the relevance to the translation is obvious; otherwise only chapter and verse are given. The notes cover all types of biblical inlay: neutral, dynamic, and allusive. (For more on the use of scriptural citation, see Brann, *The Compunctious Poet*, 40–46; and Kozodoy, "Reading Medieval Hebrew Love Poetry," 118–21).

Numbers next to the Hebrew poems refer for convenience to the editions edited by Dov Yarden—S: secular and L: liturgical—unless otherwise indicated. All editions of the poet's work have been consulted, including Haim Schirmann's anthology, and variant manuscript versions of the text are noted where relevant. Superscriptions, originally in Arabic, are drawn from both Yarden and Schirmann, and in both cases involve descriptions offered by a copyist, not by the poet himself.

The order of the poems in this volume to a certain extent follows the lead of Schirmann's popular selection of the poet's work in Hebrew (Schocken, 1944,

1967). The overall intent is to create a plausible fiction of Ibn Gabirol's development—away from the court and its poetry, and toward a more contemplative, visionary verse.

Personal Poems and Poems of Court

This part consists of what are generally known as "secular poems," though that term is somewhat misleading; it is used primarily to distinguish this body of work from Ibn Gabirol's "liturgical poems," and it in no way indicates an absence of religious concern. Broadly speaking, the social context of this verse was that of the Andalusian Hebrew courts, and most of the court genres are represented here, including nature poems, wine poems, love poems, boast poems, poems of friendship and praise, poems of complaint and separation, poems of wit, satirical, ascetic and contemplative poems, and elegies. The original Hebrew employs the bipartite line, monorhyme, and quantitative meters that, along with the genres, were brought into Hebrew from Arabic medieval literature by Dunash Ben Labrat, Shmuel HaNagid, and others.

My selection is drawn from the two-volume Yarden edition, which is arranged by genre, and the Brody-Schirmann edition, which is based on the manuscript (eventually labeled Schocken 37) that David Tzemah discovered in Iraq. In that manuscript the poems are arranged in order of decreasing length (a method employed in the Quran): first non-liturgical verse, then eulogies, and finally a group of liturgical poems. Brody-Schirmann arrange the poems by an alphabetical indexing of the poems' rhyme-letter (a common medieval method) and their volume contains 276 poems, 25 of doubtful authorship. Yarden's edition contains 294 poems. Part I also includes several poems recently discovered among the manuscripts and fragments of the Cairo Genizah.

TRUTH SEEKERS TURN (108:S)

This poem is offered as a prologue to the English translation; in the Hebrew manuscript it appears as an ordinary part of the secular diwan, and Yarden classifies it as a poem of self-praise (*fakhr*, in the Arabic tradition). Western readers are often put off by this convention of boasting, but it is important to keep in mind that it takes place in the context of a highly developed, nuanced tradition that goes back through the history of Arabic poetry to the pre-Islamic odes, where self-praise (or praise of one's tribe) was an integral part of the multivalent qasida, or ode. Scholar Salma Jayyusi notes that the skillful use of *fakhr* was considered in the medieval context one of the four prerequisites of good poetry—the other three being mastery of eulogy, satire, and description (*The Legacy of Muslim Spain*, 370). One might also read the boast as a helpful stimulant to the poetry, or as the product of a euphoria that the verse itself brings about (or even as Norman Mailer–like "advertisements for oneself," repugnant at times, but embodiments of the poet's essential strength as well). In any event, the boast was a consciously employed rhetorical strategy that served to intensify the expression and experience of a given set of values, with which the poet, or his community—in this case his spiritual/intellectual community—is identified. This is not to say that the boasts are not indicative at times of arrogance, or that they do not betray what J. Stetkevych calls "a confessed or unconfessed anxiety of self-justification" (*Zephyrs of Najd*, 28)—only that the poet's use of this strategy was sophisticated and would not have bothered a medieval audience in quite the same way that it might trouble readers today.

The Arabic superscription to this poem reads: "A poem about one who doesn't know the craft of poetry."

Line 1: The Hebrew is singular—"poem" or "song," but the meaning is clearly collective.

2: Literally, "brutish among the people"—as in Psalms 94:8: "Consider ye brutish among the people; And ye fools, when will ye understand?" The word for "brutish" in the Psalms—*ba'ar*—is glossed by the standard biblical commentaries as "foolish" or "ignorant," and that is the reading I have followed here. The speaker in this poem, then, is turning to those who do not possess the wisdom embodied in the very fabric of his verse.

5: Cf. Deuteronomy 32:47: "For it is no vain thing for you; because it is your life."

8–9: "Kills the soul," i.e., it destroys him. The Hebrew here plays on the idiom, which means "to kill," as in Proverbs 1:19: "So are the ways of every one that is greedy of gain; it taketh away the life of the owners thereof." This invokes the frequently anthologized lines of the Arabic poet Di'ibel Ibn 'Ali, "the devil of poets," quoted in Ibn Ezra's *Book of Remembrance and Discussion*: "The bad poem will die before its author, whereas the good poem will live even if its speaker dies" (Halkin: 47a/Halper: 80). And Schopenhauer, whom Pines and Klausner say is the western philosopher closest to Ibn Gabirol's philosophical system and temperament, notes: "Bad books are intellectual poison; they destroy the mind" (Schopenhauer, 65). For a marvelous incorporation of the notion of the poem's immortality, consider Nabokov's Englishing of Pushkin's Russian adaptation of Horace's Ode III, 30: "Not all of me is dust. Within my song, / safe from the worm, my spirit will survive, / and my sublunar fame will dwell as long / as there is one last bard alive. / / Throughout great 'Rus my echoes will extend" (*Horace in English*, 225).

10: Cf. Exodus 12:2: "the beginning of months," and the additional prayer for the new month, "the beginning [or head] of months to the people is given." The Hebrew calendar is partly lunar, hence the prominence of the moon in the regulation of the social and religious order, and the importance of the sighting of the new moon, upon which a blessing is said. According to the *Sanhedrin* 42a, "Whoever pronounces the benediction over the new moon in its due time welcomes, as it were, the presence of the *Shekhinah*" (the feminine divine presence). "In the mishnaic period, proclamation of the new month by the rabbinical court was celebrated with dancing and rejoicing. . . . [Generally speaking,] the rite takes the moon as a symbol of the renewal in nature as well as of Israel's renewal and redemption" (*Encyclopedia Judaica*, 12:291). The moon also figures prominently in Ibn Gabirol's personal mythology (see, for instance, "I Am the Man" and *Kingdom's Crown*, XI). Like many of the poet's so-called conventional images, this one brings in its wake a charged field of associations.

I'M PRINCE TO THE POEM (109:S)

Probably the earliest poem included in this selection, written when the poet was sixteen. (Ibn Gabirol's diwan might include still earlier work, as it appears that his elegies for his father may have been written when the poet was fourteen.) By then Ibn Gabirol had already written poems to Shmuel HaNagid in Granada and been commissioned to write four elegies for Hai Gaon, the great Eastern rabbi and head of the academy in Pumbedita.

Line 1: There are two variant readings for "prince"—"singer" and "song"—and Schirmann uses all three at different points in his career. Cf. Ecclesiastes 10:7, Proverbs 19:10, Esther 1:3 (NJPS), 2 Samuel 19:7.
2: The instrument in the Hebrew is *kinnor*, indicating, generally, "a string instrument played by hand," probably a lute or a kind of lyre or small harp. Cf. 1 Samuel 16:16 (NJPS), 1 Samuel 16:23, Psalms 68:26. Both AV and RV use "harp." Arthur Waley wrestled with the same terminological problem in his translations from medieval Chinese (*Madly Singing*, 301–2).
3: Cf. 2 Samuel 12:30.
5: Literally, "Here I am," which echoes the young Samuel's reply to God, when he is called to prophesy. Cf. Samuel 3:4, 8.
6: The English image departs some from the Hebrew, for which there are two variant versions. Schirmann reads: "My heart understands (*ban*) like the heart of [a man of] eighty"—or, to maintain the rhythm of this translation, "and my heart is like eighty with wisdom." Yarden has: "My heart within me (*bi*) is like the heart of [a man of] eighty." Cf. Yerushalmi, *Berakhot* 7:4: "And they went on to appoint Rabbi Elazar Ben Azariah to the Yeshivah at the age of 16 and his head was covered with silver." Also, *The Haggadah*: "R. Elazar Ben Azariah said: 'Lo, I am like a man of seventy.'"

MY WORDS ARE DRIVEN (116:S)

Line 1: All manuscripts and the Bialik-Ravnitzky and Brody-Schirmann editions have the first word of this well-known poem as *melitzati* (literally: "my fine speech"—or, as Bialik glosses, "my poems" or "my poetry"); Yarden has *'al-itzati* ("my rejoicing"). (See his article on the problem, *Shirei HaHol*, vol. II, page 583.) Either way, what makes the poet happy, what gives him pleasure—range and ease in poetry, or the ability to enjoy his youth—is absent, and he has already acquired his reputation as a sulker. Cf. Job 18:18: "He shall be driven from light into darkness and chased out of the world."

2: Cf. *Yebamot* 47a: "Israel at this is persecuted and oppressed." **3:** Cf. Proverbs 14:13: "Even in laughter the heart acheth; and the end of mirth is heaviness."

5–6: Cf. Genesis 23:2, Ezekiel 24:16, 23.

7–8: The Hebrew *havatzelet* can be either a lily, a meadow-saffron (crocus), or, in some biblical translations, a rose; cf. Song of Songs 2:1: "I am a rose of Sharon, a lily of the valley"; Ecclesiastes 11:9: "Rejoice, O young man, in thy youth"; Song of Songs 5:13: "His cheeks are as a bed of spices, as banks of sweet herbs."

9–10: Cf. Psalms 57:7: "They have prepared a net for my steps, My soul is bowed down"; Psalms 146:8: "The Lord raiseth up them that are bowed down."

11–12: It should be kept in mind that soul, here, refers to the seat of appetite, the senses, and passion; the heart (understood as "mind"), in this medieval scheme, is the seat of wisdom and control. The speaker explains that his soul has been restricted by his heart and therefore it—the soul—grew angry. Cf. Ecclesiastes 1:18: "For in much wisdom is much vexation; And he that increaseth knowledge increaseth sorrow"; Proverbs 23:23: "Buy the truth and sell it not; Also wisdom, and instruction, and understanding." E. Zemach (*KeShoresh Etz*, 46) points out that this line possibly alludes to an important liturgical poem of disputed authorship and date, *"Anosh mah yeezkeh"* ("How can a man be pure"), line 19: "If he brings *wrath* [anxiousness/fretfulness] through murder and deceit, his days are prematurely cut . . . If virtue be his striving and delight, he will bear fruit in ripe old age" (trans. Petuchowski, *Theology and Poetry*, 98–110).

13–14: Cf. Isaiah 8:21; Psalms 37:7: "Resign thyself to the Lord"; (NJPS) "Be patient and wait for the Lord"; Isaiah 30:26; Jeremiah 30:17: "I will heal thee of thy wounds, saith the Lord, because they have called thee an outcast: 'She is Zion, there is none that careth for her.'"

15–16: Cf. Job 21:15; Psalms 119:143.

17–18: "The day is full (full of work, i.e., long)"—is Schirmann's reading, i.e., he can't bear the distress much longer. Yarden's text has *rad*, "is falling," which implies that time is running out. Cf. Job 6:11: "What is my strength that I should wait?"; Genesis 29:7: "It is yet high day."

19–20: Literally, "a man will die in pain whose soul is afflicted with plague." Cf. Jeremiah 8:22: "Is there no balm in Gilead?," Jeremiah 46:11 and 51:8: "Take balm for her pain."

FORGET ABOUT "IF" AND "MAYBE" (103:S)

Lines 1–4: Cf. Lamentations 3:29: "Let him put his mouth in the dust, if so be there may be hope," and the Arabic of Muslim Ibn al-Walid: "And time takes back what it gives" (*Al'iqd*, 2,3 148, in Yarden). Or, "time is cruel/evil."

5: Literally, "contends with me." Cf. Job 10:2.

9: Cf. Proverbs 31:25: "Strength and dignity are her clothing; and she laugheth at the time to come."

11–12: Cf. Job 39:22: "He mocketh at fear and is not frightened"; Job 30:9: "And now I am become their song, yea, I am a byword unto them."

13–14: See, "And Don't Be Astonished."

17–18: Isaiah 6:1: "I saw the Lord sitting upon a throne high and lifted up, and his train filled the Temple"; *Berakhot* 10a: "Just as the Holy One, blessed be He, fills the whole world, so the soul fills the body."

19–20: Psalms 5:5: "Evil shall not sojourn with thee"; Psalms 15:1: "Who shall sojourn in Thy Tabernacle?"

21–24: The Hebrew phrase here and in lines 25–26 reflects the structure of the Arabic idiom calqued in the Hebrew, and the English follows suit, the slight strangeness notwithstanding. Cf. Isaiah 42:14: "Now will I cry like a travailing woman, gasping and panting at once"; Psalms 137:1: "By the rivers of Babylon, there we sat down, yea, we wept."

25–28: Cf. Psalms 137:6; and *Pirkei Avot* 6:1: "Get yourself a companion [fellow disciple]."

29–34: Cf. Jeremiah 20:9: "Then there is in my heart as it were a burning fire shut up in my bones"; Jeremiah 42:5: "The Lord be a true and faithful witness"; Job 30:15: "Terrors . . . chase mine honor as the wind"—where Ibn Janaah reads "honor" as "soul" or "life"; Deuteronomy 15:9: "Beware lest you harbor base thoughts . . . so that you are mean to your fellow kinsman and give him nothing" (NJPS). "Begrudge his success" glosses the Hebrew, which states that he was neither "stingy" nor "evil" nor a "churl," i.e., that he was generous with his wisdom.

35–38: Cf. Psalms 110:1: "I will make thine enemies thy footstool"; Isaiah 10:6: "to tread them down like the mire of the streets"; Isaiah 49:23: "They shall bow down to thee with their face to the earth, and lick the dust of thy feet"; Psalms 60:10: "Upon Edom do I cast my shoe."

39–40: Cf. Lamentations 3:12: "He hath bent his bow and set me as a mark for the arrows"; Isaiah 9:18: "The people also are as the fuel of fire."

PROLOGUE TO THE BOOK OF GRAMMAR (226:S)

This translation is drawn from Ibn Gabirol's *Sefer Ha'Anaq*, a long didactic poem about Hebrew grammar that the poet wrote when he was nineteen. All that remains of the poem is the prologue (the beginning of which is translated here) and the first forty lines of the book itself. The prologue follows an *alef-bet* acrostic, duplicated in the translation—with the final three letters of English set off in a triplet at the end. (The Hebrew breaks the acrostic at one point, using two *sins* instead of a *samech*, so that there are twenty-three instead of twenty-two entries in the acrostic. The English follows suit and breaks the acrostic there as well, omitting the letter 'q' and then collapsing the acrostic at the end to avoid padding the Hebrew.)

The revival of the study of Hebrew (linguistics and grammar) was an important part of the general renascence of Hebrew letters in the tenth and eleventh centuries. The first major figure in this "scientific" revival was Sa'adiah Gaon, who writes in the introduction to his Hebrew dictionary (*Sefer HaEgron*) that the people should speak Hebrew "in their coming in and their going out, and in all their occupations, and in the bedroom and to their infants and children." (For more on this subject see A. S. Halkin's article, "The Medieval Jewish Attitude toward Hebrew.")

Line 1: Cf. Psalms 68:35: "Ascribe ye strength unto God"; Psalms 96:6: "Honor and majesty are before him."

2: Cf. Isaiah 40:12: "And meted out heaven with the span."

3: Cf. Isaiah 57:19: "The Lord that createth the fruit of the lips"; Exodus 4:11: "Who hath made man's mouth?"

4: Cf. Song of Songs 3:11: "the crown wherewith his mother hath crowned him."

5: Cf. Ecclesiastes 12:9: "He also taught the people knowledge"; Isaiah 40:14: "And taught him knowledge."

6: Cf. Job 37:14: "Consider the wondrous works of God."

7: Cf. *Hullin* 60b, where "the Small" is added to a man's name to indicate humility. Ibn Gabirol called himself *Shelomoh HaQatan*, i.e., Solomon the Small (or the Lesser). (See notes to "The Palace Garden.") For detailed discussion of the Hebrew poets' use of biblical typology, see Brann, *The Compunctious Poet*, 23–58.

9: Cf. Numbers 27:17: "The congregation of the Lord."

10: Cf. 2 Kings 19:30: "and the remnant that is escaped."

11: Cf. Sa'adiah Gaon, *Sefer HaEgron*: 27–44, in Aloni, 158–59, where Sa'adiah tells of the people of Israel's exile "to all lands and the islands of the sea, and there wasn't a single nation that didn't encounter our refugees . . . we learned their languages." He says that the Jews spoke "Ashdodi" and Greek, and the language of Persia and Egypt, but not the holy tongue. Ashdod was a Philistine town on the Mediterranean coast of biblical Palestine, today the Israeli port town of the same name, between Gaza and Jaffa.

13–14: Cf. Nehemiah 13:24: "And their children spoke half in the speech of Ashdod, and could not speak in the Jews' language, but according to the language of each people"; Job 19:13: "Mine acquaintances are wholly estranged from me."

15–16: "Edom" in the world of Andalusian Hebrew poetry is Rome. "Edomite" in this case is probably the Romance precursor to Spanish. "The tongue of Qedar" is Arabic. Cf. Song of Songs 1:5: "I am black but comely . . . as the tents of Qedar, as the curtains of Solomon." Also Isaiah 21:16.

17: Literally, "in the enclosures of their heart sinking into the depths of the abyss."

18: Literally, "sinking like lead." Cf. Exodus 15:10: "They sank as lead in the mighty waters."

19–20: Cf. Jeremiah 45:3: "For the Lord hath added sorrow to my pain"; Jeremiah 20:9: "And if I say: 'I will not make mention of Him, nor speak any more in His name,' then there is in my heart as it were a burning fire shut up in my bones."

21–22: Cf. Jeremiah 48:36: "Therefore my heart moaneth for Moab like pipes"; Isaiah 16:11: "My heart moaneth like a harp for Moab." The Hebrew plays on the root k-n-r in *kinnor* (harp) and *yam kinneret* (the Sea of Galilee, or the harp-shaped sea).

23–24: Literally: "They didn't know prophecy [the books of the Prophets] or the Book [Torah], or how to read a letter or scholarly composition." Cf. Isaiah 29: 11–12: "And the vision of all this is become unto you as the words of a writing that is sealed, which men deliver to one that is learned, saying: Read this, I pray thee, and he saith: 'I cannot, for it is sealed'; and the writing is delivered to him that is not learned, saying: Read this, I pray thee, and he saith: 'I am not learned.'"

25–26: Cf. Exodus 15:4: "Pharaoh's chariots and host hath He cast into the sea . . . they went down into the depths like a stone"; Jonah 1:13: "The men rowed hard to bring it to the land, but they could not."

27–28: Cf. Isaiah 42:7: "To open the blind eyes, to bring out the prisoners from the dungeon."

29–30: Cf. Exodus 4:11; Psalms 63:12; Psalms 38:14; Ruth 2:12: "May the Lord reward your deeds" (NJPS).

31–32: Cf. Job 32:6: "And Elihu . . . said: 'I am young and ye are very old'"; Isaiah 51:20; Deuteronomy 28:20. The acrostic is broken here, as in the Hebrew.

33: Cf. Deuteronomy 30:17: "But if thy heart turn away"; Job 4:12–16; "Now a word was secretly brought to me and mine ear received a whisper thereof; in thoughts from the vision of the night, when deep sleep falleth on men, fear came upon me and trembling, and all my bones were made to shake."

36: Cf. Proverbs 8:1–3: "Doth not wisdom call, and understanding put forth her voice? In the top of high places . . . beside the gates, at the entry of the city."

38: Cf. Psalms 119:173: "Let thy hand be ready to help me."

39–40: Literally, "Get up and do not say I am only a youth." Cf. Jeremiah 1:5–7: "I have appointed thee a prophet unto the nations [said the Lord]. Then said I: 'Ah, Lord God! behold, I cannot speak; for I am a child.' But the Lord said unto me: Say not: I am a child"; Job 32:9: "It is not the great that are wise nor the aged that discern judgment."

41–42: Literally, "My horn was exalted." Cf. 1 Samuel 2:1; Genesis 24:50: "The thing proceedeth from the Lord."

44: Cf. Ecclesiastes 2:3; "xyst" obviously strains some to maintain the acrostic, but not too much. (In the original the reference is to Leviticus 27:8 and the vow of one offering at the temple: "according to the means of him that vowed shall the priest value him.") A xyst (pronounced ZIST) was, in ancient Rome, a garden walk lined with trees. It prefigures images in the poem's second section (not translated), where Ibn Gabirol describes his *'Anaq* as a garden full of myrtle, roses, and tall trees (ll. 30–31 in Yarden). It also points ahead to the extended and highly charged descriptions of gardens later in the diwan. "In Spain," says the scholar James Dickie, who has written extensively on gardens and garden architecture in Andalusia, "one can never get very far away from Ancient Rome." (Jayyusi, *Legacy*, 1024).

46: The "language of Cain" is, literally, "the holy tongue"; I've sought to avoid the repetition of the phrase (from line 8) and freely interpolated this epithet. It was generally believed in the medieval world that Hebrew was the language given to Adam and spoken until Babel. (The Talmud, in *Sanhedrin* 38b, presents a minority view stating that it was Aramaic.) See also Lewis Glinert on "Hebrew" in *The Encyclopedia of Jewish Thought, Miqra'ot Gedolot* to Genesis 11:1, Rashi and Ibn Ezra, and Angel Sáenz-Badillos in Brann, *Languages of Power in Islamic Spain* (59–68). In any event, the allusion is in keeping with Ibn Gabirol's fiery nature and the redemptive thrust of much of his work. A similar passage in al-Harizi's *Takhkemoni* reads "Our tongue which was a delight to every eye is considered a brother of Cain" (that is, notes Sáenz-Badillos, *Hevel* [Abel], which also means "nothing").

MY CONDITION WORSENED (22:S)

This and the following three poems are classified by Yarden as poems of friendship, and they reflect the medieval experience of *philia* (which ranges, as A. W. Price puts it in his *Love and Friendship in Plato and Aristotle*, "more widely than our friendship ... It includes 'the very strongest affective relationships that human beings form,' such as family relations and even love-affairs,' but ... also ... 'casual but agreeable acquaintance'," 11) rather than the conventions of the period's love poetry. Their hyperbole involves a playful extension and underscoring of the desire for good company, but there are clearly erotic elements in the poet's longing for the pleasure or completion that the friendship provides. The poems themselves, then, become embodiments of that pleasure.

The superscription to this poem in Yarden reads: "And al-Mutawakkil Ibn Qabrun (Yequtiel) wrote to him and invited him to visit while he was ill and he answered him with these verses." Yequtiel was in his nineties at the time.

Line 2: Cf. Genesis 49:3.

6: Cf. Psalms 78:38: "But He ... forgiveth iniquity."

8: Abu Nuwas, the great ninth-century Arabic poet has: "God knows I only left off visiting you for fear of my enemies and those who keep an eye on me. / If I could come I would—crawling on my face or walking on my head" (*'Abbasid Belles-Lettres*, 213).

10: Cf. 2 Kings 2:22: "So the waters were healed."

ALL MY DESIRE (15:S)

The superscription in Brody-Schirmann reads: "And this about a man who was late in coming to see him because he [the poet] was ill."

Lines 1–2: Cf. Genesis 4:7; Job 16:7.3–4: Cf. Isaiah 16:11: "Wherefore my heart moaneth like a harp for Moab ..."; Jeremiah 31:20: "Therefore my heart yearneth for him"; Isaiah 38:15 (NJPS): "All my sleep had fled,"—literally, "I will drive away my sleep."

7–8: Cf. Jeremiah 7:31; Ezekiel 38:18: "And it shall come to pass in that day, when Gog shall come against the land of Israel, saith the Lord God, that my fury shall arise up in My nostrils."

10: In an extended discussion of Andalusian "deep song," Lorca quotes the following verse, from his *Mariana Pineda*, described there as "very Andalusian and very Gypsy": "If my heart had / windowpanes of glass / you would look in and see it / cry drops of blood." He adds, "when our songs reach the very extremes of pain and love they become the expressive sisters of the magnificent verses of Arabian and Persian poets" (*Deep Song*, 36)—which recalls the passage in the Andalusian anthology *Al-'Iqd al-Fariid* attributed to al-Asma'ai: "Al-Asma'ai asked a Bedouin: 'Why are elegies the most noble of poems?' And he replied: 'Because we say them (compose them) when our hearts are on fire.'" (in I. Levin, vol. II: 9).

THE APPLE: I (25:S)

"Apple" (*tufaahah*) in Arabic is feminine, hence the description here. Line 4: Schirmann has a variant reading: "first touched by my hands."

Line 8: Cf. Genesis 27:34: "[Esau] cried with an exceeding great and bitter cry and said [to Isaac]: Bless me, even me also."

9: Cf. Psalms 72:3: "Let the mountains bear peace to the people."

10: As in many of the apple poems, the bite into the apple is associated with a kiss, as the two words involved in the association—*nashakh* (bit) and *nashaq* (kissed)—differ in one letter only, which also look like one another. Cf. Midrash Rabbah 78:9: "'And Esau ran forth toward Jacob and kissed him'; He (Esau) didn't come to kiss him (*lenashqo*), but to bite him (*lenashkho*)."

THE ROSE (65:S)

The superscription in Brody-Schirmann reads: "And a love poem of his." Yarden places it among the poems of "friendship and praise."

Lines 1–2: Cf. Song of Songs 5:13: "His cheeks are as a bed of spices"; Nahum 2:4: "The shield of his mighty men is made red"; Judges 11:1: "Now Jephthah the Gileadite was a mighty man of valor"—"an able warrior" (NJPS).

3–4: Cf. Psalms 38:3: "For Thine arrows are gone deep into me"; Isaiah 26:17: "Like as a woman with child that . . . is in pain and crieth out in her pangs"; Isaiah 65:14: "But ye shall cry for sorrow of heart."

5–6: Cf. Micah 6:6–7: "Shall I come before Him with burnt-offerings, with calves of a year old? Will the Lord be pleased with thousands of rams . . . Shall I give my first-born for my transgression, the fruit of my body for the sin of my soul?"; Isaiah 6:6:7: "Then flew unto me one of the seraphim, with a glowing stone in his hand, which he had taken with the tongs from off the altar; and he touched my mouth with it, and said: Lo this hath touched thy lips; and thine iniquity is taken away, and thy sin expiated."

SEE THE SUN (158:S)

An elegy for his patron Yequtiel, who was murdered by rivals at the Tujibid (Saragossan) court in 1039, when Yequtiel was ninety-nine. The loss was catastrophic for Ibn Gabirol, who had little means of his own and had held Yequtiel in the highest esteem. This is one of his more famous short poems, distinctive in part for its combination of genres—the nature poem and the elegy, its merging of a private sensation of loss with a larger, cosmic response to that loss (and all inevitable loss), and for its perfect embodiment of the natural scene in the cadence and modulations of the poem.

Line 1: The syntax and vocabulary here are reminiscent of the atmosphere and the reversal enacted in Genesis 27:27, where Jacob fools his blind father Isaac by dressing up as his brother Esau and thereby gaining his birthright: "See the smell of my son is as the smell of a field."

2: Cf. Isaiah 1:18: "Though your sins be as scarlet, They shall be as white as snow; Though they be red like crimson, They shall be as wool." The Hebrew word for "crimson" is *tola'a*, which also means worm, as in the worm of the co-chineal insect, from which crimson is made (and from which the word derives: it is a doublet of carmine, from the Sanskrit *krmi[s]*, worm). Crimson, then, carries overtones of Yequtiel's glory, of the blood shed in his murder, and of the worms that "eat through the shrouds" of the dead in the earth. Cf. also Isaiah 14:11: "Thy pomp is brought down to the nether-world; and the noise of thy psalteries; the maggot is spread under thee, and the worms cover thee."

3: The Hebrew verb employed here is used in Scripture only with regard to the dead. Cf. 1 Samuel 31:8: "And it came to pass on the morrow, when the Philistines came to strip the slain," and 2 Samuel 23:10. For "edges," cf. Numbers 35:5, 24:17.

4: Cf. Daniel 8:8: "the four winds of heaven," i.e, the four directions.

6: Cf. Isaiah 16:3: "Make thy shadow as the night in the midst of the noonday"; Psalms 91:1: "O Thou that . . . abidest in the shadow of the Almighty"; Psalms 36:8: "And the children of men take refuge in the shadow of Thy wings."

7: The intense progression of colors is often central to the effect of Ibn Gabirol's poetry: here the movement is from implied daylight to red to violet to grayish black. Cf. Isaiah 50:3: "I clothe the heavens with blackness, And I make sackcloth their covering"; Jeremiah 4:28: "For this shall the earth mourn, And the heavens above be black."

8: Cf. 2 Kings 19:1, "And it came to pass, when King Hezekiah heard it, that he rent his clothes, and covered himself with sackcloth."

THEY ASKED ME AS THOUGH THEY WERE MYSTIFIED (51:S)

Line 1: "Like clouds," i.e., like clouds that bestow rain generously over the land.

3: Cf. Isaiah 14:17: "That opened not the house of his prisoners."

4: Cf. Exodus 35:22; Jeremiah 11:22.

Halper (*JQR* NS IV, 153) discusses the comparison in Arabic poetry of the liberal man to rain and rivers; almost all words denoting "moisture," he says, signify "liberality." Abu Nuwas, for example, writes: "The clouds would be embarrassed to look at / your generosity and compare it to their own"; al-Mutanabbi: "People's gossip has not checked your generosity; / Who would block the course of sudden heavy rain?" (Ajami, *Neckveins*, 56, 61).

ON LEAVING SARAGOSSA (III:S)

The Arabic superscription reads: "Another of his poems, from the time he was leaving Saragossa." This qasida is reminiscent in many respects of Shmuel Ha-Nagid's "On Leaving Córdoba" (see my note there, *Selected Poems of Shmuel HaNagid*) and employs many of the same literary maneuvers as that poem, including similar word play and the loosely adapted three-part qasida structure: an attention-getting introduction that surveys a place of ruin or abandonment (here his present predicament; in the pre-Islamic qasida an abandoned campsite), the journey (in this case a desire for a journey, away from the unsympathetic community), and the boast and praise (the object of the qasida—couched here in a vow to pursue wisdom). Each of these poems was written early in the poet's career as he fled the city of his youth and headed toward a new life elsewhere. Although both poems are drawn from a common stock of conventional images and a similar biographical situation, the characters that emerge are worlds apart: HaNagid's poem is addressed to a friend and expresses an Aristotelian ambition to greatness; Ibn Gabirol's poem is addressed to no one in particular, or to a hypothetical sympathetic reader, and sets up the solitary pursuit of wisdom as its goal. While Ibn Gabirol appears to be emotionally out of control, in fact the poem is cunningly built through a series of paradoxes and mirroring devices that lend it a particular brilliance. The shift from self-praise to mockery of others (*hijaa'*) is characteristic of the poet's Arabic models. E. Zemach has a fine analysis of the poem in *KeShoresh 'Etz* (66).

Lines 1–2: The English reverses the order of the Hebrew lines, for rhythmic effect. Cf. Psalms 69:4: "I am weary with my crying, my throat is dry"; Lamentations 4:4: "The tongue of the sucking child cleaves to the roof of his mouth for thirst"; Psalms 137:6: "Let my tongue cleave to the roof of my mouth, if I remember thee not . . . Jerusalem."

3–4: Cf. Psalms 38:11: "My heart fluttereth, my strength faileth."

5–6: Cf. Psalms 132:4: "I will not give sleep to mine eyes, nor slumber to mine eyelids."

7–8: Cf. Psalms 79:5: "How long will thy jealousy burn like fire?"; Psalms 89:47: "How long shall thy wrath burn like fire?"; Job 6:11.

9–10: Cf. Jeremiah 6:10: "To whom shall I speak and give warning?"

11–12: Cf. Lamentations 1:21: "There is none to comfort me"; Psalms 73:23: "Thou holdest my right hand."

13–14: Cf. Psalms 142:3: "I pour out my complaint before Him"; Psalms 62:9: "Pour out your heart before Him"; Numbers 23:13: "Thou shalt see but the utmost part of them."

15–16: Cf. Job 32:20: "I will speak that I may find relief"; *Yoma* 75a: "'Care in the heart, boweth it down' [Proverbs 12:25]. R. Ammi and R. Assi [explained it differently], one said: One should force it down, the other said: One should tell thereof to others"—wherein the two rabbis vocalize the word for "boweth it down" in different ways and derive different meanings from it.

17–18: Cf. Psalms 65:8: "who stillest the roaring of the seas, the roaring of their waves"; Psalms 122:6; Isaiah 60:5.

19–20: Cf. Zechariah 7:12: "Yea, they made their hearts as an adamant stone"; Isaiah 7:4: "Fear not, neither let thy heart be faint [soft]."

23–24: Cf. Numbers 16:9: "Is it but a small thing?"; Jonah 4:11: "Sixscore thousand persons that cannot discern between their right hand and their left hand."

25–26: Cf. 1 Kings 2:34: "He was buried in his own house in the wilderness"— there is an internal rhyme of *niqbar* (buried) and *midbar* (wilderness, desert), with *midbar* in this instance also meaning a graveyard.

27–28: Cf. Psalms 69:30: "But I am afflicted and in pain"; Psalms 25:16: "For I am solitary and afflicted"; Psalms 119:141: "I am small and despised."

29–30: A play of roots in the Hebrew between *re'a* (friend) and *ra'ayoni* (my idea) leads into the complex patterning of the entire poem: the poet longs for a friend and finds only his mind; in his mind is wisdom; by wearing away his existence (his body) he can come closer to the object of his desire (wisdom and friend), which he finally finds in himself-not-himself, i.e., Solomon the elder (of Ecclesiastes' wisdom literature), not Solomon the Younger, or the Small (see "Prologue to the Book of Grammar," note to line 7). This sort of mirroring is repeated in numerous places in the poem. Of course also in his mind are his enemies, and so the hall of mirrors is not free of paranoia.

31–32: Psalms 102:10: "I have . . . mingled my drink with weeping"; Psalms 80:6: "Thou hast . . . given them tears to drink in large measure." This is also a conventional image in Arabic poetry, e.g., *A Thousand and One Nights* 5:759: "I have already wept blood" and the anthology *Al-'Iqd* 191, 19–22: "And we wept the blood of tears."

33–34: Cf. Ezekiel 5:12: "With famine shall they be consumed."

35–36: Cf. *Yebamot* 112a: "Three [classes] of women must be divorced . . . One who declares . . . 'Heaven is between me and you'"; Nehemiah 9:6: "The heaven of heavens with all their hosts."

37–38: Cf. Genesis 23:4: "I am a stranger and a sojourner"; Job 30:29: "I am become a brother to jackals, and a companion to ostriches"; Lamentations 4:3: "My poor people has turned cruel like the ostrich of the desert" (NJPS)—a verse that is followed by the allusion of line 1: "The tongue of the sucking cleaves."

39–40: Cf. Proverbs 26:12: "Seest thou a man wise in his own eyes? There is more hope of a fool than of him."

41–42: Cf. Jeremiah 8:14: "and given us water of gall to drink"; Job 20:16: "He shall suck the poison of asps."

43–44: Cf. Jeremiah 9:7: "Their tongue is a sharpened arrow, it speaketh deceit. One speaketh peaceably to his neighbor with his mouth, but in his heart he layeth wait for him"; Genesis 43:20: "If you please, my Lord, said [Joseph's brothers]." (NJPS)

45–46: Cf. Job 30:1: "But now they that are younger than I have me in derision, whose fathers I disdained to set with the dogs of my flock."

47–48: Cf. Isaiah 1:18.

49–50: The allusion here involves a characteristic reversal of the terms involved in the scriptural allusion to Numbers 13:33: "And there we saw the Nephilim, the sons of 'Anak [the giant], and we were in our own sight as grasshoppers, and so we were in their sight." HaNagid has a structurally similar image in his response to a poem of support sent to him by Isaac Ibn Khalfon (see also note to "Your Soul Strains and You Sigh," line 22): "They're snakes in your eyes and their own / but in mine they're little green worms . . . for what can a goat (*tayyish*) do to a lion (*layyish*)?" (*Ben Tehillim*, #58)

51–52: Literally, "When I take up my parables [or images] they quarrel"—cf. Job 27:1: "And Job again took up his parable"; also Joel 4:6–8.

53–54: Literally, "this language [of yours] is the language of Ashqelon"—a non-Hebrew coastal city in Scripture, near Ashdod, likewise non-Israelite. Cf. Joshua 13:3, and Nehemiah 13:24: "In those days also I saw the Jews that had married women of Ashdod and their children spoke half in the speech of Ashdod and could not speak in the Jews' language"; also 2 Kings 18:25: "Speak . . . to thy servants in the Aramean language; for we understand it; and speak not with us in the Jews' language"; Jeremiah 5:15. See "Prologue to the Book of Grammar," note to line 11.

55–56: The Hebrew of line 56 involves another of the poem's striking internal rhymes (see note to lines 25–26, 97–98, and 101–2): *qilshoni* (my pitchfork) *leshoni* ([is] my tongue/language). The English is developed further to account for the workings of the ornament. Cf. Psalms 64:4: "Who have whet their tongues like a sword"; Jeremiah 9:7: "Their tongue is a sharpened arrow"; 2 Samuel 22:42. See also *Aggadot 'Olam haQatan* (*Beit Midrash*, Book V, 59): "Said Rav, a man's tongue resembles the sea . . . the sea stinks and the tongue stinks, the sea spits out and the tongue spits out . . . the sea kills and the tongue kills, the sea drives out mire and mud and the tongue drives out mire and mud." This expression of contempt for his rivals and other people in general is part of the rhetorical strategy taken over from Arabic poetry, though, again, it seems particularly suited to Ibn Gabirol.

57–58: Cf. Jeremiah 6:10: "Their ear is dull, and they cannot attend"; Hosea 10:3.

59–60: The reference is dual, involving both biblical and Arabic literature. The primary allusion is to Judges 8:21: "And Gideon arose . . . and took the crescents that were on their camels' necks." But the camels in the poem may also be associated with the pre-Islamic qasida, in which these noblest of animals take the poet/hero across the desert (see line 25–26 again) wasteland; there the camels are contrasted to the other animals also alluded to in the early qasidas. Here the other "animals" are the people—snakes, oxen, ostriches, creatures lower than dogs, and so on. So while not exactly a journey, this section of the poem alludes to some of the conventions of that second part of the tripartite qasida structure.

61–64: Cf. Job 29:23: "And they opened their mouths wide as for the latter rain"—where latter rain, in the Hebrew *malqosh*, echoes the pitchfork (*qilshoni*) of lines 55–56. Also Exodus 30:23: "Flowing myrrh . . . sweet cinnamon."

65–66: Cf. *Nega'aim* 12:6: "Woe to an evil person, woe to his neighbor"; Psalms 120:5.

67–68: Cf. Proverbs 2:5; Deuteronomy 18:11; Leviticus 20:27; Hosea 4:1.

69–70: Cf. Micah 1:8: "For this will I wail and howl"; Jeremiah 4:8: "For this, gird you with sackcloth, lament and wail"; Joel 1:13.

71–72: Cf. Isaiah 58:5: "Is such the fast that I have chosen . . . Is it to bow down his head as a bulrush, and to spread sackcloth and ashes under him?"; *Ta'anit* 2:9: "The first three fasts are on Monday, Thursday, and Monday"—biblical market days and the weekdays on which the Torah is read.

73–74: Cf. Ecclesiastes 9:4: "For to him that is joined to all the living, there is hope."

75–76: Cf. Zechariah 4:10: "For who hath despised the day of small things . . . the eyes of the Lord . . . run to and fro through the whole world."

77–78: Cf. Jonah 4:3: "It is better for me to die than to live"; Psalms 116:15: "Precious in the sight of the Lord is the death of His saints."

79–80: Cf. Proverbs 7:25; Job 31:33.

81–82: Cf. Psalms 7:17: "His mischief shall return upon his own head"; Psalms 35:13: "My prayer, may it return into my own bosom."

83–84: Cf. Habakkuk 2:16: "Thou art filled with shame instead of glory."

87–88: The *shibbutz* (in the Hebrew) is from Ruth 4:1, literally: "Ho, such a one, turn aside, sit down here," where Boaz addresses the kinsman and the elders of the city. The constellation referred to specifically is the Great Bear (the sons of the bear).

89–90: Cf. Genesis 27:40: "Thou shalt shake his yoke from off thy neck."

93–94: Cf. Job 7:15: "Till I prefer strangulation, death, to my wasted frame" (NJPS); Psalms 71:3: "Be thou to me a sheltering rock."

95–96: Cf. Genesis 27:46: "I am weary of my life."

97–98: Another instance of the conspicuous word play referred to above. This time the two terms involved are *sesoni* (my joy) and *asoni* (my downfall or disaster, i.e., death), which is then reversed in the following hemistich.

99–100: Cf. Ecclesiastes 2:21: "For there is a man whose labor is with wisdom"; Proverbs 5:11: "And thou moan when thine end cometh, when thy flesh and thy body are consumed"; Psalms 71:9: "When my strength faileth [is consumed], forsake me not."

101–2: Yet another instance of conspicuous consonant shifting. In line 101 the terms are *anahah* (sigh) and *hanahah* (repose/rest/assumption); in 102 *rezoni* (my leanness—from his asceticism or perhaps his illness) and *mezoni* (my food, nourishment)—implying spiritual nourishment and/or the world to come. The *anaha/hanahah* combination is found at least twice in Ibn Gabirol's diwan and once in HaNagid's.

103–4: Cf. Ecclesiastes 1:13: "I applied my heart to seek and to search out by wisdom"; Proverbs 2:3–5: "Yea, if thou call for understanding, lift up thy voice for discernment; if thou seek her as silver, and search for her as for hid treasures; then shalt thou understand the fear of the Lord, and find the knowledge of God."

105–6: Cf. Job 12:22: "He uncovereth deep things out of darkness"; Psalms 119:18: "Open Thou mine eyes, that I may behold wondrous things out of Thy Law."

107–8: Cf. Ecclesiastes 2:10: "This was my portion from all my labor."

THE MOON WAS CUT (186:S)

Line 1: Cf. Isaiah 14:14; Job 22:14: "He walketh in the circuit of heaven."

2: Cf. Exodus 28:17–19 for the names of the gems, which might also be rendered "emerald/smaragd" and "crystal."

3: Literally, "and there is a star that takes refuge in its shadow"—which alludes to Judges 9:15: "Take refuge in my shadow."

4: The English is a free rendering of the Hebrew that reads: "and the sight of it was like the sight of the letter *yod* with a dot in it." The image of the *yod* with the *dagesh* (dot for emphasis) in it—which in fact does look like the moon and a star—has many parallels in Hebrew and Arabic medieval poetry. Shmuel HaNagid compares the moon to a *yod*, and the Arab poet Alsari Alrafa writes: "And the moon was like the letter *nun* formed in gold / written onto dark blue paper." See Schimmel, *Calligraphy*, chapters 2 and 3 for many parallels in Islamic verse.

5: Cf. Job 4:15: "Then a spirit passed before my face that made the hair of my flesh to stand up."

6: This, too, is a free rendering of the possibly untranslatable image that plays on letters of the Hebrew alphabet. Literally the line reads: "in their remembering the three letters." The "three letters" are those that follow the *yod* in spelling out the Tetragammaton, the unpronounceable name of the Lord—the letters of which are *yod* [with a dot in it], *heh, vuv, heh* (YHVH). So in seeing the moon and the star, the sages or the "men of understanding" instantly filled in the remaining letters and saw there the signature or mark of God on his handi-work. See George Herbert's poem, "Love-Joy": "As on a window late I cast mine eye, / I saw a vine drop grapes with J and C / Anneal'd on every bunch."

MY HEART THINKS AS THE SUN COMES UP (193:S)

Line 1: Cf. Isaiah 10:7: "Neither does his heart think so."
4: Cf. Genesis 38:18: "What pledge shall I give thee?" See also Exodus 22:25.

THE PALACE GARDEN (39:S)

The Arabic superscription reads: "And he also said [this], and it was called 'The Bustan' (The Garden), and it is among his finest poems." Compelling discussion of this complex, ambiguous, and quietly spectacular qasida can be found in Bargebuhr (*Alhambra*, 99, 231) and Scheindlin (in "Ibn Gabirol's Poem of the Palace") and in his article in Sperl's *Qasida*, with translation of the poem, 123, 141). Taking the poem at face value, it is a panegyric for an unnamed patron— that is, a poem in praise of a patron whose favor the poet now seeks. It describes the patron's palace and the gardens within it, then moves on to the virtues of the patron himself. But as is often the case with Ibn Gabirol, the materials of the poem and the description of an apparently realistic surface soon lead one into a maze of metaphysical implication. Like many of Ibn Gabirol's poems, this one enfolds a kind of obsession with patterning, mirroring, and layering—draw-ing much of its imagery from scriptural passages associated with King Solomon, the poet's namesake (see "Prologue to the Book of Grammar," line 7, note, and "On Leaving Saragossa," note to line 27). In *The Face of Spain*, Gerald Brenan describes this sort of pattern as "not a string of identical things repeated, but a design in which each separate element increases in some mysterious way the potency of the others." He notes the arabesque patterns' "apparent complexity of nature" and underlying "law of order and eternal recurrence." For more on the nature and effects of the patterning involved in such a building, and its Solomonic echoes, see Grabar, *The Alhambra*, 16–17, 99–101, 170–78, and Dickie (*The Legacy of Muslim Spain*, ed. Jayyusi, 624–25), who says that the function of pattern in the Alhambra is "to trap and enmesh the eye," thereby drawing the spectator into a more profound and active encounter with the architecture and its inscriptions. Scheindlin ("Ibn Gabirol," 40) also notes relevant parallels in Arabic literature and Scripture: Sura XXVII of the Quran, for example, tells of

Solomon's magical powers in transforming the Queen of Sheba's throne and of his constructing a palace that magically confuses nature and artifice (the glass floor so closely resembles water that the queen lifts her skirt as she crosses it); in Arabic panegyrics, palaces are often described as rivaling those built by Solomon. For more on Solomon's magical powers, see *The Encyclopedia of Islam* ("Sulayman") and the index to Ginzberg's *Legends of the Jews*: "Solomon, a cosmocrator; Solomon, dominion over the whole of creation; Solomon, magic ring of; Solomon, palace of."

Lines 1–2: The opening recalls the Song of Songs 7:12: "Come, my beloved, let us go forth into the field; let us lodge in the villages [or, in NJPS: among the henna shrubs—i.e., in the country]" and establishes both the sensual and allegorically messianic mood of that biblical (Solomonic) book, confusing them in traditional fashion. Schirmann notes that the Hebrew phrase, literally "friend to the luminaries"—in the translation, "friend to the spheres"—is peculiar, and seems to mean: "lover of light" (nature's light and order). Bargebuhr provocatively points out (*Alhambra*, 102) that the term "lover of light" or "light's friend," though hyperbolic, has parallels in the Gnostic vocabulary of Mani, where the "Friend of the Luminaries" is the "First Man's" first helper, created during a "Second Creation." (See Barnestone, *The Other Bible*, 44, and Jonas *The Gnostic Religion*, 217, 221.) While there is no direct line from the Gnostics to Ibn Gabirol, there are numerous similarities: for the light–dark dichotomy, see "I Am the Man"; for the body–soul struggle see "Heart's Hollow," "And Don't Be Astonished," and others; for the macrocosm–microcosm structure see this poem and *The Improvement of the Moral Qualities*; for the relation to the cycle of birth and suffering see "If You'd Live Among Men." In addition, Susan Stetkevych comments, with regard to the poetics of *badii'a*, with which Ibn Gabirol is identified (see notes to "The Garden"), that Abu Tammaam's qasidas are characterized by a "consciously constructed antithetical structure [that] is not only suggestive of a dialectical form (*jadal*) of theological dispute (*kalaam*), but also reflects the subtle penetrations of Manichaean dualism (*thanawiyya*) into 'Abbasid thought" (*Abu Tammaam*, 32). It is at least of interest, then, that this turns out to be a poem about the nature and dynamics of "creation" and "re-creation." For more on this notion see Harry Berger, Jr., *Second World and Green World*, 3–40.

3–4: Cf. Song of Songs 2:11–12: "For lo, the winter is past. The rain is over and gone . . . and the voice of the turtle [dove] is heard in our land"; Jeremiah 8:7: "turtle and swift"—the translation of the biblical *sis* is disputed, and might also be rendered as "crane" and in some instances "swallow." "Swifts" are more in keeping with what happens in spring; Ezekiel 26:13: "I will cause the noise of thy songs to cease." Sperl notes that the revival of spring is one of the standard motifs in panegyrics of this sort and is structurally parallel to the cultural revival embodied in the caliph/patron ("Islamic Kingship and Arabic Panegyric," 22).

5–8: Cf. Psalms 91:1: "O though that dwellest in the covert of the most high and abidest in the shadow of the almighty"; Leviticus 23:40: "goodly trees," or "citron," for "citrus." A short list of fruits cultivated in medieval Spain would include: figs, apples, six kinds of melons, pears, pomegranates, oranges, citron, lemons, grapes, palms (which were difficult to grow), bananas, almonds, quince, chestnuts. Flowers grown there included: spikenard, cloves, gilly flowers, cinnamon, jasmine, narcissus, violets, roses, saffron (crocus). For greater detail see Imamuddin, *Muslim Spain*, chapter 5.

9–10: The English collapses some of the Hebrew description. Cf. 1 Kings 6:7: "[Solomon's] house . . . was built of stone made ready at the quarry"; 1 Kings 7:10: "And the foundation was of costly stones, even great stones," etc., for the remainder of the description of Solomon's "house." Also Psalms 47:10 and 97:9.

11–12: Cf. 1 Kings 6:5: "And against the wall of the house he built a side-structure round about"; Song of Songs 2:1: "a rose of Sharon"—the line is in some dispute and might simply mean, "flower-filled courtyards" or "courtyards were magnificent with flower-beds." Scheindlin (in Sperl) has "and a flat place made smooth, around which are places that make splendid all the courts."

13–14: Or "the buildings there"; literally, for arabesques and screens, "openings and openings and closings."

15–16: Cf. Esther 1:6; Genesis 15:5.

17–18: Cf. Psalms 45:9: "Out of ivory palaces"; 2 Chronicles 9:10–11: "And the servants of Solomon . . . brought sandal-wood and precious stones . . . for the king's house." The Hebrew *heikhalei-* (halls of/palaces of) carries with it an overtone of the mystical Heikhalot literature, which is echoed in some of Ibn Gabirol's liturgical verse, furthering the confusion of secular and sacred splendor. Again, see the Quran, Sura XVII: 43.

19–20: Cf. 1 Kings 6:4: "And for the house he made windows, broad within and narrow without."

21–22: Song of Songs 3:9: "King Solomon made himself a palanquin" (NJPS); Ezekiel 8:12: "Every man in his chambers of imagery." *Maskit* is uncertain: "Mosaics" is inferred from what follows.

23–24: Cf. Job 37:12: "turned round about by His guidance"; Numbers 11:7: "Now the manna was like coriander seed, and the appearance thereof as the appearance of bdellium [or crystal]"; Song of Songs 5:14: "His body is as polished ivory overlaid with sapphires"; Esther 1:6: "a pavement of green, and white, and shells, and onyx marble." Scheindlin has "an ornament among rooms."

27–28: Cf. Proverbs 31:6–7. The key confusion of the natural and artificial intensifies here and prepares us for the garden sequence and the poem's climax, an evaluation of the patron's role.

29–30: Cf. Ecclesiastes 7:3: "By the sadness of the countenance the heart may be gladdened"; Psalms 118:5: "Out of the straits I called upon the Lord"; Psalms 116:3: "The straits of the netherworld got hold upon me."

31–32: Or: "I was soon lifted." Cf. Exodus 19:4: "I bore you on eagles' wings, and brought you unto Myself."

33–34: Cf. 1 Kings 7:13, 23–25: "And King Solomon sent and fetched Hiram out of Tyre . . . and he made the molten sea . . . it stood upon twelve oxen"; *Yoma* 58b: "Concerning the sea which Solomon made." Also the Quran, Sura XXXIV:12.

35–36: Cf. 1 Kings 7:29: "And on the borders . . . were lions, and oxen, and cherubim"; Psalms 104:21: "The young lions roar after their prey, and seek their food from God." This is the passage that gave Bargebuhr reason to think that the palace in question was an early part of the Alhambra, which he claimed was built for Shmuel HaNagid's son Yehosef. (Bargebuhr's claim is hard to support, at least on chronological grounds; Scheindlin argues that it is even harder to accept on linguistic grounds—i.e, that Bargebuhr is misreading the Hebrew.)

Abu Ishaq of Elvira, an eleventh-century Arabic poet who vehemently objected to the Granadan (Berber) king having appointed Yehosef HaNagid, i.e., a Jew, to the position of chief vizier, wrote a long poem against the younger Nagid and the Jews of Granada: "They slaughter beasts in our markets / and you eat their *trefa* [food unfit for a Muslim]. Their chief ape has marbled his house and led the finest spring water to it. . . . Slaughter him as an offering . . . for he is fat as a ram" (trans. B. Lewis, in Stillman, 216). Sultan 'Abd Allah of Granada writes of the decline of Muslim–Jewish relations after Shmuel HaNagid's death: "For a time there was peace and well-being. The treasury was filled, and for several years no dissension was heard and no disorder seen. Then things went wrong. The Jew [Yehosef]—may Allah curse him—played false." He then quotes an intimate of the Sultan on Yehosef: "He has eaten your money . . . and he has built a finer palace than yours" (trans. B. Lewis, in Stillman, 219–20). Whether or not the patron in the poem at hand is Yehosef HaNagid and the palace an early incarnation of the Alhambra, one gets a sense of the wealth, splendor, and power involved.

Oleg Grabar states that there are eleventh-century elements of the Alhambra walls, and that the lions in the fountain likewise appear to be eleventh or twelfth century in style. He sums up the situation well, noting that it is possible that the architects of the Alhambra "sought inspiration from the memory and remains of the palace erected in the eleventh century by the Jewish viziers of Granada, but it seems more likely that the ideas which find expression in the Alhambra belong to a generalized mood of mediaeval Islam and of the Middle Ages as a whole" (Grabar, *Alhambra*, 170). While he values Bargebuhr's work, Grabar is inclined to consider this poem a literary exercise rather than a description of a specific palace. My own sense of the situation—no more than an educated guess—is that the poem refers to Shmuel HaNagid and an idealized account of his residence (see Ashtor, vol. II, 126–29).

37–38: Cf. Proverbs 5:16; Habakkuk 3:8.

41–42: Cf. Ezekiel 46:14; Hosea 13:15; Ezekiel 36:25

43–44: Cf. Isaiah 55:13.

45–46: Cf. Song of Songs 4:10; Song of Songs 4:16; Esther 2:12: "So were the days of their anointing accomplished, to wit: six months with oil of myrrh, and six months with sweet odors, and with other ointments of the women, when then the maiden came unto the king . . . unto the king's house"; Song of Songs 3:6: "perfumed with myrrh."

47–48: Cf. Psalms 104:12: "Beside them dwell the fowl of the heaven, from among the branches they sing."

49–50: Cf. Song of Songs 4:13. Debates of this sort between flowers are common in medieval Arabic poetry and were carried into Hebrew as well (Ratzhaby, "Flowers," 375; *'Abbasid Belles-Lettres*, 166). While the debate here clearly echoes the playful tradition absorbed from Arabic literature, the confusion of inanimate / animate and the emphasis on "degree" feed organically into the design of the poem as a whole. Earlier Hebrew sources also contain arguments of a similar sort between plants (Judges 9:7–15, *Bereshit Rabbah* 93:5).

51–52: Cf. From the morning liturgy: "Be thou blessed, O our Rock, our King and Redeemer, . . . Creator of ministering spirits, all of whom stand in the heights of the universe, and proclaim with awe in unison aloud the words of the living God . . . All of them are beloved, pure [clear, excellent], and mighty."

55–56: Cf. Leviticus 5:7; Isaiah 59:11: "We all growl like bears, and mourn sore like doves"; Nahum 2:8: "And her handmaids moan as with the voice of doves." My reading of these obscure lines follows Scheindlin (Sperl, *Qasida*, 145). One might also understand a conflict between pigeons on the one hand and ring-necked doves on the other.

59–62: The "debate" has moved from the flowers (inanimate) to the doves (animal / non-rational) to a new factor, "deer," though it isn't clear whether or not the poet means the artificial deer (lining the watercourses) or whether he is using "deer" and "virgins" as epithets for the young men and women at court, including the servants. The text is ambiguous, though the progression in the entire poem so far seems to be from the natural and wild to the artificial-resembling-the-natural (and set above it) to the vegetable, then the non-rational animal, then a lower order of rational (with much in common with the nonrational and vegetable). Likewise we have gone from outdoors, to indoors, to outdoors-within-the-artificial-and-controlled, where the above progression is picked up. Scheindlin has a slightly different analysis of the progression, but his focus is similar. The important thing to keep in mind, he notes, is that the debates here cross "the boundaries of genus" and "the patio contains representatives of all categories of medieval thought.... Thus, the patio actually contains a microcosm of the universe, ... in which the poet imagines a competitive spirit with each part vying for supremacy" ("Ibn Gabirol's Poem of the Palace," 38). Cf. Song of Songs 2:9: "My beloved is like a gazelle or like a young hart"; Isaiah 10:15: "Should the axe boast itself against him that heweth therewith?"

63–64: At this point in the progression the course of nature is interrupted, with a construction that recalls Joshua's stopping the sun in its course (Joshua 10:12–13: "Then spoke Joshua to the Lord ... and he said in the sight of Israel: 'Sun, stand thou still upon Gibeon, and thou, Moon, in the valley of Aijalon.' And the sun stood still, and the moon stayed.") This is the *takhallus* (the Arabic term for the transition in the qasida to the object of praise), which will lead into the climax of the poem—praise of the patron. It is important to note, at this juncture, that it is the poet who tells the sun to stop, who manipulates the natural, even as he does so to praise the patron's superiority to that nature. On top of the hill, in the magnificent palace, at the summit of the chain of being established in the palace's microcosm are the poet and the patron. The remainder of the poem now works out their respective roles. Cf. Psalms 104:9: "Thou didst set a bound which they should not pass over." Scheindlin notes that this theme of the poet's power paradoxically being greater than that of his patron is common in world literature. He cites Horace's *Odes*, IV:9, which, like the Horation parallel to "Truth Seekers Turn," highlights the immortality brought about by excellent poetry: "Many a great hero was living before / Agamemnon, but they all unlamented / and unknown, are smothered by night that / never ends: They have no sacred poet" (trans. J. Clancy); Pope has a wonderful imitation of this: "Vain was the chief's and sage's pride / They had no poet and they dyd! / In vain they schem'd, in vain they bled / They had no Poet and are dead!"

67–68: Cf. Proverbs 14:19.

69–70: Cf. Proverbs 8:15: "By me kings reign, and princes decree justice." This and the following verses do indeed sound like they might be referring to a figure like Shmuel HaNagid.

71–72: Cf. Micah 5:7: "And the remnant of Jacob shall be among the nations ... as a lion among the beasts of the forest."

73–74: Schirmann places lines 75–76 before 73–74. Cf. Genesis 23:6: "Thou art a mighty prince among us"; 2 Samuel 19:28: "My lord the king is as an angel of God"; Lamentations 2:9: "Yea her prophets find no vision from the Lord"; Nehemiah 5:8: "Then held they their peace, and found never a word."

75–76: Cf. Psalms 23:1: "The Lord is my shepherd; I shall not want"; 1 Samuel 30:19: "There was nothing lacking to them, neither small nor great"; 1 Samuel 25:15–16.

77–78: Cf. Proverbs 17:27; 1 Samuel 26:21; Exodus 35:22; Psalms 76:12; Isaiah 19:21; Psalms 22:26.

79–80: Cf. Deuteronomy 34:7: "And Moses was a hundred and twenty years old when he died: his eye was not dim, nor his natural force abated"; Deuteronomy 11:17: "He shut up the heaven, so that there should be no rain." Perhaps the most important allusion in the poem, though not a direct *shibbutz*, is to Proverbs 16:15: "In the light of the king's countenance is life; and his favour is as a cloud of the latter rain." This allusion, which hovers over the (assumed) border between secular and sacred splendor, material and spiritual wealth and well-being, is followed by another more explicitly esoteric allusion:

81–82: Cf. *Sefer Yetzirah* (*The Book of Creation*) 3:7: "He made the letter *alef* king over breath, and He bound a crown to it" ("bound to it the highest *Sefirah*"). This is the same word employed in the title of Ibn Gabirol's masterwork, *Kingdom's Crown*; *Tosefta Sotah* 3:18: "All are kings with crowns bound to their head."

83–84: Cf. Ecclesiastes 1:7: "All the rivers run into the sea."

85–86: The line reads literally: "He is one as-against the creatures." Cf. Isaiah 51:2: "For when he was but one I called him." The final praise of the patron sounds suspiciously like Ibn Gabirol's praise of himself in other poems—the extended progression now revealing the poet as dependent upon the patron's "rain" and, at the same time, the vehicle through which the patron is himself ornamented (or "properly equipped"). In this way the poet is superior to him, since his own "second creation" or even "third creation," artifice upon artifice, embodies the patron's magnificence and virtue. Just as the biblical Solomon was able to overcome nature and penetrate the secrets of creation, confusing the artificial and natural, so too Solomon the Small, at least in his verse, can create a literary microcosm that embodies similar qualities and makes the patron "immortal." At this point Scheindlin rightly gestures in the direction of several of Ibn Gabirol's more explicitly religious and mystical "creation" poems (e.g., "I Love You," "Haven't I Hidden Your Name," "He Dwells Forever," and "You Lie in My Palace"). Scheindlin also picks up on articles by Sarah Katz and Yehuda Liebes, which explore Ibn Gabirol's relation to the *Sefer Yetzirah*, including his legendary involvement with the creation of a golem and his identification with King Solomon the magician. In short, as the patron can recognize the poet and grant him his favor, he can also withhold and deny the existence of the poet's powers and worth. More important, however, the dynamic can be reversed, and the poet can either use his gifts to give life and commemoration to the patron's glory, or he can withhold his words, the flow from his fountain, and leave the patron unacknowledged and essentially incomplete. So the poem passes through the various permutations of the poet-patron-nature-art relationship, hovering and shifting, shimmering within the overtones set up by the magician/poet.

WINTER WITH ITS INK (189:S)

Line 1: The tight musical weave of the Hebrew throughout the poem, but especially at the start, matches the look of the letter and the garden: *Katav setav bedyo metarav uvirveevav, uv'et-beraqav hame'eerim vekkaf 'avav.* Cf. Psalms 72:6: "May he come down like rain upon the mown grass, as showers that water the earth." Winter implies the Mediterranean rainy season, as in the Song of Songs 2:11: "For, lo, the winter is past, the rain is over and gone." Generally it can be taken to refer to the months October–March. See Targum Onkelos to Genesis 8:22. Cf. also *Pirkei Rabbi Eliezer* 5:23: "But when the Holy One, blessed be He, wanted to bless the growth of the earth . . . , he opened his treasure of good in the heavens and sent down rain to the earth; these rains were masculine waters and the earth immediately conceived, as a bride is made pregnant by her first husband. There grew there the seeds of blessing."

2: Cf. Psalms 45:2: "My tongue is the pen of a ready writer."

5: The vocabulary of craftwork here and in the following lines is drawn from accounts in Exodus of Bezalel's building the tabernacle. (See introduction— "Bezalel"—and note to "I Love You," lines 14–15. Cf. Exodus 35:30–35 and 38:23. There is an echo as well of the vocabulary used to describe the preparations for the defense of Jerusalem in 2 Chronicles 26:15.)

5–6: Cf. 1 Samuel 2:3: "By Him actions are weighed."

7: Scheindlin translates *hamdah* as "longed for," though he notes that most editors explain that the word in this context meant "envied." Bargebuhr has "delighted in." Ratzhaby offers several parallels for "envied" in medieval Arabic poetry; he also cites numerous parallels for the image of the flowers as stars or embroidery. The biblical "longed for" (as in "desired" or "coveted"— cf. Exodus 20:14, Deuteronomy 7:25, and Proverbs 6:25) seems to me to convey the more complicated overtones of *hamdah*, which implies both envy and desire, and maintains the erotic elements of the personification.

8: Literally, "like its (the sky's) [or his] stars." Scheindlin comments: "The sky writes a letter to the ground in the form of flowers, and the earth responds with a gift in the form of stars. On the level of the imagery, the reciprocity is perfect. But this ideal rhetorical reciprocity is only a trick of the poet's imagination, for although the flowers are real, the stars are not" (*Wine*, 10). In other words, the larger harmony between the heavens and the earth exists in the mind, or in the art, of the poet, who likens the flowers to stars and seeks an explanation for the correspondence he senses. The power from above is, then, a divine artificer, and the creative force below is fashioned and fashions in its image. Other writers have suggested a slightly different, but convincing reading, in which the sky (male) writes a love letter to the earth (female) with its rain. In response to the calligraphy of the sky, the earth embroiders a message of longing along its furrows, reflecting or representing the stars. This is one of the most famous of all medieval Hebrew poems, a small masterpiece without doubt, though it is open to several interpretations. Regardless of how one reads it, the central dynamic is between upper world—lower world, and the so-called ornamental arts are central to its equation. (For more on the image of the primal calligrapher, and the calligraphed manuscript–garden comparison in poetry, see A. Schimmel, *Calligraphy and Islamic Culture* 4 and 121–23.) She cites, for instance, the comparison of the diacritical marks—which were written in colored ink—and flowers.

Bialik notes Brody's comment to the effect that Ibn Gabirol carries out an elegant reversal of the conventional images in the Arabic and Hebrew poetry of the time: the pen of the ready writer is usually likened to lightning, the hands of the patrons to clouds, and the stars to flowers, whereas here the polarity of these images is reversed.

THE GARDEN (181:S)

Yarden classifies this as a nature poem, as it deals directly with the passage from winter to spring in a garden, and its images resemble those used by numerous Arab poets writing in a similar vein. Nevertheless, poems of this sort constitute a subgenre of the wine poem: their subject is the *place* of the drinking session. The wine itself is mentioned only in passing, usually as part of one of the many metaphors used in the description of the garden. Nykl and Israel Levin refer to the medieval Arabic anthology *Al-Badii'a fi Wasf a-Rabii'a* (The Wonders of the Description of Spring), and they note that this anthology contains poems by Andalusian poets alone—none of the Eastern poets are included. The implication is that the Andalusian climate and setting were particularly suited to the genre, that spring there is stunning, and that in this respect the local poets bettered their Eastern counterparts. (For more on this topic, see Jayyusi, "Nature Poetry in Al-Andalus and the Rise of Ibn Khafaja," in *The Legacy of Muslim Spain*, 367–97.) While the nature poem is essentially a minor genre, Ibn Gabirol transcends the limits of the convention; his garden poems are in fact some of his finest works, and they are central to a thorough reading of his oeuvre. For as the garden is the place where members of the court society meet, and where visual, verbal, and musical aspects of its arts are combined, so the garden poetry embraces and often addresses all of these constituent elements of Jewish-Andalusian society.

Alongside its sensual immediacy, its intricate patterning and fullness of presence-in-place, however, this particular garden poem also establishes a curious and slow-release sort of distancing effect—an abstract, even metaphysical dimension. This impression is strengthened when one examines the poem structurally and follows out some of the scriptural associations of its *shibbutzim*. Excellent discussion of the poem's design can be found in Zemach, who notes, for instance, the symmetry of the opening four lines of the Hebrew (eight in the English), with each terse hemistich containing four words. A new syntactical ornament breaks this symmetry—each hemistich of line 5 in the Hebrew contains 5 words, in a chiastic conditional construction of 2 x 3 : 3 x 2. Likewise the progression of pronouns in the poem is of interest, though here there is some controversy (see line 17). Further, the reference to God (first and last line only) serves to frame the processes observed in the poem, and there is also a progression of coloration, from white through darker and "deeper" colors. Throughout this rather deliberate employment of a conceptual grid there is subtle and intense movement—a combination that clearly recalls the visual arabesques of the period. It is precisely this sort of complexity that often renders the identification of Ibn Gabirol's poems by genre misleading.

Parallel in many ways to the theory of ornament followed out in these translations is S. Stetkevych's discussion of the ornamental style known in Arabic literature as *badii'a* (see *Abu Tammaam and the Poetics of the 'Abbasid Age*). Stetkevych traces the word to its root and verb, *abda'a*, to invent, to bring something new into creation, akin to one of the names for God, the Originator: "I would like to propose," she says, "that . . . the *badii'a* style is first and foremost the *intentional, conscious encoding* of abstract meaning into metaphor and further, the expression in poetry of the entire scope of the metaphorical and analytical process that characterized Mu'tazilite speculative theology (*kalaam*), and in a broader sense, the whole cultural and intellectual framework of the era of Mu'tazilite hegemony. . . . The large number of . . . rhetorical devices in *badii'a* poetry is not a mere proliferation due to infatuation . . . . but rather the product of a constant and ineluctable awareness of the logical and etymological relationship between words, and the intention to express this awareness" (*Abu Tammaam*, 8, 30). As the term metaphysical was originally a pejorative in the history of English poetry, so the root *b-d-'a* in Arabic also yields the word for heresy (*bid'ah*), and Arabic literary history records very mixed feelings about the modern poets' inventiveness and break with tradition.

Ibn Ezra referred to Ibn Gabirol as the first Hebrew poet to adopt the *badii'a* approach. Ibn Qutayba says that Muslim Ibn al-Walid (d. 823) was the first Arab poet to employ the style, "the first to make meanings subtle and speech delicate" (Adonis, *Arab Poetics*, 50).

The superscription to the poem in Brody-Schirmann reads: "In which the various ornaments (*badii'a*) are employed in the most supple fashion, with power and originality; a poem that describes the garden beds and the changing conditions of the sun in relation to them."

Line 1: Cf. Song of Songs 5:2: "My head is full of dew, my locks with the drops of night"; Exodus 15:8: "The floods stood upright as a heap"—where Ibn Gabirol uses the scriptural figure from Moses' song of the sea, which celebrates deliverance from Israel's Egyptian oppressors, to describe the miraculous solid state of the water; Scripture refers to "floods," Ibn Gabirol to "dew"; Psalms 33:7: "He gathereth the waters of the sea together as a heap."

2: Cf. Psalms 147:18: "He sendeth forth His word, and melteth them."

3–4: Literally, "it trickles through me." The Hebrew uses the same word (*yitfu*—literally, drip) to characterize the action of the dew and the "juices" of the vine. Cf. Joel 4:18: "The mountains shall drop down sweet wine"; also Amos 9:13, and the great Muslim prose writer, al-Jaahiz, on *nabiidh*, date wine: "When *nabiidh* soaks into your bones, spreads to every organ and suffuses into your brain, it clarifies your mind, redeems your spirit [from care], relaxes you in body and soul . . . . it seeps into your soul and mingles with your blood" (Pellat, 54); Ibn al-Walid: "[Wine] diverts a man's spirit from that which grieves him, and makes miserly tongues give expression to kindliness"; and Abu Nuwas: "[Wine] flows through their limbs like healing through a sick body" (*'Abbasid Belles-Lettres*, 230–31).

6: Cf. Exodus 26:11, where "clasps" are part of the ornamental equipment of the sanctuary.

7: Cf. Ezekiel 8:17: "And, lo, they put the branch to their nose"; Deuteronomy 33:10: "They shall put incense before Thee" (literally, "before Thy nose"); the Hebrew for "fragrance" recalls the myrrh perfume of the Song of Songs (3:6) and the incense offered on the altars of Exodus (30:7).

8: Cf. Zechariah 1:8: "I saw in the night, and behold a man riding upon a red horse, and standing among the myrtle trees." Zemach notes that this passage, which is read with messianic associations, is the only place in Scripture where "myrtle" appears as a plural. Yarden suggests that "myrtle" is simply a generic term for "flowers," or that one is walking among the flowering myrtle trees or bushes. In classical literature the myrtle is sacred to Venus and an emblem of love.

9–10: Cf. Psalms 58:9. There is some dispute over how to read the word *tzitz*—which is used twice. The first time it means "flower" or "blossom" (Isaiah 40:6 and Numbers 17:23; 1 Kings 6:18: "And the cedar on the house [The Temple] . . . was carved with knops and open flowers"). In interpreting the second usage, most editors draw from the reference to Jeremiah 48:9: "Give wings unto Moab." Ibn Janaah in his *Book of Roots* states clearly that the word means "wings." The line says that one who walks about in the garden will be lifted into the air on a petal—or the wing of a petal—so as not to crush the flower-beds. This is the first of a series of extravagant descriptive metaphors, though in fact it seems like a fairly realistic description of the effect of a garden on someone who enters it in spirit. This sort of quiet but hallucinogenic intensity runs through the poem as a whole. Dickie notes that archeological excavations carried out in Spain have revealed that the walking paths in some of these gardens were raised some 50–80 cm. above the level of the flower beds, so that the person walking there had the illusion of "treading upon a carpet woven with flowers"—without, of course, crushing them ("The Hispano-Arab Garden," 245).

11–12: Cf. Isaiah 61:10: "As a bride adorneth herself with her jewels"; Isaiah 3:18. The great Arab poet al-Mutanabbi writes: *wa-fi 'anaq alhasnah yithasan al 'iqd* ("On the neck of the beautiful woman the necklace is made more beautiful"), which has a similar subject and chiastic structure. The image of the sun as a bride is taken from Arabic poetry.

14: Cf. Leviticus 26:17: "And ye shall flee when none pursueth you."

15–16: Cf. 2 Kings 23:11 "And he took away the horses that the kings of Judah had given to the sun . . . and he burned the chariots of the sun with fire." The combination of images in these lines recalls *Kingdom's Crown*, particularly cantos XIV and XVI. Zemach suggests the source of the image is the Greek myth of Apollo, the sun god, who gallops with chariots of fire across the sky. The story, he says, might have reached the Jewish poets through Arabic sources, but he also notes related images in *Pirkei Rabbi Eliezer* 6 and other Jewish sources that show Greek influence: "The sun rides in a chariot, and rises crowned like a bridegroom and rejoicing like a strong man [to run his course], as it is said: 'He is like a bridegroom coming forth from his chamber' [Psalms 19:6]. The sun's rays and aspect that face downward and look to the earth are made of fire, and its rays and aspect that look upward are made of ice. If it weren't for the ice, which extinguishes the aspect of fire, the earth would be devoured in its fire, as it is said: 'His going forth is from the end of the heaven, and his circuit unto the ends of it; and there is nothing hid from the heat thereof' [Psalms 19:7]. In the winter it turns its downward aspect up. And if it weren't for the fire which warms the ice, the world would not survive the cold, as it is said: 'He casteth forth his ice like crumbs; who can stand before his cold?' [Psalms 147:17]. These are the limits of the suns paths." See also Goodenough on the figure of Helios and his chariot in Judaism, especially 168–73.

17: Yarden has "as you pass through the gardens."

20: Cf. Psalms 68:14: "The wings of the dove are covered with silver, and her pinions with the shimmer of gold."

21–22: *Sanhedrin* 91:b: "Antoninus said to Rabbi: Why does the sun rise in the east and set in the west? He replied, 'Were it reversed thou wouldst ask the same question.' 'This is my question,' said he. 'Why does it set in the west?' He answered: 'In order to salute its Maker.'" Also *Kingdom's Crown*, Canto XV.

24: Zemach notes that in the Jewish wedding ceremony the groom marks the taking of the bride into the sphere of his protection by drawing her in under a tallit or a hat or a coat (which is red in some communities)—biblical precedents for which are found in Ruth 3:9 and Ezekiel 16:8.

THE FIELD (182:S)

The Arabic superscription in Schirmann reads: "And he offered this description of the abundant rainfall and the appearance of the first grasses." There are detailed discussions of this poem in Bargebuhr and in Zemach. Once again the poem registers an "upper-world/lower-world" correspondence, again the poet depicts a battle between darkness and light, and again the poem involves a stunning reversal of polarities.

Line 1: Cf. 2 Samuel 22:12: "And He made darkness pavilions round about Him, gathering of waters, thick clouds of the skies"; Job 6:5; 1 Samuel 6:12.

2: For "angry with sorrow" cf. Genesis 40:6–7 and Nehemiah 2:2–3. The implication is that there is a combination of sorrow, or a mourning for the seemingly dead or dying trees and plants, and an anger at that state of things. This sets up Zemach's analysis of the poem's Orphic lyricism and of its focus on resurrection. Bargebuhr discusses the concatenation of metaphorical causes in the poem and the impression they create of a Solomonic magic.

3: Some editors read this line as "like the masts of a ship." The translation is based on Brody-Schirmann and refers to the difference between the heavy storm clouds of line 1, 'avei-shehakim, and lighter cirrus clouds implied by the word 'anaan. Zemach discusses the distinction.

4: Again there are variant readings for this line: Zemach reads "like hunters blasting at rams' horns." The Hebrew alludes to Joshua 13:3 ("lords") and Joshua 6:4–9 ("blast with the ram's horn").

5: Cf. Jeremiah 4:28: "For this shall the . . . heavens above be black"; Isaiah 5:30: "and the light is darkened in the skies thereof."

6: Cf. Job 38:7–9: "When the morning stars sang together . . . when I made the cloud the garment thereof—and thick darkness a swaddling band for it"; Job 6:3. The point is that the light of the stars no longer shines through directly.

7: Cf. Malachi 3:20: "But unto you that fear My name shall the sun of righteousness arise with healing in its wings"; Psalms 139:9.

8: Cf. Job 26:8: "He bindeth up the waters in His thick clouds, and the cloud is not rent under them"; Genesis 7:11: "On the same day were all the fountains of the great deep broken up, and the windows of heaven were opened";

Proverbs 3:20: "By His knowledge the depths were broken up, and the skies drop down the dew." The clouds split and the earth broke open.

9–10: Some versions of the poem have another two lines here from the Schocken 37 manuscript. Schirmann, however, says they are a later addition, and he omits them. The lines refer to the heavy clouds, and read: "How they stood, massed against it, while swift as an eagle they once had fled." Cf. Exodus 39:3: "And they did beat the gold into thin plates, and cut it into threads, to work it in the blue and the purple and the scarlet."

11: Cf. Deuteronomy 32:22: "And burneth unto the depths of the nether-world"; Psalms 38:3: "Thine arrows are gone deep into me," i.e., the rain penetrated the field.

12: Cf. Psalms 65:10–11: "With the river of God that is full of water; Thou preparest them corn, for so Thou preparest her; Watering her ridges abundantly, settling down the furrows thereof, Thou makest her soft with showers; Thou blessest the growth thereof."

13–14: Cf. Proverbs 27:25: "When the hay is mown and the tender grass showeth itself, and the herbs of the mountains are gathered in"; Job 40:20: "Surely the mountains bring him forth food and all the beasts of the field play there"; Deuteronomy 29:28: "The secret things belonging to the Lord our God; but the things that are revealed belong unto us."

15: The Hebrew has the same *stav*, here, the idea being that the poem traces the progress of the seasons.

16: Cf. Isaiah 55:12: "And all the trees of the field shall clap their hands."

THE BEE (184:S)

This poem treats the recitation of the most important prayer in the Jewish liturgy, the *Shema*, whose first part reads in the JPS translation as follows (from Deuteronomy 6:4): "Hear, O Israel: the Lord our God, the Lord is one." The other parts of the prayer are drawn from Deuteronomy 6:5–9, Deuteronomy 11:13–21, Numbers 15:37–41. Following the dictates of the midrash and Talmud, the final syllable of the word "one" (*ehad*) and the end of the first syllable of the word "remember" (*tizkeru*, Numbers 15:40) are emphasized, for reasons outlined below. An interesting and plausible, if unusual, reading of the poem is offered by Avraham Bar Yosef in his *Poems from the Middle Ages* (93–97). In that reading the bee is an image of the People of Israel. Its song, the *Shema*, epitomizes the principles of Judaism, namely, its monotheism and its deliverance from enemies and bondage into the Promised Land. Honey in this scheme is the Torah, the creature is small but of singular importance, and its merit distinguishes it from the nations of the world. In Schirmann the poem is placed with the poems whose authorship is uncertain.

Line 1: Cf. Judges 5:12: "Awake, awake, Deborah; Awake, awake, utter a song." The line employs the wording from the "Song of Deborah"—"utter a song"— as it puns on the name Deborah (Devorah), which also means "bee."

2–3: Cf. *Berakhot* 13b: "It has been taught: Symmachus says: Whoever prolongs the word *ehad* (one), has his days and years prolonged. R. Aha b. Jacob said: [He must dwell] on the [letter] *daleth*. R. Ashi said: Provided he does not slur over the [letter] *het*. R. Jeremiah was once sitting before R. Hiyya b. Abba, and the latter saw that he was prolonging [the word *ehad*] very much. He said to him: Once you have declared Him king over [all that is] above and below and over the four quarters of the heaven, no more is required." *Berakhot* 15b: "R. Hama b. Hanina said: If one in reciting the *Shema* pronounces the letters distinctly, hell is cooled for him"; *Berakhot* 61b: "Rabbi Akiba was arrested and thrown into prison [for studying Torah when the Roman government had issued a decree forbidding the Jews to study and practice the Torah] . . . When R. Akiba was taken out for execution, it was the hour for the recital of the *Shema*, and while they combed his flesh with iron combs, he was accepting upon himself the kingship of heaven. His disciples said to him: Our teacher, even to this point? He said to them: All my days I have been troubled by this verse, '*with all thy soul,*' [thou shalt love the Lord thy God with all thy soul and with all thy heart and with all thy might] [which I interpret,] 'even if He takes thy soul.' I said: When shall I have the opportunity of fulfilling this? Now that I have the opportunity shall I not fulfill it? He prolonged the word *ehad* until he expired while saying it." Also *Pirkei Rabbi Eliezer* 4: "One unifies his name . . . and recites the *Shema Yisrael.*" The line reads, literally, "uniting and extending in 'one.'" Shulamit Elitzur suggests the image of the *dalet* may refer to an old pronunciation of the soft *dalet*, which may have sounded like the Arabic equivalent, closer to a hard "th," as in the word "the" (*Leshonenu La'am*, 39, 7/8), and hence like the buzz of the bee.

4: "Remember" appears in the third paragraph of the prayer: "So that you may remember and perform all my commandments." Cf. Yerushalmi, *Berakhot* 2:4: "One needs to stress [the letter *zayin*] so as to remember." The play is on the Hebrew *tizkeru* (remember) and *tiskeru* (to lease/hire/bribe), which of course should not be confused. Emphasizing the "z" brings the worshipper back to the sound of the bee and the proper intention of the prayer and commandments.

5: Cf. Song of Songs 4:11: "Honey and milk are under thy tongue."

6: Much like Ibn Gabirol's play on Deborah/*devorah* (bee), *Deuteronomy Rabbah* 1:6 contains an extended play on *devarim* (words) and *devorim* (bees): "Just as the honey of the bee is sweet and its sting is sharp, so too are the words of the Torah; any one who transgresses them receives his punishment . . . But any one who fulfils the Torah merits long life. . . . Another explanation: . . . Just as the bee reserves honey for its owner and for the stranger its sting, so to Israel the words of the Torah are the elixir of life, but to the other nations the poison of death." Also Cf. Deuteronomy 6:19: "To thrust out all thine enemies from before thee"; Job 20:12,14: "Though wickedness be sweet in his mouth, though he hide it under his tongue . . . Yet his food in his bowels is turned, it is the gall of asps within him."

7: Cf. 1 Samuel 15:17: "And Samuel said [unto Saul]: 'Though thou be little in thine own sight, art thou not head of the tribes of Israel?'"

8: Cf. Deuteronomy 21:17: "The right of the first-born is his," where Ibn Gabirol plays on the Hebrew phrase and bends it toward meaning: "the choicest sentence/portion is yours."

9: The images relate to the question of food that is kosher, or pure. *Bekhorot* 7b: "The Divine Law expressly permitted honey. For it was taught: R. Jacob says: *Yet these may ye eat of all the winged swarming things*: This you may eat, but you are forbidden to eat an unclean winged swarming thing. . . . An unclean fowl that swarms you must not eat, but you may eat what an unclean fowl casts forth from its body. And what is this? This is bees' honey." Cf. also Daniel 10:11, where Daniel is referred to as a "precious" man ["greatly beloved"], and Ibn Janaah, *Sefer HaShorashim*, h-m-d, where the reference to Daniel is explained as meaning "a man of great virtues and good qualities."

10: Cf. Deuteronomy 14:11: "Of the clean birds you may eat."

ISN'T THE SKY (191:S)

Line 3: Literally, "its stars like lilies," without the embellishment.

4: Cf . Song of Songs 7:3: "Thy navel is like a rounded goblet [or 'the basin of the moon'], wherein no mingled wine is wanting; thy belly is like a heap of wheat set about with lilies." Cf. also Exodus 24:6.

THE LILY (188:S)

The superscription reads: "And someone asked him to describe a flower and he improvised the following."

This riddle-like epigram has drawn widely different interpretations, ranging from D. Magid's suggesting that the poem is a riddle about the bulb of a lily, to Bialik-Ravnitzky's saying it is about the (red) lily itself, to others' saying that it is about the white flower and the long green leaves of the lily or narcissus, to the more convincing recent reading by Shulamit Elitzur in "Epigrams and Riddles," where she claims that the previous writers, in their straining to find complication, had failed to see the obvious, i.e., the poem is about the unopened bud of a lily. Its body (the inside of the bud) is like its dress (the leaves or sepal wrapping the bud): both are greenish white. It is not yet a flower. In its tight, closed state, it is likened to a bride on her wedding night, and to a young girl with her hands (the sepals) clasped over her head (the unopened flower). The variant reading of the penultimate line is reflected in this double-exposure approach to the verse. The first reading is Elitzur's.

Line 1: Bialik-Ravnitzky read: "Don't you know the lily."

4–6: The final image is confusing and has a variant reading (in Bialik-Ravnitzky and Yarden): "like a virgin (young girl) wailing." Brody-Schirmann have "dancing." I have included both. Cf. 2 Samuel 13:19: "Tamar put ashes on her head, and rent her garment of many colors that was on her; and she laid her hand on her head and went her way, crying aloud as she went"; Jeremiah 2:36–37: "Thou shalt be ashamed of Egypt also, as thou wast ashamed of Asshur. From him also shalt thou go forth, with thy hands upon thy head."

NOW THE THRUSHES (199:S)

Lines 1–2: The Hebrew has a general term for "songbirds," drawn from Isaiah, *benot 'agur.* "Thrush" picks up on that bird's distinction for song, as the prosody of the translation enfolds an homage to Hardy and his sense of the line. Cf. Jeremiah 8:7: "And the turtle and the swallow and the crane observe the time of their coming"; Isaiah 38:14: "Like a swallow or a crane, so do I chatter; I do moan as a dove"; Psalms 48:5: "For, lo, the kings assembled themselves"; Ezekiel 17:6; Jeremiah 31:18. The gist of the Hebrew is that the birds sing naturally, without having been taught. The implicit contrast is with the court singers who would likely be in attendance at the garden gatherings, or, by extension, the poets.

3–4: It's natural for birds to sing and men to drink, though the learned latter need some coaxing. Cf. Song of Songs 6:11: "I went down into the garden of nuts, to look at the green plants of the valley, to see whether the vine budded, and the pomegranates were in flower"; Exodus 18:9.

5–6: Cf. Zechariah 9:18.

7–8: The natural (untaught) approaches the courtly (taught) and the circle comes round. Cf. *Genesis Rabbah* 13:2: "All the shrubs of the field and trees were as though speaking to one another." See also Ginzberg, *Legends,* (vol. V, 60–61): "The conception that the animals and all created things chant praise to God is genuinely Jewish, and is not only poetically expressed in the Bible, but occurs quite frequently in talmudic and midrashic literature. . . . The language of trees was understood not only by R. Johanan b. Zaccai . . . but also by the Gaon Abraham. . . . Hippolytus . . . explicitly states . . . that according to the Jewish view 'all things in creation are endowed with sensation, and that there is nothing inanimate'"; Exodus 12:27: "And the people bowed the head and worshipped"; 1 Kings 22:24: "Which way went the spirit [*ruah*—which also means 'wind'] of the Lord from me to speak?"; Psalms 103:16: "For a wind passeth over it, and it is gone"; Job 37:21: "But the wind passeth, and cleanseth them"; Numbers 5:14.

THE APPLE: II (183:S)

The superscription reads: "And another of his poems on an apple, describing its fine beauty." Bialik-Ravnitzky refer to the poem as a riddle, with the solution being "an apple"—again, feminine in the Arabic. The gender is maintained in this poem, with the word for "figure," *gizrah*, also being feminine. Bialik sees the apple here on the branch, moving and flashing in the sunlight.

Lines 1–6: The colors and gems are drawn from numerous sources, including Exodus 28:17 and Leviticus 13:49: "If the plague be greenish or reddish in the garment . . ." The biblical terms have not been precisely identified, and the translation makes somewhat free use of them in order to account for the dominant element in the Hebrew, namely, the acoustic weave and the representation of the greenish, reddish, and gold-like color scheme. Ibn Janaah defines *baraq* ("beryl") as a yellowish gem.

7–13: Cf. Deuteronomy 28:22: "The Lord will smite thee with consumption, and with fever, and with inflammation, and with fiery heat, . . . and with mildew"; Esther 1:6: "upon silver rods [rolls, or rolled silver]"; Song of Songs 5:14: "His hands are as rods of gold"; Exodus 27:17: "All the pillars of the court round about shall be filleted with silver."

14–17: Cf. Judges 21:12.

18–22: Cf. Judges 20:24–5; 1 Samuel 4:18—where the word for "neck" (*mafreqet*) implies "link" or "joint."

23–26: The Hebrew is more collapsed, the last four lines reading, simply, "and kisses their lips."

THE LIGHTNING (180:S)

The superscription reads: "And this in which he describes the descent of fine rain on the garden." What begins as a nature poem shifts through a description of illness and into a love poem.

Lines 1–2: Literally, "Lightning [*baraq*], which has the appearance [or: the color] of *bareqet*, send to the garden of myrtles [flowers] a nursemaid [cloud/*meineqet*]." For more on *bareqet*, the gem, see note to "The Apple: II," lines 1–6. Cf. Number 11:7, where *'ayin*, which normally means "eye" also means "color," and Exodus 28:17, where the gems of the breastplate are mentioned.

3: Cf. Song of Songs 5:13: "His cheeks are as a bed of spices."

5–6: There are variant readings of these lines: I have followed Schirmann (*Hebrew Poetry in Spain*, 218). Yarden reads, literally: "Lightning, strike toward the myrtle, for [the cloud] is sent and stands over against you knocking." Cf. Isaiah 55:10–13: "For as the rain cometh down and the snow from heaven . . . and make [the earth] bring forth and bud . . . so shall my word be that goeth forth out of My mouth . . . Instead of the thorns shall come up the cypress, and instead of the brier shall come up the myrtle"; Psalms 144:5–6.

7–8: Cf. Psalms 65:10: "Thou hast remembered the earth, and watered her"; Isaiah 29:8: "Or as when a thirsty man dreameth, and, behold, he drinketh."

9–10: Cf. Job 37:14: "Hearken unto this, O Job; stand still and consider the wondrous works of God."

11–12: Literally, "Aaron's dashing blood." Cf. Song of Songs 5:2: "My head is filled with the dew, my locks with the drops of the night"; Leviticus 17:2–6: "And the priest shall dash the blood against the altar of the Lord."

13–14: Cf. Genesis 40:10: "And as it was budding, its blossoms shot forth"; Leviticus 19:28: "Ye shall not . . . imprint any marks upon you"; Exodus 28:11: "Thou shalt make them to be inclosed in settings of gold"; 2 Chronicles 2:13: "in gold and in silver . . . in fine linen, and in crimson"; Esther 8:15: "a robe of fine linen and purple."

15–16: Cf. Jeremiah 44:21; Numbers 17:5; Song of Songs 3:6 and 5:13; Job 26:8: "He bindeth up the waters in His thick clouds; and the cloud is not rent under them."

17–18: Cf. Deuteronomy 28:22, "The Apple: II," lines 7–13. I.e., they are green and red but are not sick and "have no fever."

19–22: "Your slave," or "handmaid," meaning, "my soul." Cf. 1 Samuel 25:24; Genesis 49:11: "Binding his foal unto the vine, and his ass's colt unto the choice vine." Also, Abu Mihjan al-Thaqafii, an early Islamic warrior-poet: "When I die, bury me beneath a vine, that its roots may give drink to my bones" (*'Abbasid Belles-Lettres*, 223); Omar Khayyam: "Ah, with the Grape my fading Life provide, / And wash the Body whence the life has died, / And lay me, shrouded in the living Leaf, / By some not unfrequented Garden-side" (*The Ruba'iyat*, XCI, trans. FitzGerald). The image was common in Arabic poetry.

23–24: Literally, "Don't shake out your lap at those who torment you [your friends]"—cf. Nehemiah 5:13.

25–26: Literally, "with the light cast by a graceful gazelle on you, if she spoke, your neck would probably break." Cf. Proverbs 5:19; 1 Samuel 4:18, as in notes to "The Apple: II," lines 18–23, where the same word for "neck" is used.

27–28: Cf. Song of Songs 2:7: "I adjure you, O daughters of Jerusalem, by the gazelles, and by the hinds of the field, that ye awaken not, nor stir up love, until it please"; Song of Songs 8:6: "For love is as strong as death, jealousy is cruel as the grave; the flashes thereof are as the flashes of fire, a very flame of the Lord. Many waters cannot quench love, neither can the floods drown it."

THE LIP OF THE CUP (195:S)

Another example of a poem that transcends its generic limits: what seems to be a straightforward, descriptive wine poem in a light mode ends up as both a metaphysical poem about the nature of poetry and a poem about the superiority of Ibn Gabirol's own verse to that of Shmuel HaNagid. Many of the familiar motifs associated with the wine poem are evident here—the wine is like fire, it flashes like lightning or like glimmering jewels, it establishes an atmosphere of sensuality and blurs boundaries of various sorts. But beyond this, the poet constructs a series of oppositions that lift the poem onto another and more charged plane of meaning: water–fire, cold–hot, interior–exterior, and body–dress are contrasted, and this contrast carries overtones of an argument about art and poetry. The poem begins with a metonymic image linking the lip of the cup with the lip of the poet (in the Hebrew this is a more conspicuous pun, as the word for "lip," *safah*, is also the word for "language"). By extension, then, the wine which speaks (through the poet) and the words of the poet become one.

The superscription reads: "What he said about a morning drinking session and the lightning."

Lines 1–4: Cf. Proverbs 24:26: "He kisseth the lips that giveth a right answer"; Leviticus 10:2: "And there came forth fire from before the Lord, and devoured them [Nadab and Abihu, the sons of Aaron]"; Sanhedrin 52a: "it devoured *them* but not their garments"; Numbers 11:3: "the fire of the Lord burnt among them"; Exodus 3:2: "And he looked, and, behold, the bush burned with fire, and the bush was not consumed"; Genesis 49:11: "He washeth his garments in wine, and his vesture in the blood of grapes."

5–8: Cf. Isaiah 64:3: "Neither hath the eye seen a God beside Thee"; Genesis 1:26: "Let us make man in our image"; 1 Samuel 18:22: "And Saul commanded his servants: 'Speak with David secretly'"; Joel 1:5: "Awake, ye drunkards, and weep, and wail, all ye drinkers of wine, because of the sweet wine, for it is cut off from your mouth"; Job 13:11: "Shall not His majesty terrify you?"—where Avraham Ibn Ezra explains in his commentary that the word for "majesty" (which can also mean "torch" or "beacon," cf. Judges 20:40) indicates fire.

9–12: Cf. Isaiah 40:18: "To whom then will ye liken God? Or what likeness will ye compare unto Him?"; Judges 5:31: "The sun when he goeth forth in his might."

14: "Flow" here is *devari*—literally, "my word," or "my substance"; "the man who steals my desire" is the friend who drinks the wine, which arouses desire, and also, by implication, someone who steals from the poet's sweet discourse.

19–20: These lines are extremely hard to unravel in the original; Schirmann's text reads: "It gloried in a golden mouth over a tooth: 'You'll gather chains'"—though the second half of the line might also refer to another element in the poem that "gathers chains of gold." Cf. Exodus 28:14–15: "And thou shalt make . . . two chains of pure gold." My reading here, which is open to debate, is based on Yarden's textual emendation of *'av* (cloud) for *niv* (tooth).

21–22: Cf. Deuteronomy 3:8–9: "Mount Hermon . . . the Amorites call it Senir." Mt. Hermon is the highest mountain in Israel (formerly Syria). *Targum Onkelos* calls it "the mountain of snow"; *Targum Yonatan* calls it "the mountain of snow on which snow falls through winter and summer alike." In other words, the water of the rain (or cloud—or, according to Yellin in his book of poetics, the wine; in a note to poem 121 of Todros Abulafia he says it refers to the night) was like the snow of Senir.

These lines employ the Arabic rhetorical figure known as *istitraad* (leap, or digression). At least one Arabic theorist has explained that the figure is often exploited in the context of a discussion of poetry and the relations between poets, or poet and patron (Yellin, 302–4). In Arabic, the device calls for a return to the original subject, and the digression is sudden, says Yellin, like a flash of lightning. He notes that the figure is rarely used in Hebrew Andalusian verse, and that Ibn Ezra mentions the verse in question, but catalogues it instead as *takhallus*, that is, a transitional figure (perhaps because in Ibn Gabirol's case it brings the poem to a close, and is more like a spear through the heart than a stinging aside). Says Ibn Ezra: "This poet (Ibn Gabirol) employed a fine transitional device and moved from a description of the dark night and cold cloud to a condemnation of poetry: 'cold as the snow of Senir, or the poetry of Samuel the Kehati' [i.e., of the priestly family; HaNagid refers to himself as "heir of Kehat" in his long wine or boast poem, "Have You Heard How I Helped the Wise," *Selected Poems*, 67, the poem which may have prompted Ibn Gabirol's comment.] This is the poem for which he had to apologize, and he did so often in a long poem . . . of apology that begins '*Qum hazeman*'—Arise, Time, put on your ornaments'" (*Book of Discussion*, 281). In that long poem, which is not translated here, Ibn Gabirol claims that he was misunderstood and slandered by someone who interpreted the poem incorrectly and had it in for him. We do not know the details of the quarrel between the two poets, but, as another poem in this volume indicates ("Tell the Prince," p. 84), it seems that the poem of apology was not well received. Ibn Ezra also has this to say about Ibn Gabirol: "This young man, may he rest in peace . . . would easily take the great to task and he often did so, heaping mockery and scorn upon them" (*Book of Discussion*, 71).

Various writers have speculated on the complicated relationship the two poets no doubt had—with the older and far more powerful HaNagid serving, for a time, as both patron and poetic model for the young star-poet, who was notoriously difficult and arrogant. Bargebuhr suggests that Ibn Gabirol belonged to a rival, probably Saragossan school of Andalusian intellectuals opposed to HaNagid, and this may well have been the case, but the two poets nonetheless needed each other in one way or another. Ibn Gabirol has several early poems of praise addressed to HaNagid, but there are no extant poems of reply from HaNagid to Ibn Gabirol—or at least none that are identified as such. Nor do we have any proof that the two actually ever met—though it seems likely that in fact there was a good deal of contact between them in Granada. Whatever the actual circumstances of the quarrel may have been, this poem seems to represent the beginning of the end for their relationship.

I'D GIVE UP MY SOUL ITSELF (197:S)

This translation maintains (with some leeway) the monorhyme of the original, including the doubled rhyme of the first two lines. It is another classic instance of the poet's lifting a poem in a lighter genre (the wine poem, which initially seems to be a poem of desire as well) into a much more resonant and evocative mythopoetic register.

Lines 1–2: Cf. Exodus 21:28–30: "If an ox gore a man . . . If there be laid on him a ransom, then he shall give for the redemption of his life whatsoever is laid upon him"; Psalms 49:8–9: "No man can by any means redeem his brother, nor give to God a ransom for him—for too costly is the redemption of their soul, and must be let alone forever"; Job 9:7. Ibn Gabirol complicates the associations of the scriptural allusion, where the ransom is paid for one who has committed a crime for which he was sentenced to pay with his life. Here the speaker is willing to pay for the serving boy's beauty (or the wine he offers), and the redemption takes on the menacing associations of the biblical context.

3–4: Cf. Proverbs 7:21: "With her much fair speech she causeth him to yield, with the blandishment of her lips she enticeth him away"; Proverbs 31:6–7: "Give strong drink unto him that is ready to perish, and wine unto the bitter in soul; Let him drink, and forget his poverty, and remember his misery no more"; Isaiah 46:2.

5–6: Cf. Proverbs 23:31–33: "Look not thou upon the wine when it is red, when it giveth its color in the cup, when it glideth down smoothly; at the last it biteth like a serpent, and stingeth like a basilisk. Thine eyes shall behold strange things, and thy heart shall utter confused things. Yea, thou shalt be as he that lieth down in the midst of the sea, or as he that lieth upon the top of a mast." The griffon is a kind of vulture (Leviticus 11:13) and the name, by design in this translation, carries overtones of the griffin, the mythological creature.

7-8: The Hebrew has a homonym here: "Can a *heres* (sun) be put in *heres* (clay / potsherd)?" The English intensifies the rhyme and alliteration but doesn't attempt to reproduce the pun. Cf. Isaiah 45:9: "Woe unto him that striveth with his Maker, as a potsherd with the potsherds of the earth!"; Psalms 22:16.

9-10: The slippery syntax of these lines (where the subject of "its" is twice suspended and initially unclear in the Hebrew) extends and complicates the allusion of the first stanza, where the wine poses a threat with its smooth talk. Cf. Psalms 13:3; Proverbs 31:6-7, above, lines 5-6.

11-12: Bashan appears in Deuteronomy as a region in what is today northern Jordan and Southern Syria. Cf. Hosea 2:20: "And I . . . will make them lie down safely." Og's sixty fortified cities were proverbial: Cf. Deuteronomy 3:1-11: "Og the king of Bashan came out against us, he and all his people, unto battle at Edrei. And the Lord said unto me: 'Fear him not'; . . . So the Lord our God delivered into our hand Og also, the king of Bashan. . . . And we took all his cities . . . threescore cities. . . . All these were fortified cities, with high walls, gates, and bars. . . . For only Og King of Bashan remained of the remnant of the Rephaim; behold, his bedstead was a bedstead of iron . . . nine cubits was the length thereof, and four cubits the breadth of it." Rephaim means, literally, ghosts, though in this biblical verse it refers to a tribe of giants. To fathom the enormity of the powers of the wine in this poem, it helps to recall the figure of Og in the Aggadah. There we read that "Og was born before the Flood and was saved from it by Noah on the promise that he and his descendants would serve Noah as slaves in perpetuity. Sihon and Og were giants, their foot alone measuring eighteen cubits. . . . During his reign he founded sixty cities, which he surrounded with high walls, the lowest of which was not less than sixty miles in height." (*Encyclopedia Judaica*, vol. 12, 1341-42)

TELL THE BOY (218:S)

For more on the charged issue of Hebrew love poetry and homoeroticism, see my *Selected Poems of Shmuel HaNagid*, 167-68. Conflicting views are presented in N. Roth, "'Deal Gently with the Young Man': Love of Boys in Medieval Hebrew Poetry of Spain" and "The Care and Feeding of Gazelles: Medieval Arabic and Hebrew Love Poetry"; H. Schirmann, "The Ephebe in Medieval Hebrew Poetry"; D. Pagis, *Hebrew Poetry of the Middle Ages and the Renaissance*, 45-71; Scheindlin, *Wine, Women, and Death*, 77-89, especially 86-89; and M. Huss's Hebrew article, which is summarized in the notes here to "You Lie in My Palace on Couches of Gold." See also Boswell, *Christianity, Social Tolerance, and Homosexu-*

ality, 133–34, 186–200, 243–66; Dronke, *Medieval Latin and the Rise of European Love-Lyric*, 19–32, 48–97; Blackmore and Hutcheson, *Queer Iberia*; Murray and Roscoe, *Islamic Homosexualities*; and Wright and Rowson, *Homoeroticism in Classical Arabic Literature*.

Lines 1–4: The image is the conventional one of the bright (blond) hair set against the red cheek, which the poet finds miraculous. The original leans heavily on the knowledge of that convention and asks simply: "How can noon embrace the morning?"

5–6: Cf. 2 Samuel 19:20–21: "Let not my lord impute iniquity unto me. . . . For thy servant doth know that I have sinned." Agur (pronounced AgOOR) is one of the names for the biblical Solomon (Proverbs 30:1 and *Song of Songs Rabbah* 1:10), who says: "Grace [charm] is deceitful and beauty is vain [literally: vapor]" (Proverbs 31:30).

8: Cf. Job 5:9 and 9:10: "God who doeth great things past finding out."

BE SMART WITH YOUR LOVE (211:S)

Schirmann (*History*, 298) suggests that, while Ibn Gabirol's other love poems involve the young poet trying his hand at the genre and embracing its "ideal," this poem, precisely because it breaks with the conventions of erotic verse (see Huss and notes to "You Lie"), might accurately reflect the poet's experience.

Line 1: Literally, "Consider and love," with the Hebrew word for "consider"— or "be smart" in this translation—also meaning "set limits" or "check." Schirmann has: "Consider well, my friend." Cf. Deuteronomy 13:15: "Thou shalt inquire and make search."

2: Literally, "find scale [balance] for your love and a circle [boundary]." Cf. Proverbs 4:26; Proverbs 16:11.

3: Literally, "while I looked into the limits [or 'that which has been searched out' or 'the deep things'] of love"—using the same roots (*h-q-r/a-h-v*) as line 1. Cf. Job 8:8; Job 11:7; Psalms 145:3. The poet is cautioned to be moderate, and his own inclination, as we know, is to inquire and seek out the metaphysical dimension in things. The essential word play on the root *h-q-r* pivots on the dual meaning of "be smart" and involves a measure of self irony, which becomes clear in the following lines.

4: Adina, in Isaiah 47:8, means, literally, "a woman given to pleasure" or "the gentle," though it is also a name.

5: Cf. Proverbs 27:5.

7–8: Cf. Psalms 74:6 (NJPS): "with hatchet and pike they hacked away at its carved work"; Joel 4:13: "Put ye in the sickle for the harvest is ripe."

9: Literally, "in the might of love."

10: Cf. 1 Samuel 25:39: "And when David [the son of Jesse] heard that Nabal [the husband of Abigail—in Hebrew, *Avi-guy'il*, in this poem *Avigal*, for the rhyme,] was dead, he ... [David] sent and spoke concerning Abigail, to take her to him to wife."

ALL IN RED (268:S)

The superscription reads: "A witty stanza of his."

Lines 1–2: "Red" might refer to the clothes or the color of the young man's hair. The English reverses the order of the first two lines, which are somewhat obscure in the original and involve a play on the syllable *dom*, which on its own means "silent" or "mute." In the same first two lines Ibn Gabirol also weaves it through the words *adom* (red), *Edom* (Edom, or Rome—see below), and then *Sedom* (Sodom). Cf. Isaiah 63:1–2: "Who is this that cometh from Edom, with crimsoned garments from Bozrah? ... Wherefore is Thine apparel red, and Thy garments like his that treadeth in the winevat?"; Genesis 25:14, *Targum Yonatan*, which involves a play on the names of Ishmael's sons. Edom is normally an epithet for Christianity, and it is also traditionally associated with the Messiah (see "You Lie" and *admoni*). For the Hebrew reader, then, religious associations are raised in the diction of the first three lines, only to be punctured with the final line's explicitly sexual allusion. This combination of allusions might suggest that the poem is addressed to a Slav servant or saki, that is, a European convert to Islam, whom Ibn Gabirol is telling not to worry—he (the poet) is harmless. Also cf. Jeremiah 47:6: "O thou sword of the Lord ... Put up thyself into thy scabbard, rest, and be still"; Psalms 37:7: "Resign thyself (*dom*) unto the Lord."

3–4: Literally, either "By God" (*l'el*) or "It is in my hand to"—where it appears that he is maintaining the religious overtones, playing on the idiom "*l'el yadi*" (it is in my power). Cf. Genesis 31:29: "It is in the power of my hand to do you hurt." Cf. Genesis 19:1–5 for the "men of Sodom."

SHARDS (230, 232, 233, 234, 235, 236, 237:S)

This poem in English is a collage assembled from a string of fragments that appear at the back of Yarden's volume I of the secular poems. The full poems appear in Brody-Schirmann and in Yarden vol. II. Some are of doubtful attribution to Ibn Gabirol. I offer this collage to bring out (sometimes deceptive) overtones much like those of fragments from *The Greek Anthology*.

Line 11: Or "try the passes of the deep."

THE APPLE: III (187:S)

Another apple poem, this one a riddle.

Lines 1–2: Its flesh is silver-white beneath the skin.

4: Or, as though it blushed with shame when it saw us looking at it.

5: Dov Septimus notes a variant version of the line—*hadufah* [for *redufah*], which yields: "like a girl being seized [by the breast] by men." This, he suggests, is based on *Berakhot* 10b (Septimus, 3).

6: Cf. Psalms 71:13: "Let them be ashamed and consumed . . . Let them be covered with reproach."

YOU'VE STOLEN MY WORDS (126:S)

Line 1: Cf. Joshua 7:11: "[They] have stolen and dissembled also"; Jeremiah 23:30; Leviticus 19:11.

2: Cf. Psalms 80:13: "Why hast thou broken down her fences?"; Psalms 89:41; *Berakhot* 63a.

4: Literally: "Did you hope to find [through stealing my poems] help in trouble?"

5: Cf. Deuteronomy 30:12: "It is not in heaven, that thou shouldest say: 'Who shall go up for us to heaven, and bring it unto us, and make us to hear it, that we may do it?'"

7: Cf. 2 Kings 3:18.

8: Cf. Daniel 12:5, and Radaq on *ye'orot*, where he explains that the word normally means "channels," but also refers to the Nile and the Tigris rivers. In Daniel it is "rivers."

THE ALTAR OF SONG (132:S)

Superscription: "About one who claimed for himself some of the poet's work."

Lines 1–2: Cf. Hosea 14:5; Job 16:19; Genesis 41:19: "Presently there followed . . . seven other cows, scrawny, ill-formed, and emaciated" (NJPS).

3–4: Literally, "your knees are weak." Cf. Isaiah 35:3: "Strengthen ye the weak hands, and make firm the tottering knees."

5–6: Cf. Proverbs 1:2–3: "To comprehend the words of understanding; to receive the discipline of wisdom, justice, and right and equity." Line 6, literally, is: "Don't ascend on the altar of poetry by degrees [steps]."

7–8: Cf. Exodus 20:23: "Neither shalt thou go up by steps unto Mine altar, that thy nakedness be not uncovered thereon"; Deuteronomy 25:11: "And the wife of one draweth near to deliver her husband out of the hand of him that smiteth him, and putteth forth her hand and taketh him by the secrets [the private parts]."

TELL THE PRINCE (6:S)

This poem of complaint marks the break between HaNagid and Ibn Gabirol (see Introduction, "Corridors" and note to "The Lip of the Cup").

Line 1: Cf. 1 Chronicles 5:2: "For Judah prevailed above his brethren, and of him came he that is the prince (*nagid*)."

2: Cf. Psalms 87:3: "Glorious things are spoken of thee."

3: Cf. Psalms 28:7: "In Him hath my heart trusted, and I am helped."

4: Cf. Psalms 22:6: "In Thee did they trust, and were not ashamed"; Psalms 119:116: "And put me not to shame in my hope"; Job 6:20: "They were ashamed because they had hoped."

5: Cf. Song of Songs 7:2: "O prince's daughter"; Song of Songs 5:6: "I opened to my beloved; but my beloved had turned away, and was gone."

WHAT'S TROUBLING YOU, MY SOUL (112:S)

The superscription to this poem reads: "And he said upon [about?] leaving Andalusia." It isn't clear, however, when it was written or what the circumstances surrounding its composition were. Nor is it clear where he went. Perhaps the poet is referring to his *desire* to leave Muslim Spain, where his work clearly did not find a sympathetic audience, and go to Egypt, Palestine, or Babylonia. In any event, the poem is a curious combination of sacred and secular strategies: in its gentle opening address it resembles his liturgical poems to the soul; in its reference to the coarse people who plague him and in its use of the curse toward the end of the poem it is clearly a secular poem of complaint, with the familiar stench of self-praise. Yehuda Liebes singles it out as an example of the deceptive way in which poetic categories figure in Ibn Gabirol's work. In essence, Liebes concludes, "there are no boundaries in Ibn Gabirol." Like many of Ibn Gabirol's poems, this one is addressed to *yehidah*, "the only one," an epithet for the soul.

Lines 1–2: Cf. Genesis 21:17: "And the angel of God called to Hagar . . . 'What aileth thee?'"; Psalms 22:21; Isaiah 47:5.

3–4: Literally, "you drag around the wing of your grief," like a wounded bird.

5–6: Cf. Job 14:22: "But his flesh grieveth for him, and his soul mourneth over him."

7–8: Cf. Isaiah 22:16: "Thou hast hewed thee out here a sepulchre."

9–10: Cf. Psalms 62:6: "Only for God wait thou in stillness, my soul"; Lamentations 3:26: "It is good that a man should quietly wait for the salvation of the Lord."

11–12: Cf. Lamentations 3:50: "till the Lord look forth and behold from heaven"; Psalms 123:1: "Thou that art enthroned in the heavens."

13–14: Cf. Isaiah 26:20: "Come, my people, enter thou into thy chambers, and shut thy doors about thee; Hide thyself for a little moment, until thy indignation be overpast."

17–18: Cf. Genesis 15:1: "Thy reward shall be exceeding great."

19–20: Cf. Proverbs 24:21: "Meddle not with them that are given to change"; Ezra 9:2; Psalms 106:35. Literally, don't meddle in the ways of the world. The image of the prison is drawn from later in the poem and elsewhere in medieval Hebrew verse.

23–24: Cf. Jeremiah 4:30: "In vain dost thou maketh thyself fair; thy lovers despise thee, they seek thy life."

27–30: Cf. Lamentations 2:19: "Pour out thy heart like water before the face of the Lord"; Hosea 14:2: "Return, O Israel, unto the Lord thy God"; Psalms 23:3: "He restoreth my soul"; 1 Kings 8:33.

31–32: Cf. Genesis 41:14: "Then Pharaoh sent and called Joseph, and they brought him hastily out of the dungeon."

33–34: Cf. Ezekiel 21:36: "I will deliver thee into the hand of brutish men"; Psalms 119:163: "I hate and abhor falsehood."

36: Erased from memory, crossed out.

39–40: Cf. Leviticus 7:12: "He shall offer with the sacrifice of thanksgiving."

43–44: Cf. Isaiah 54:11: "O thou afflicted, tossed with tempest."

47–50: 1 Kings 19:20–21; Psalms 45:11; Song of Songs 1:4; 2 Samuel 1:23.

51–52: Cf. Psalms 119:143: "Trouble and anguish have overtaken me"; Isaiah 44:8: "Fear ye not, neither be afraid"; Song of Songs 6:5.

53–54: Cf. Job 9:8.

55–56: Cf. Isaiah 38:17: "For Thou hast cast all my sins behind Thy back"; 1 Kings 14:9; Genesis 45:9.

57–58: Literally, "the beautiful land," meaning the Land of Israel.

59–60: Cf. Judges 5:21: "O my soul, tread thou down with strength"; Isaiah 33:10: "Saith the Lord: . . . I will lift myself up"; Isaiah 2:11: "The Lord alone shall be exalted in that day."

61–62: Cf. Jeremiah 31:12: "They shall not pine any more at all." Leviticus 26:16; Deuteronomy 28:65.

63–64: Cf. Isaiah 2:6: "For thou hast forsaken thy people."

67–68: Cf. Psalms 91:1: "Thou that . . . abidest in the shadow of the Almighty"; Isaiah 49:2.

69–70: Cf. Psalms 39:13: "I am a stranger with Thee, a sojourner"; Psalms 119:19; Proverbs 14:30: "Envy is the rottenness of the bones."

75–76: Literally, "they took refuge in their exile." Cf. Zephaniah 3:12: "They shall take refuge in the name of the Lord"; Psalms 68:5: "Extol Him that rideth upon the skies."

78: Literally "the curse of Ben Avi"—i.e., Barak Ben Avinoam, the military leader incited by Deborah to rout the Canaanites, a battle commemorated in the "Song of Deborah," cf. Judges 5, especially 5:23: "Curse ye, Meroz . . . curse ye bitterly the inhabitants thereof."

79–80: Cf. Deuteronomy 29:22: "And the whole land thereof is brimstone, and salt, and a burning"; Deuteronomy 32:22: "A fire . . . devoureth the earth with her produce."

81: Cf. Ecclesiastes 10:16: "Woe to thee, O land, when thy king is a boy."

83: Cf. Deuteronomy 18:2: "They shall have no inheritance among their brethren."

85: Cf. Psalms 21:3: "Thou hast given him his heart's desire."

88–100: From here on the poem is in Arabic dialect written out in Hebrew characters. The initial words of each line, *lahafa ʻala*, might also be translated as "I grieve for," "woe for," or "Oh for." See also al-Maʻarri's similar complaint in Nicholson, 46: *"Lahafa ʻala nafsi . . ."* (My soul grieves for having returned [to my country], instead of dying in Baghdad).

THE PEN (Brody-Schirmann 5)

Lines 1 and 4: Cf. Jeremiah 9:7: "Their tongue is a sharpened arrow, it speaketh deceit; one speaketh peaceably to his neighbor with his mouth, but in his heart he layeth wait for him." The first word of the Hebrew, *ʻarom* (naked), puns on *ʻaroom*, which means clever (like the snake in the Garden of Eden). For more on the use of martial imagery and writing in Arabic poetry see Schimmel, *Calligraphy*, 118–19.

WHAT'S WITH YOU (144:S)

Brody-Schirmann classify this as a poem whose authorship is in doubt.

Line 2: Cf. Habakkuk 3:4: "And there is the hiding of his power." Literally, "women [or 'men'] of hiding."

3: Cf. Jonah 4:7: "But God prepared a worm when the morning rose the next day, and it smote the gourd, that it withered"; *Baba Bathra* 6:2.

6: Cf. Genesis 14:18: "And Melchizedek King of Salem . . . was priest of God the Most High." Ginzberg (*Legends*, IV: 169–70) summarizes the various midrashim that tell the story of King Solomon, who, after having built the Temple, was banished from his home by Asmodeus the King of the Demons.

Deprived of his realm, he became a wandering beggar. "Nor did his humilia-
tion end there; people thought him a lunatic, because he never tired of assur-
ing them that he was Solomon, Judah's great and mighty king."

GOD-FEARING MEN (M.Y. #14, 43)

This is one of several poems by Ibn Gabirol that were recently discovered in the
St. Petersburg Firkovitch Collection. Ezra Fleischer presents them in the journal
Mehqerei Yerushalayim (M.Y.) 14. Fleischer notes that the poem works both on the
objective ethical level of many of the medieval epigrams and, on the subjective
level, as a poem about Ibn Gabirol's personal situation (hence the liberty taken
in the final line of the translation).

Line 2: Cf. Psalms 36:7: "Thy righteousness is like the mighty mountains."
5: Literally, "But the evil"; Cf. Psalms 37:10.
7–8: Cf. Zechariah 10:8: "And they shall increase as they have increased." The
line in the Hebrew is actually a complete *shibbutz*. The translation replaces the
familiarity (to the medieval reader) of the scriptural verse with the familiarity
of the medical detail, which has the added advantage of returning the poem
to the plane of the subject.

YOUR SOUL STRAINS AND YOU SIGH (100:S)

Zemach has a powerful cosmological reading of this poem in his volume on Ibn
Gabirol. Essentially he claims that the poem is a microcosm of the larger philo-
sophical and cosmological schemes that Ibn Gabirol works out in *Kingdom's
Crown* and *The Fountain of Life*. The poet seeks to elevate his soul beyond the
material world and even the stars, and hopes to reach the tenth sphere—the
sphere of intelligence which is just below the throne of God. The thrust here is
a more embodied version of what appears in *The Fountain of Life*: III: 56–57:

'You must ascend in your mind [intellect] up to the highest level of ideation
[the intelligibles] and cleanse and purify your intellect of all sensory impu-
rity, and free it from captivity in nature, and reach by virtue of your mind's
power the outer limit of all that is possible to reach of the truth of the
ideational until at last you will be stripped almost entirely of sensory sub-
stance, as though you did not know it at all. And then it will be as if you
contained the entire physical world in your essence, and you will place the
whole of it in a single corner of your soul . . . and then the spiritual sub-
stances will be as though in your hands, and you will see them as though
they were before your eyes as they really are, surrounding you and above
you, and you will see your own true substance as though you were made

of the very same substance; and sometimes that you are only part of them, because of the bond between you and between physical being; and sometimes it will seem to you that you are the sum total of all these substances and that there is no difference between you and them, because of the oneness between your substance and theirs and the adherence [conjunction] of your form to their forms.' To this the student replied: 'I have done as you instructed me to do, and I rose up the ladder of intellect and wandered in the pleasant groves and found that the sensory was inferior to the ideational [intelligible], and imperfect, and I saw that all of the physical world sailed there like a ship on the sea or a bird in the air.'

(See Wolfson, 296–97.) Zemach divides the poem into three parts: part one consists of seven (Hebrew) distichs (fourteen lines in the English) and brings us through the seven planets; part two consists of thirteen distichs (twenty-four lines in the English) and takes us through the twelve signs of the zodiac and the sphere of day; and part three consists of eleven distichs (twenty-six lines in the English) and takes us into the ten elements of the sphere of intelligence and God above (Zemach, 90–91).

Yarden's edition has the following superscription: "And this is one of his most original and moving creations." Schirmann has: "A poem in which he condemns the flaws of his time and enumerates the virtues of wisdom."

Lines 1–14: The first fourteen lines of the poem consist of a challenge posed by the poet's friends (real or imaginary—Bialik and Ravnitzky suggest it is the divided poet once again giving voice to the conflicting sides of the "argument with himself"). The friends rework the notion presented in Ecclesiastes 1:18: "For in much wisdom is much vexation and he that increaseth knowledge increaseth sorrow." Cf. Psalms 74:23; Job 8:2; Psalms 42:6; Psalms 62:6; Psalms 37:7; Isaiah 34:10. Zemach notes in these and the next four lines the rhythmic and tonal associations of an oceanic feeling on the one hand (the element of water) and the conflicting yearning to rise and be always (*tamid*—which is also the name of one of the sacrificial offerings) in pursuit of wisdom and its heights (like the element of fire) on the other. The English is gauged accordingly. Line 2 might also be translated: "it [the soul] moans."

5–8: Cf. Psalms 24:1–2; Job 38:4. Lines three and four can also be read in a more literal fashion: "You imagine yourself to be like fire whose smoke will always (like an offering) ascend."

9: Cf. Psalms 21:3: "Thou hast given him his heart's desire."

10: Literally, "the Bear and her offspring"—the Big Dipper and the other constellations and stars.

11: Cf. Proverbs 4:7: "The beginning of wisdom is: Get wisdom."

12: Literally, "the heads of the earth—are its last," i.e. men of virtue and wisdom may be uplifted in their minds but in the world they won't get far and will always suffer.

13: Cf. Psalms 119:31; Isaiah 30:11; *Sefer Yetzirah* 1:1: "There are thirty-two paths of wisdom" (the twenty-two letters of the alphabet and the ten spheres).

14: Literally, "The world will spread out its finest cloth (or sheets) for you."

15–18: The poet's response begins here, with a complicated admission of suffering that he then turns against the friends. The Hebrew of the poem eddies and swirls, as the direction of the discourse shifts. Again, the English tries to reproduce this effect, following Zemach's reading. Zemach comments on the characteristically complex syntax of the passage, which he calls "elusive, convoluted, and misleading," noting that it forms an integral part of the content and development of the poem. Employing a kind of syntactical jujitsu, using the force of his friends' argument against them, Ibn Gabirol turns that argument on its head. He begins the main sentence of the stanza as though he were about to apologize for his condition and accept the friends' indictment, but by the time he works through the subordinate clause and reaches the predicate of the main sentence, it is clear that he has simply set the friends up for his strike. After that is delivered (lines 17–38), the poet will answer the friends' initial question (lines 5–10). In Hebrew the convolution is intensified by the use of roots with identical letters: *tz-m-a* (in "thirst") and *m-tz-a* (in "find"). Cf. Jeremiah 31:13: "I . . . will comfort them, and make them rejoice from their sorrow."

17–18: Cf. Psalms 42:3: "My soul thirsteth for God"; Amos 8:11–12.

19–22: Or, "search the families of the world." Cf. Numbers 12:14: "And the Lord said unto Moses: 'If her father had but spit in her face, should she not hide in shame seven days?'" Ibn Khalfon has a similar image in his "Face of the World," a poem addressed to his young friend, Shmuel HaNagid, after the latter's dismissal from an important post he held as head tax-collector in the Jewish community. The circumstances of HaNagid's ouster are murky (he was in his mid-twenties), but from the poem and its superscription one can imagine that personal politics were behind the affair. In any event, Ibn Khalfon writes his friend a poem in which he says, "the world is like the neck of a leper, so it's right to spit in its face."

23–26: Cf. Genesis 32:21: "For he [Jacob] said: 'I will appease him [Esau] with the present that goeth before me . . .'"; Jeremiah 31:34: "For I will forgive their iniquity, and their sin will I remember no more."

27–30: The Sphere of Fortune is the eighth sphere of the zodiac, which governs people's fate. At this point, Zemach notes, we are eight Hebrew lines (sixteen in the English) into the second part of the poems and, as it were, eight spheres into the poet's cosmology. Cf. Deuteronomy 3:26; Ezekiel 33:15; Jonah 4:10: "the gourd . . . which came up in a night and perished in a night"; Zechariah 14:13.

31–32: Cf. 1 Samuel 2:30: "For them that honor Me I will honor, and they that despise Me shall be lightly esteemed"; Proverbs 27:3: "A stone is heavy, and the sand weighty, but a fool's vexation is heavier than they both."

33–34: Line 33 reads literally, "Cut off the tail of those who say"—which Schirmann, Yarden, and Zemach understand sexually, based on the *Targum Yonatan* to Deuteronomy 25:18, as cut off the penis. Rashi comments there: "smiting the membrum; he cut off the membra and threw them up towards Heaven (God) [*Tanhuma*]." In the scriptural passage it means, "cut off the stragglers." Cf. also Psalms 31:24: "The Lord preserveth the faithful" and 2 Samuel 2:19.

35–38: Cf. Proverbs 31:15.

39–40: Literally, "daughters of the sun," which Yarden glosses as "the most beautiful women." Schirmann comments: "Every fine thing they touch is spoiled." Cf. Genesis 6:1–4.

42: Cf. Isaiah 34:13: "And thorns shall come up in her palaces, nettles and thistles in the fortress thereof"; 2 Kings 14:9.

43–44: Cf. 1 Samuel 18:23; Genesis 16:4–5.

45–46: Wisdom withdraws and is closed to them, like a woman, because of their coarseness. Cf. Hosea 13:8: "I . . . will rend the enclosure of their heart." R. David Qimhi comments on the scriptural verse: "Their heart which is closed and doesn't understand."

47: Zemach points out the brashness of the line, as the poet associates the synagogue ark in which the Holy Scriptures are kept and the sexual "opening" of wisdom. Brann discusses the "displacements of sacred text [Scripture]" that are "consciously designed to generate literary pleasure. But when construed as a structure of thought, such allusions can be seen as literate jokes of the tendentious variety which Freud labeled as 'cynical.' That is, they are 'blasphemous' jokes whose production is also designed to 'evade restrictions and open sources of pleasure that have become inaccessible,' except that in the case of courtier culture, it would be more correct to emend this statement to read 'evade restrictions and open sources of pleasure that have *suddenly* become accessible'" (*Compunctious Poet*, 44). Here the displacement is of a religious image, not a scriptural verse; but Ibn Gabirol's work is filled with the latter as well.

48: This line doesn't appear in the Hebrew—I've added it as an ironic extension to the previous images. Part and parcel of the wisdom they shun is knowledge of their own inadequacy.

49–50: Cf. Exodus 31:3: "I have filled him [Bezalel—the artist who designs and builds the ark and the implements for the sanctuary] with the spirit of God, in wisdom"; Isaiah 11:2; Genesis 15:18; 1 Kings 15:19.

51–52: *Exodus Rabbah* 10:4 discusses the Torah and describes it as "a mother to those who study it"; then in passing it refers to Proverbs 2:3 ("If thou call for understanding . . . lift up thy voice for discernment") and states: "Don't read 'If (*im*) thou call . . .' but 'a mother (*em*) will call . . .'"—the change involving only a difference of vocalization under the initial *alef*. As in the poem at hand, the link is between "if," "mother," and "wisdom." Also worth noting with regard to this triangular constellation is the beginning of Ibn Gabirol's poem "Forget about 'if' and 'maybe,'" where the poet is once again being advised to leave his pursuit of wisdom, though this time the advice comes from earth or the world itself.

53–54: Literally, "I've been like a talisman for her and like a necklace on her neck." Cf. Proverbs 25:12; Isaiah 3:20; Song of Songs 4:9.

55–56: Cf. Exodus 33:5: "Ye are a stiff-necked people. . . . Now put off thy ornaments from thee, that I may know what to do unto thee"; Ezekiel 16:11.

57–58: Cf. Psalms 28:7; Judges 19:6; Psalms 36:9.

59–60: Cf. Genesis 2:18: "And the Lord God said: It is not good that the man should be alone"; Job 22:13.

61–62: Cf. Psalms 91:9: "Thou hast made the Lord who is my refuge, even the Most High, thy habitation."

63–64: I.e., wisdom's lord. Cf. Numbers 24:16: "The saying of him who heareth the words of God, and knoweth the knowledge of the Most High"; Hosea 4:1; Isaiah 1:3.

DON'T LOOK BACK (273:S)

Lines 1–2: Cf. Proverbs 4:20, 26: "My son, attend to my words . . . Make plain the path of thy feet. And let all thy ways be established, Turn not to the right hand nor to the left; remove thy foot from evil"; 1 Kings 18:37: "For thou didst turn their heart backward."

3–4: Cf. Malachi 3:14: "Ye have said: 'It is vain to serve God; and what profit is it that we have kept His charge, and that we have walked mournfully because of the Lord of hosts?'"; Isaiah 22:12–13.

6: Cf. Proverbs 5:11: "And thou moan, when thine end cometh, when thy flesh and thy body are consumed."

7–8: Cf. Psalms 129:3: "The plowers plowed upon my back; they made long their furrows."

9: Literally, "Don't sin again now." Cf. Psalms 25:7: "Remember not the sins of my youth."

IF THIS LIFE'S JOY (178:S)

Line 1: Cf. Proverbs 14:13: "The end of mirth is heaviness."

2: Cf. Psalms 121:3; Isaiah 68:7.

3: Cf. Job 14:1–2: "He cometh forth like a flower, and withereth; he fleeth also as a shadow and continueth not."

4: Cf. Isaiah 30:13–14: "Therefore this iniquity shall be to you as a breach ready to fall, swelling out in a high wall, whose breaking cometh suddenly at an instant. And He shall break it as a potter's vessel is broken."

6: Cf. Ecclesiastes 2:11: "Then I looked on all the works that my hands had wrought, and on the labor that I had laboured to do; and, behold, all was vanity."

WHEN YOU FIND YOURSELF ANGRY (M.Y., #14, 38)

This is another of the poems by Ibn Gabirol that were recently discovered in the St. Petersburg Firkovitch Collection and presented by Ezra Fleischer. Fleischer notes that the poem is written in the form of an ethical parable, or proverb, and is likely directed at the poet himself.

Line 4: Cf. Exodus 32:12: "Turn from Thy fierce wrath."

5: "Lord of the sky" in the Hebrew is *adon 'eretz* (with an *'ayin*, not an *alef*)—*'eretz* being a standard medieval epithet for sky. In this case there is also the homonym pun with *eretz* (with an *alef*), which means land. Cf. Psalms 36:12: "Let not the foot of pride overtake me, and let not the hand of the wicked drive me away."

6: Cf. Proverbs 16:5: "Every one that is proud in heart [high of heart] is an abomination to the Lord; My hand upon it! [Hand upon hand] He shall not be unpunished"; Proverbs 15:25: "The Lord will pluck up the house of the proud."

I AM THE MAN (102:S)

Israel Levin calls this one of the more complicated poems in Ibn Gabirol's diwan. It cuts across inherited Arabic genres—*fakhr*, or self-praise, on the one hand, and *wasf*, the description of nature, on the other—and makes use of powerful biblical and mythological undercurrents. The transcendence of generic boundaries is so profound, according to Levin, that it results (here and in many of the other poems that involve self-praise) in the creation of a new genre of "personal" or even "crisis" poems, the characteristics of which are specific to Ibn Gabirol. (Levin suggests, in passing, that it is a late poem, written in Saragossa, though, again, we have no evidence of the poet's whereabouts in the second half of his life.) Bargebuhr offers an extended and often fascinating commentary on the poem and its precursors (*The Alhambra*, 260–327). For instance, prior to his discussion of this poem, which he calls "Ibn Gabirol's great nature poem," Bargebuhr draws our attention to the poem's not-so-obvious mood by citing the Scottish Ballad of Sir Patrick Spence, which serves as an epigraph to Coleridge's "Dejection, An Ode": "Late, late yestreen I saw the new Moon, / With the old Moon in her arm; / And I fear I fear, my Master dear! / We shall have a deadly storm." The parallel can be followed out in the whole of "Dejection," where Coleridge speaks of his "abstruse research" with which he might "steal from my own nature all the natural man . . . ." though "viper thoughts . . . coil round [his] mind." See also excellent commentary by Zemach (*KeShoresh 'Etz*), and Dvora Bregman's fresh reading, which traces the central role of light in Ibn Gabirol's mythic imagination and, in particular, in this apparently straightforward but in fact deeply strange poem. Especially important in this context is Bregman's discussion of Ibn Gabirol's active relationship to the moon in his pursuit of wisdom (*Mehqerei Yerushalayim* 10–11). See also "The Tree," lines 73–80.

The superscription reads: "And he was up late one Friday night and was looking about. And the light of the moon guided his way until the clouds thickened in the air and the horizon grew dark. As the rain began falling, the moon disappeared and he couldn't see it. Then he described this situation and recited a poem that became famous." Ratzhaby reads the superscription differently (in Bregman): "He went out to read by the light of the moon" since it was the Sabbath and reading by lamplight was forbidden. (In *Leqet Shirim* Ratzhaby has a variant reading of the superscription: he understands Sukkot [the autumn harvest holiday], not Shabbat.) Fleischer comments (Schirmann, *History*, 306) along similar lines, adding that the act of reading by the light of the moon in the middle of the month is mentioned in Avraham Ibn Ezra's *Iggeret HaShabbat*.

Line 1: The elaborate rhetorical opening alludes to Lamentations 3:1–4 and, by implication, to what follows there: "I am the man that hath seen affliction by the rod of his wrath. He hath led me and caused me to walk in darkness and not in light. Surely against me He turneth His hand again and again all the day. My flesh and my skin hath He worn out." The second half of the first line reads literally, "girded up his loins" [or "belt"] and alludes to 1 Kings 18:46: "And the hand of the Lord was on Elijah; and he girded up his loins." Also Job 38:3 and 40:7—the Lord to Job, out of the whirlwind: "Gird up thy loins now like a man." There are numerous parallels between Ibn Gabirol's poems of self-glorification and the pre-Islamic odes. Levin (*Me'il*, chapter 4) traces many of them, including the use of military and quest motifs. Here, as Bargebuhr points out, the tone is as much tragic as it is boastful.

2: Cf. Numbers 30:15: "And he causes all his vows to stand."

3: Literally, "whose heart [mind] was frightened by his heart [mind]." Schirmann glosses: "whose drive." Ratzhaby comments: "when his old heart, the seat of wisdom, saw what his new heart had vowed, it trembled in fear." See "My Words Are Driven," note to lines 11–12. Cf. Song of Songs 5:2: "I sleep, but my heart waketh," for a similar portrayal of self-division. Septimus suggests that the line alludes to several rabbinical sources (*Yalqut Shim'oni* 296, *Midrash*

Tehillim 14:1), where man is described as having two hearts, i.e., two im-
pulses, one to good, one to evil, and that what appears to be the presentation
of a modern "divided self" is in fact a standard, Neoplatonic medieval figure
(Septimus, 1).

4: Cf. Job 7:15–16: "Till I prefer strangulation [of my soul], Death, to my wasted
frame. I am sick of it" (NJPS). Also cf. al-Ma'arri: "The soul's being is in the
vile flesh." Line 6: Cf. Isaiah 48:10: "I have tried thee in the furnace of afflic-
tion." Psalms 12:7: "The words of the Lord are pure words, as silver tried in
a crucible on the earth, refined seven times." Bargebuhr quotes al-Muta-
nabbi's example of the Arabic convention of self-praise in the face of hardship:
"Time smote me with so many afflictions / that my very heart became hid in
a cover of arrows; So that when more arrows struck me / their heads broke
against one another." (Also see line 64, this poem.)

7–8: Cf. Ecclesiastes 3:2–3; Jeremiah 1:10; Isaiah 5:5: "I will break down the fence
thereof."

10: Bargebuhr reads: "as misfortune surrounds him."

11: Literally, "And the children of the daughter of days." The Hebrew expres-
sion, meaning "time and its ways," is drawn from the Arabic. The tenses in
English depart from the Hebrew, and some commentators understand these
lines to read: "He'd have made it to the limits of wisdom and right conduct
if it hadn't been for misfortune which surrounded him and fate which shut
him in."

12: Cf. Proverbs 1:7: "But the foolish despise wisdom and discipline."

13: Cf. Jeremiah 31:37.

16: Cf. Psalms 73:26.

18: Cf. Ibn Hazm: "This mortal world whose gifts to man / are loans demanded
back again"—in Bargebuhr.

21: I.e., Even if the day (fate, time) doesn't help me. Cf. Genesis 22:3: "Then
Abraham rose up early and saddled his ass"—to climb the mountain as God
had commanded.

23: Cf. Numbers 30:15–16.

25: Cf. Job 3:25: "For the thing which I did fear is come upon me, and that which
I was afraid of hath overtaken me"; Proverbs 10:24: "The fear of the wicked,
it shall come upon him."

26–27: For Yarden's and Bialik-Ravnitzky's "it was night," Schirmann has:
"While I was resting [sleeping, staying over for the night]"—opening the pos-
sibility that this might have been a dream-vision. Cf. Psalms 24:4.

29: Cf. Isaiah 59:13: "conceiving and uttering." This line in the Hebrew, like its
biblical precedent, has proven hard to decipher, and the English maintains the
ambiguity. The implication is that Ibn Gabirol saw the moon as a powerful,
even magical, guide. (See Bargebuhr, 290–94.)

32: Cf. Malachi 3:17: "I will spare them as a man spareth his own son that serveth him."

34: 1 Kings 20:38: "Then the prophet, disguised by a cloth over his eyes . . ." (NJPS)

36: Literally, "till they welled up." Cf. Jeremiah 6:7.

37: Cf. Isaiah 50:3: "I clothe the heavens with blackness."

39–40: Cf. 2 Samuel 22:12: "And he made darkness a tabernacle round about him, and water gathered together in thick clouds." (Tyndale)

41–42: Cf. Numbers 22:6, 31:8 and Deuteronomy 23:5 for the story of Balaam and the circumstances of his death.

43: Cf. 1 Samuel 17:38: "And [Saul] clad [David] . . . with a coat of mail"—before he went out to face Goliath.

48: Cf. Jeremiah 48:40: "He . . . shall spread out his wings against Moab."

49: The image of darkness as a raven appears often in Arabic poetry, from pre-Islamic verse on (Ratzhaby, "Night Visions," 87–88). Here it is lightning that sends the ravens up into the air. Zemach notes that the image might refer to the lightning zigzagging across the sky, like a bat in flight, and shattering the mass of darkness. Bregman claims that, given Ibn Gabirol's strict imagistic scheme, it isn't likely that a figure of brightness (lightning) could be compared to a bat, which is dark and treated in a negative fashion in rabbinical literature. She suggests that the image refers to the night itself, which brings up the ravens of darkness; these then scatter through the sky and block the light of the moon with clouds. The English maintains the ambiguity of the Hebrew.

53: The implication of the Hebrew is that he is like Samson bound in thick ropes or chains from which he broke free. So the poet's thoughts, will, and heart will break free from their prison of the body. Cf. Judges 15:13–14. Also Psalms 78:65.

54–55: The transition and recapitulation of the poem's earlier images here is not altogether clear, but it seems to be saying that "this is the state of mankind," to be torn from within, and shackled and bound from without, and therefore the poet had best reconsider his ambition. Bargebuhr notes that the "waiting for the moon . . . has all the pathos of the Psalmist and of Job's waiting for deliverance." Cf. Job 30:26: "Yet when I looked for good there came evil; and when I waited for light there came darkness." Also Proverbs 20:20: "Whoso curseth his father or his mother, his lamp shall be put out in the blackest darkness." Bregman comments that the poet is saying: "I will no longer struggle against fate, or time, but instead accept with humility and gratitude what comes my way, like a slave or a servant; I won't make an effort to guard the moon, because in doing so I simply bring harm to it. I will wait with submission for its shining." Bregman notes the unusual nature of this hitherto *active* relationship to the moon, which goes well beyond the conventional use of the figure: "Man has a supernal power but this power works against him; he is capable of interfering with the ways of fate, but this is forbidden, for if he employs his power he will be punished." In a telling parallel to the poem's conclusion, Bargebuhr quotes a letter of Nietzsche, where the philosopher says that he is "no longer waiting for external help, only for internal resources to be mobilized." See also Coleridge's "Dejection," lines 45–46: "I may not hope from outward forms to win / The passion and the life, whose fountains are within."

59: Cf. Psalms 123:2: "Behold, as the eyes of servants unto the hand of their master, . . . so our eyes look unto the Lord our God, until He be gracious unto us."

60: Literally, "has his spear beaten" (or "broken"). Cf. Isaiah 2:4.

61: Cf. Psalms 37:30–31: "The mouth of the righteous uttereth wisdom . . . none of his steps slide."

64: My reading draws on Zemach's comments (*KeShoresh 'Etz*, 64–65). The line might also read, literally: "though he put his holy of holies [dwelling] in the house of [among] the brightest stars [splendor]." The word in question is *nogah*, which most likely refers to Venus. (See also *Kingdom's Crown* XIV— where Venus/*nogah* is the planet that brings prosperity, peace, and renewal.) At least one scriptural association, however, also suggests the moon—cf. Isaiah 60:19–20: "The sun shall be no more thy light by day, neither for brightness (*nogah*) shall the moon give light unto thee; But the Lord shall be unto thee an everlasting light, and thy God thy glory. Thy sun shall no more go down, neither shall thy moon withdraw itself; For the Lord shall be thine everlasting light." Cf. also Proverbs 4:18–19: "But the path of the righteous is as the light of dawn [the light of *nogah*], that shineth more and more unto the perfect day [or 'noon'—NJPS]. The way of the wicked is as darkness; they know not at what they stumble."

AND DON'T BE ASTONISHED (110:S)

A boast in which the poet employs the vocabulary of Genesis and Psalms to establish his superiority over others and his place in the cosmic scheme.

Line 1: Sarah Katz suggests that the initial "And" is not merely for metrical convenience, as others have stated, but that it implies a continuation of a conversation or argument, almost a kind of talking-to-oneself that spills over into a statement to others. Cf. Genesis 43:33, where Joseph's brothers, not knowing that their brother has risen to power in Egypt, are seated at his table and "look at one another in astonishment" (NJPS). Also, *Sefer Yetzirah* 1:12, Sa'adiah Gaon's commentary, where nearly the same wording is employed for the opening: "And don't be astonished as to how He takes the fire from the water"; *Midrash Leqah Tov* (*Va'Ethanan*): commentary to "And God said"—"And a man should not be astonished by the palaces (*heikhalot*)."

2: Cf. Psalms 63:2, "my flesh longeth for thee," and Genesis 32:29, where Jacob wrestles with God and "prevails." Literally, "and is able."

3: See *The Moral Qualities*, chapter 1, for Ibn Gabirol's early discussion of the body/soul relation: "We know that some men may undoubtedly be superior to others, nay more, that one man may be equal to a large number of men— although they be of one form and one composition, except that the soul of one man is predisposed to worldly honor, with the help of the celestial bodies, and his preference for ethical practice, and because the baser part of him is obedient to the higher, i.e., his intellect exercises control over his physical nature." Bar-On comments on parallels to the ethical treatises of the Islamic Brethren of Purity (*Ikhwaan As-safaa'*), Ragib al-Isfahaani (eleventh century), and above all Abu-Bakhr Muhammad Ibn Zakriiya al-Raazi (ninth century), who was one of the most important Muslim doctors and philosophers of the time, and was the author of *Kitaab At-Tib Al-Ruhaani* (*The Book of Spiritual Medicine*), otherwise known as *The Treatment of Souls*. (See introduction, "Tiqqun Middot.") Coleridge has an interesting parallel in his "Dejection": "Ah! from the soul itself must issue forth / A light, a glory, a fair luminous cloud / Enveloping the Earth." Cf. also Jeremiah 31:22, literally: "For the Lord has created something new on earth: Feminine shall encircle male," or in NJPS (reading uncertain): "woman courts a man." "Soul" in the Hebrew is feminine, "body" masculine.

4: The sphere refers to the ninth, all-encompassing sphere in Ibn Gabirol's cosmology. See *Kingdom's Crown* XXIII. Also cf. "Forget About 'If' and 'Maybe'": "And I'm a sphere, it's true— the planets circle through me"; or *KeShemesh meromim*: "The dome of the skies is held in my heart / while the world is held in the dome of the skies." Two English parallels that come to mind are Emily Dickinson's: "The Brain is wider than the Sky" and the Donne quoted in the introduction ("Metaphysics"). See also *The Fountain of Life* III:56 (in the introduction). Bar-On again notes parallels to the Brethren of Purity (Epistle 26): "The sages say, that man is a microcosm." See also *Agadat 'Olam Qatan* (*Microcosmos*), 57: "All that the Holy One, blessed be He, created in his world he created in man. The heavens are the head of a man, the sun and the moon his eyes, the stars the hairs on the head of man."

THE TREE (95:S)

Bialik-Ravnitzky comment: "The poem deals with the poet's despair in the face of time's favors, all of which, even brotherhood and friendship, prove insubstantial, while in fact there is only one consolation for the poet in his sorrow: his addiction to wisdom and study night and day."

Lines 1–2: Haim Brody notes that this expression is taken from the Arabic. Cf. Job 33:3: "My words shall utter the uprightness of my heart"; Job 5:25.

3–4: Cf. Proverbs 1:4; Proverbs 2:11; Ecclesiastes 1:18: "For in much wisdom is much vexation; and he that increaseth knowledge increaseth sorrow"; *A Choice of Pearls* 9:8: "According to the disposition of the heart is the anxiety [grief] one experiences"; Job 3:25: "For the thing which I did fear is come upon me, and that which I was afraid of hath overtaken me"; Lamentations 2:22.

5–6: Cf. Genesis 31:25; Jeremiah 10:20; Job 17:11.

7–8: Cf. Psalms 17:5: "My steps have held fast to Thy paths."

9–10: Cf. Psalms 75:9: "For in the hand of the Lord there is a cup, with foaming wine, full of mixture, and He poureth out of the same; Surely the dregs thereof, all the wicked of the earth shall drain them, and drink them."

11–12: Psalms 147:3.

13–14: Proverbs 28:3; Job 27:6.

15–16: Cf. Isaiah 11:8: "And the sucking child shall play on the hole of the asp"; Genesis 49:17: "Dan shall be a serpent in the way, a horned snake in the path, that biteth the horse's heels."

17–18: Cf. Isaiah 60: 20: "And the days of thy mourning shall be ended."

19–24: Cf. Exodus 19:4; Isaiah 40:31: "But they that wait for the Lord shall renew their strength; they shall mount up with wings as eagles"; Radaq on Psalms 103:5 ("Who satisfieth thine old age with good things; so that thy youth is renewed like the eagle"): "And so R. Sa'adiah Gaon wrote that the eagle flies over all other birds of the air and high up into the heavens and falls into the ocean, and it nears the heat of the primary fire and casts itself into the sea because of the heat and is renewed and its wings rise and it returns to the days of its youth, and it does this every ten years for one hundred years and when it reaches the age of one hundred it rises in its way and falls into the sea and there it dies"; Genesis 2:12.

25–26: Cf. Lamentations 1:3.

27–28: Cf. Exodus 35:35, and Bezalel's work.

29–30: Cf. Job 33:19: "He is chastened also with pain upon his bed, and all his bones grow stiff."

31–32: See line 2, above, Lamentations 2:22; Job 3:25; Proverbs 19:7: "All the brethren of the poor do hate him; How much more do his friends go far from him."

33–34: Cf. Judges 15:14.

35–36: Literally, he hides his eyes from his own nakedness. Cf. *Nega'im* 2:5: "All plagues does a man examine except for his own plagues"; *Ketubot* 105b: "No man sees himself in the wrong"; Isaiah 1:15; Habakkuk 2:15.

39–40: Cf. 1 Samuel 26:8.

41–42: Cf. Deuteronomy 32:24, Onkelos, where *merirav* (bitter destruction) is read as "evil winds." Rashi says *meriri* is the name of a demon that causes destruction.

43–44: Cf. Amos 9:11: "In that day will I raise up the Tabernacle of David that is fallen, and close up the breaches thereof"; Psalms 80:13; Job 38:32.

45–46: Cf. Job 37:16: "Dost thou know the balancing of the clouds, the wondrous works of Him who is perfect in knowledge?"

47–48: Al-Ma'arri has similar lines: "Mine is a nobility that sets the Pleiades beneath its foot" (*'Abbasid Belles-Lettres*, 329). Cf. Isaiah 63:6; Job 9:9; Amos 5:8. Davidson and Loewe offer a list of what these books may have been, tracing them back through a scribal error that surfaced in a book by Yohanan Allemano, the teacher of Pico della Mirandola (fifteenth century). That book, a commentary on the Song of Songs, cites the list offered by an Arabic philosopher, Abu Afla'ah (c. 1100), as "seventeen philosophical essays of King Solomon, the Jew." "King," here, is *al-malik*, a corruption of "Malagite," *al-malaqi*, which is one of the ways Ibn Gabirol was known, as he was born in Malaga. The list includes (in Loewe's translation): *The Book of Experiments, The Book of Old Age, The Book of Apothegms (?), The Book of Perfection, The Book of Causes, The Book of Divine Unity, The Book of the Methods of Inquiry, The Book of the Occasioning of Permanence (?), The Book of the Will, The Book of the Exposure of Falsity, The Book of Rectitude, The Book of Medical Remedies, The Book of Belief, The Book of the Concept of Election, The Book of Sustained Application, The Book of the Schools of Philosophy*, and *The Book of Teleology*. Allemano adds four more books from another source (see Loewe 24–26.): *The Book of Celestial Visions, The Book of Iamblichus (?), The Book of the Work of the Deity, The Book of Moral Choice*. Of the books on the list, only two, it seems, are extant: *Moral Choice*, which we know as *On the Improvement of the Moral Qualities*, and *The Book of Apothegms (?)*, which we know as *The Choice of Pearls*; the remainder have been lost and are not mentioned elsewhere. The twenty-second book credited to him would then be his *Fountain of Life*. Posthumously one would add his diwan (and perhaps the lost biblical commentary).

49–50: Cf. *Sefer Yetzirah* 1:14: "He selected three letters from among the elementals and fixed them in his Great Name. . . . With them he sealed the six directions."

53–54: Cf. Jeremiah 36:23: "And it came to pass, when Jehudi had read three or four columns, that he cut it with a penknife, and cast it into the fire."

55–56: Literally, "from its nostrils." Cf. Job 41:12: "Out of his nostrils goeth smoke"; 2 Samuel 22:9.

59–60: Cf. Job 9:8: "Who . . . treadeth upon the waves of the sea."

61–62: Cf. Numbers 23:10: "Who hath counted the dust of Jacob."

65–66: Cf. Zechariah 6:7: "Get you hence! Walk to and fro through the earth."

67–68: Cf. Isaiah 60:11: "Thy gates also shall be open continuously"; Psalms 52:4:

"Thy tongue deviseth destruction; like a sharp razor, working deceitfully"; Psalms 119:164: "Seven times a day do I praise thee"; Proverbs 24:16.

69–70: I.e., I don't sleep, and my nights run into my days.

71–72: Cf. Psalms 104:2: "Who covereth thyself with light as with a garment"; Ibn Hasdai, *"HaLetzvi Hen"*: "to put on the mantle of dark like a garment."

73–74: Cf. 1 Kings 20:41: "And he hastened and took the headband away from his eyes."

75–76: Bregman comments (455): "A primal negative power, the Creator's enemy." Cf. Ezekiel 29:3.

79–80: Cf. Exodus 34:30–33: "And when Aaron and all the children of Israel saw Moses, behold, the skin of his face sent forth beams; and they were afraid to come nigh him . . . and when Moses had done speaking with them, he put a veil on his face."

81–82: Cf. Exodus 33:8: "All the people rose up, and stood, every man at his tent door."

83–84: Cf. Nahum 3:17.

85–86: See HaNagid's "Gazing Through the Night" for a similar set of pastoral images, which were common in Arabic poetry as well.

87–88: Cf. 2 Kings 23:11.

89–90: Cf. Leviticus 14:9.

91–92: Cf. Isaiah 14:12: "How art thou fallen from heaven, O daystar, son of the morning"; 2 Samuel 21:19: "The staff of whose spear was like a weaver's beam."

95–96: Cf. Jeremiah 46:11: "In vain dost thou use many medicines; there is no cure for thee."

97–98: Cf. Genesis 41:6: "And, behold, seven ears, thin and blasted with the east wind."

99–100: *Ketubot* 13:2: "He who went overseas, and someone went and supported his wife—Hanan says, 'He [who did so] has lost his money, [literally: has placed his money on the antlers of a deer].'"

101–2: These lines are in dispute, and it isn't clear where the friends' comments end. My reading follows Bialik-Ravnitzky.

103–4: See "I am the Man," line 6.

105–6: Cf. Isaiah 53:2–3. The entire passage from Isaiah reads like a description of Ibn Gabirol: "He shot up right forth as a sapling, and as a root out of a dry ground; he had no form nor comeliness, that we should look upon him, nor beauty that we should delight in him. . . . A man of pains, and acquainted with disease, and as one from whom men hide their face; he was despised, and we esteemed him not"; Job 30:18.

109–10: Cf. Song of Songs 1:4: "The king hath brought me into his chamber."

111–12: Cf. Genesis 19:11: "They wearied themselves to find the door"; Psalms 119:130: "The opening of thy words giveth light."

115–16: Literally, "every man without heart"; cf. Proverbs 9:16.

117–18: Cf. Judges 9:3; Job 28:12, 15: "But where can wisdom be found . . . it cannot be gotten for gold."

119–20: Literally, "when those who stray and work evil." Cf. Isaiah 2:12: "The Lord of hosts hath a day upon all that is proud and lofty, and upon all that is lifted up, and it shall be brought low"; Psalms 83:14–16: "O my God, make them like the whirling dust, as stubble before the wind . . . so pursue them with Thy tempest"; Psalms 148:8: "stormy wind, fulfilling His word."

121–22: Cf. Psalms 9:20–21: "Let not man prevail; let the nations be judged in Thy sight. Set terror over them, let the nations know they are but men"; Psalms 149:5: "Let the saints exult in glory"; Psalms 37:2: "For they shall soon wither like the grass, and fade as the green herb."

IF YOU'D LIVE AMONG MEN (176:S)

Bargebuhr calls this "an Islamic poem in the Hebrew language" and quotes "the pessimistic and somewhat gnostic" al-Ma'arri, the poet he feels had the greatest influence on Ibn Gabirol: "I see but a single part of sweet in the many parts sour / and wisdom that cries: Beget no children, if thou art wise." (trans. Nicholson).

Line 1: The first line is deceptive in the Hebrew, as it appears to say: "if you want to live among [with] men of this world." The ambiguity is maintained in the English. Schirmann glosses: "to be among men who live eternal life." Yarden reads: "If you want, among men of this world, to live in eternity in the world to come." Fleischer (in Schirmann, *The History of Hebrew Poetry*, Vol. I, 298) comments: "between life and eternity," which can be understood as "under the Throne of Glory," where the souls of the righteous are placed in *Kingdom's Crown*. The Hebrew implies both an ability to suffer the men of this fleeting world (*heled*) and a desire to live a life beyond them in, or for, eternity (also *heled*, here, relying it would seem on the Arabic, *khuld*, which means infinite duration, eternity, Paradise, the world to come). While this would seem to be an example of ascetic verse in the Arabic manner, the ambiguity of the Hebrew seems to carry with it an additional overtone of the immortality that strong poetry and a good name will bring, as in "Truth Seekers Turn."

Cf. Psalms 17:14–15: "[Deliver my soul from the wicked . . .], from men, by Thy hand, O Lord, from men of the world, whose portion is in this life, and whose belly Thou fillest with Thy treasure; Who have children in plenty, and leave their abundance to their babes. As for me, I shall behold Thy face in righteousness; I shall be satisfied, when I awake, with Thy likeness"; Psalms 49:2; Psalms 96:48; Job 11:17.

2: Cf. Isaiah 33:14: "Who among us shall dwell with the devouring fire? Who among us shall dwell with everlasting burnings?"; Nahum 2:4: "The chariots are fire of steel."

3–4: This line might also read: "Take lightly what the world . . ." Cf. Isaiah 23:9; Psalms 49:13; 2 Kings 19:10; Psalms 49:17; Proverbs 3:13–16. The Andalusian Arabic poet Ibn 'Abd al-Rabbihi (860–940) has: "No matter how great my poverty—I will not sit in grief; no matter how great my wealth—I will not rise above men. I am a man who despises the world and desires neither fortune nor child."

5: Cf. Genesis 16:4: "Her mistress was despised in her eyes" (the story of Hagar and Sarah); Proverbs 13:18: "Poverty and shame shall be to him that refuseth instruction."

6: As Bargebuhr points out, this line is heretical in the Jewish tradition, where the commandment is to "be fruitful and multiply" (Genesis 1:28). Cf. 1 Chronicles 2:30: "But Seled died without children." Seled was in the line of Judah (see 1 Chronicles 2:3f.).

8: Cf. Psalms 78:27: "He caused flesh also to rain upon them as the dust."

WHY ARE YOU FRIGHTENED (175:S)

Bialik notes the Arabic superscription: "And this on the elevation of the soul." Schirmann has: "And this on the same matter [the ascetic life—*tazahud*]."

Line 1: Cf. Psalms 42:12: "Why are thou cast down, O my soul? And why moanest thou within me?"; Deuteronomy 1:17.

2: Cf. 2 Kings 8:1: "Sojourn wheresoever thou canst sojourn."

3: Cf. 1 Kings 18:44: "Behold, there ariseth a cloud out of the sea, as small as a man's hand." In the Hebrew the line is put as a question: "If you consider the world to be as small as a hand, where can you go?"

4: Literally: "Where, afflicted and stormy, will you turn?" Cf. Isaiah 54:11: "O thou afflicted, tossed with tempest."

5: Cf. 1 Kings 2:42: "On the day thou goest out, and walkest abroad any whither, thou shalt surely die"; 2 Kings 5:25; Psalms 61:8: "May he be enthroned [sit] before God forever!"

7–8: Cf. Zechariah 7:3; Jeremiah 31:15.

9–10: Bialik-Ravnitzky point out that these lines can be read several ways. One reading takes "your desire" or "lust" to refer to bodily appetite the soul is faced with. Another possible reading would be: If the soul's desire [for wisdom and understanding], which the poet would pursue in his wandering, is held in a fortified city, the desire will nevertheless be satisfied with a little effort. The translation follows the first reading, which is also that of Schirmann, who glosses: "It is possible to overcome the desire." Cf. Ecclesiastes

9:14–15: "There was a little city, and few men within it; and there came a great king against it, and besieged it." The *Targum* to these verses interprets them as a parable: "The evil inclination [*yetzer ha-ra‘* which in Hebrew has a root that is close to *mivtzar* (fortress), and *tatzuri* (to lay siege)] entered into the body of man and it built on him a place to sit so that it might lure him away from the straight path before God and trap him in the enormous nets of Gehinnom. . . . But there is also found in the body the desire for good [*yetzer ha-tov*] which is miserable and wise and which overcomes the evil desire with its wisdom and saves the body from the judgments of hell [Gehinnom]." Cf. also 2 Kings 3:19: "You shall smite every fortified city"; Psalms 10:3: "For the wicked boasteth of his heart's desire."

11–12: Cf. Deuteronomy 18:1: "[They] shall have no portion or inheritance"; Judges 5:12: "Awake, awake, Deborah; Awake, awake, utter song."

A KITE (117:S)

Bialik-Ravnitzky describe this as "a complaint about a patron-friend who left him when he was in need and separated himself from him." The Arabic superscription in Brody-Schirmann, however, suggests a somewhat different emphasis: "And he said this about the ascetic life." The poem seems to be modeled on Psalm 142, especially verses 1–5, though the allusions to Job are also central (see Introduction, "I, Ideal"). The "kite" of the title and line 16 is a bird (possibly of the falcon family), mentioned in Leviticus 11:14, literally, "the swooper."

Line 1: The Hebrew is singular—"wound," though it refers both to the physical sores caused by his illness and the general sense of woundedness the poet had. Cf. Jeremiah 15:18: "Why is my pain perpetual and my wound incurable?"

2: Cf. Judges 16:17; Isaiah 40:29; Exodus 32:18.

3: Cf. Psalms 142:1–5: "Maschil of David, when he was in the cave; a Prayer. With my voice I cry unto the Lord; with my voice I make supplication unto the Lord. I pour out my complaint before Him, I declare before Him my trouble; . . . Look on my right hand, and see, for there is no man that knoweth me; I have no way to flee; No man careth for my soul. . . . Attend unto my cry; for I am brought very low. Deliver me from my persecutors; for they are too strong for me. Bring my soul out of prison, that I may give thanks unto Thy name."

4: Cf. Genesis 8:9; Lamentations 1:3; Exodus 31:17.

5–6: Cf. Psalms 73:26: "My flesh and my heart faileth"; Isaiah 33:4.

7: Literally, "the size of my sin [or 'punishment'], great pain, and separation." The noun referring to the poet's isolation, *perud*, usually refers to forced separation from friends, and may explain the apparently contradictory readings implied by the two superscriptions. Given Gabirol's temperament, it is likely that much of his isolation was rooted in a combination of choice (the contemplative life) and character (he both put people off and, it isn't a stretch to imagine, invited quarrels). The English "estrangement" tries to account for that combination. Cf. Psalms 32:10: "Many are the sorrows of the wicked."

8: Cf. I Samuel 6:20: "Who is able to stand before the Lord?"

9–10: Cf. Job 7:12: "Am I a sea, or a sea-monster, that thou settest a watch over me?"; Job 6:12: "Is my strength the strength of stones? or is my flesh of brass?"; Isaiah 48:4: "Because I knew that thou art obstinate, and thy neck is an iron sinew and thy brow brass."

11–12: Cf. Lamentations 3:5; Deuteronomy 2:19.

13–14: C. Job 10:6: "Thou inquirest after mine iniquity, and searchest after my sin"; 2 Chronicles 24:6.

15–16: The soul here is not a sparrow, but a hawklike, predatory bird. Cf. Psalms 25:18: "See mine affliction and my travail"; Psalms 124:7: "Our soul is escaped as a bird out of the snare of the fowlers."

AND HEART'S HOLLOW (173: S)

The Arabic superscription from Schirmann-Brody reads: "And this which speaks in dispraise of Time."

Lines 1–4: Cf. Job 11:12:1 "A hollow man shall get understanding" (NJPS).

6: Literally, "find evil" or "come to a bad end." "Corruption" picks up on Schirmann's gloss to the previous lines.

7: This line might also be understood: "Man in the ground rejoices in nothing."

8–9: The implied metaphor of rebellion and struggle in this line is that of servant–body opposing master–soul (or master of the world, i.e. God); Cf. Proverbs 30:22–23: "For a servant when he reigneth . . . And a handmaid that is heir to her mistress"; I Kings 16:9–10 and 2 Kings 9:31: "Is all well, Zimri, murderer of your master" (NJPS).

10–11: Cf. Micah 7:6–10: "For the son dishonoreth the father, the daughter riseth up against her mother . . . A man's enemies are the men of his own house. But as for me, I will look unto the Lord. . . . He will bring me forth to the light . . . Who said unto me: Where is the Lord thy God? Mine eyes shall gaze upon her; Now shall she be trodden down as the mire of the streets." The English reverses the order of the Hebrew images in these lines.

13: "The overthrow of the social hierarchy mirrors the reversal of the cosmic hierarchy in the minds of the Philistine masses, who think only of the life of the body, and for whom the life of the soul is as nothing" (Scheindlin, *Wine*, 175).

14: Cf. Ecclesiastes 8:15: "And this [mirth] shall accompany him in his labor all the days of his life"; Job 7:5: "My flesh is clothed with worms and clods of dust."

15–16: Cf. Ecclesiastes 3:20–21: "All go unto one place; all are of the dust, and all return to dust. Who knoweth the spirit of man whether it goeth upwards, and the spirit of the beast whether it goeth downward to the earth?" Also Ecclesiastes 12:7: "And the dust returneth to the earth, and the spirit returneth unto God who gave it. Vanity of vanities, saith Kohelet, all is vanity."

The original has "dust returns to dust," or "clay returns to clay"; "slime" in the penultimate line, picks up on Micah 7:10 (above, line 10).

I LOVE YOU (74:S)

Yehuda Liebes calls this line for line one of the most thoroughly analyzed works in all of post-biblical Hebrew literature. Essentially the debate concerns the nature of the poem and its philosophical or theological implications. According to the Arabic superscription it is "an answer to a student who has asked about the nature of existence." Bialik-Ravnitzky refer to another source where it is described by R. David Qimhi as a poem about "the mysteries of creation." Liebes reminds the reader of the obvious, that the poem is catalogued as a secular poem of friendship (though this is the editor's classification, not the poet's) and is in fact typical of such poems in many respects. He then goes on to develop a compelling reading of what he calls a truly astonishing poem—one that deals simultaneously with "flesh-and-blood" love and, as the superscription suggests, the nature of existence. Accordingly, Liebes foregrounds the *address* and notes its Socratic dimension—a relationship between student and teacher that begins in erotic attraction and develops into a kind of modeling of the excellent type and, finally, a love between equals. He then discusses parallels between the poem and Ibn Gabirol's relationship to the golem—which involves an act of creation in imitation of God. Revealing the poem's sources in *Sefer Yetzirah* (the Book of Creation), in Sa'adiah Gaon's commentary to that book, and in several Platonic and Neoplatonic philosophical texts, he shows that the pursuit of wisdom imitates in a sense the creation of a new being. There is an aggadic story according to which Ibn Gabirol did in fact create a golem: "And they said of R. Shelomoh ben Gabirol that he created a woman, and she waited on him. When he was denounced to the authorities, he showed them that she was not a perfect creature, and [then] he turned her to her original [state]—to the pieces and hinges of wood, out of which she was built up" (from Shelomoh del Medigo's *Matzref le-Hokhmah*, in Idel, *Golem*, 233). Liebes goes on to compare the poem to the philosophical treatise *The Fountain of Life* and notes that "in the relationship between the teacher and the pupil the secret of creation is given expression."

Line 1: Cf. Genesis 22:2: "Take now thy son, thine only son, whom thou lovest, even Isaac, and get thee into the land of Moriah"; Isaiah 43:4: "Since thou art precious in My sight, and honorable, I have loved thee."

3: Cf. Deuteronomy 6:5, from which the *Shema* is taken: "And thou shalt love the Lord thy God with all thy heart, and with all thy soul, and with all thy might." (See "The Bee.")

5–7: Cf. Ecclesiastes 1:13; Ecclesiastes 7:23–25: "I said: 'I will get wisdom'; but it was far from me. That which is far off, and exceeding deep; who can find it out? I turned about, and applied my heart to know and to search out, and to seek wisdom and the reason of things." Also, Psalms 72:6. Liebes points out that Sa'adiah Gaon's introduction to the *Sefer Yetzirah* also describes the first principle and the secret of creation as "far off and deep." Sa'adiah raises the issues again in his major philosophical work, *The Book of Belief and Opinion*, where he notes that King Solomon was able to understand the issue only because he ascended from the level of philosophy to that of prophecy. As we have seen, Ibn Gabirol often identified with his biblical namesake and was also familiar with Sa'adiah's influential book.

8: Cf. Isaiah 44:18; Psalms 82:5.

11–13: The Hebrew is particularly difficult to paraphrase, and the English is raveled accordingly. Liebes suggests that the "sages" of the poem are in fact the sages of the Neoplatonic Gnostic Gospels in particular the *Gospel of Truth* ("The Book of Creation and R. Shelomoh Ibn Gabirol," 120–23; Schlanger is also quoted as suggesting that the lines refer to thinkers "with gnostic tendencies"). "Owes all" in line 12, is based on a reading by Zemach, but is usually understood to mean "for the sake of." Cf. Proverbs 16:4: "The lord hath made everything for his own purpose." Also, *Berakhot* 6:8: "He who drinks water to quench his thirst recites [the blessing]: 'For all was created at his word.'" See also *The Fountain of Life*, 410: "Unity [oneness] overcomes (the) all and extends through (the) all, and sustains (the) all." Line 13 might also be understood as saying that the secret, or mystery, of all creation resides in each person [in all], in their power to create. This individual aspect of "all" is used in Isaiah 43 (verse 7), a chapter Ibn Gabirol alludes to several times in the course of the poem. For this reading I am indebted to Zali Gurevitch.

14: Literally, "He longs to appoint (or place, establish) there-is as [like] there-is," or "being as near-being." Bialik-Ravnitzky comment: "'Primary matter,' which in *The Fountain of Life* is called 'foundation,' which has no true existence of its own, but is 'like-existence,' longs to and desires to couple with 'form,' so that the Creator will give it true existence, and this desire of matter to take on form is very great . . . and according to the ancients is the reason for the eternal movement in creation." Yarden glosses: "All things long for God to establish them in being that resembles the true being, which is the Lord." There is extensive discussion of this line and its possible readings in Liebes and

Zemach (in Malachi). My reading generally follows out Liebes's analysis and leans on background material from *The Fountain of Life* (especially Book V:29, 32, see introduction) for its vocabulary. Liebes locates the source of the view of creation presented in the poem first of all in the most well-known of Plato's works in the Arab world of the middle ages, the *Timaeus* (29–30): "Let me tell you then why the creator made this world of generation . . . he desired that all . . . should be as like himself as could be."(92c—trans. Jowett).

The second link in Liebes's probe takes him to Pseudo-Aristotle and the Neoplatonic *Theology of Aristotle*: "All intellectual things possessing any sort of desire are after (or one step below) that which is intelligence alone and lacks desire. And when the intelligence gains possession of some desire, it goes out on account of that desire in any way it can, and does not remain in its initial position, for it longs to act and to ornament the things it has seen with the mind. As a pregnant woman upon whom pain has come to give birth to that which is in her womb—so is intelligence when drawn by the form of desire— its desire is to bring into action the form within it, and it craves and strives to attain this with great effort, while toil and pain take hold of it, and it brings it forth (the form) into action as a result of its desire for the concrete world" (Liebes, "The Book of Creation and Ibn Gabirol," 119). "Ornament" is used here in the manner explained in the introduction to this volume (see, "Embracing Evasion").

The third pivot on which Liebes turns his study of the poem is the term "All." The background to this complex of images he traces to the Valentinian *Gospel of Truth*, which refers to "the Father, the perfect one, the one who made the all, while the all is within him and the all has need of him, since he retained its perfection within himself which he did not give to the all. The Father was not jealous. . . . As is the case of one of whom some are ignorant, who wishes to have them know him and love him, so—for what did the all have need of if not knowledge regarding the Father?—he became a guide, restful and leisurely. He went into the midst of the schools (and) he spoke the word as a teacher. There came the wise men—in their own estimation— putting him to the test. But he confounded them because they were foolish. They hated him because they were not really wise. . . . Since the perfection of the all is in the Father, it is necessary for the all to ascend to him" (*Nag Hammadi*, 38–40). Liebes identifies this "all" with "light," as in the "Light of the World" (John 1:3–4). For Ibn Gabirol, Liebes claims, the "all" is God's wisdom out of which the world was shaped. Liebes finds other parallel uses of the term as well, and then concludes with a poem by Ibn 'Arabi, the great Andalusian Islamic philosopher-poet (1165–1240), whose poetry was likewise charged with inseparable erotic and religious dimensions: "And all is in need, not what is satisfied, / This is the truth, and we've spoken plainly. / If I've mentioned the rich, I mean those who lack nothing / And here now you know what I mean. / All is linked with all—nothing exists without it. / Accept this matter which I have told you."

16–18: Cf. Isaiah 43:7: "Everyone that is called by My Name whom I have created for my glory, I have formed him, yea I have made him."

19–20: Cf. Numbers 22:8: "Lodge here this night and I will bring you back word." There are two readings of the last line and numerous interpretations of their meaning. Literally, "Now, get [*qnei*] a sign to set it [him] up aright" and "Now, offer [*tena*] a sign to set it [him] up aright." Sachs, Bialik-Ravnitzky, and Liebes prefer the latter; all others—including all extant manuscripts—have the former. Arguing that the next word in the poem, *mofet* (sign, example), appears numerous times in Scripture after the verb *natan*, from which *tena* is formed, Liebes suggests that a copyist's error may have changed *tna* to *qnei* (in Hebrew only the initial letter is different)—but that in the Gabirolian context, the thrust is similar: create or form signs with your behavior that will embody what you have learned from the teacher. Cf. Exodus 7:9: "Show a wonder"; 1 Kings 13:3: "And he gave a sign the same day"; Deuteronomy 13:2. Both readings further allude to *Sefer Yetzirah* 1:4: "And put the matter straight and set the creator in his proper place." Cf. also Ezra 2:68 (which appears in *Sefer Yetzirah* 1:4): "And some of the heads of fathers' houses, when they came to the house of the Lord which is in Jerusalem, offered willingly for the house of God to set it up in its place" (or the NJPS: "to erect the House of God in its site"), where once again the subject of the Hebrew is a "second creation," this time of Solomon's destroyed temple.

In distinction to other scholars who stress the passive philosophical aspects of the poem, in which the student is expected to find proof or support, perhaps in the literature, for the teacher's claims, Liebes is convinced of the fundamentally erotic nature of the line. As God's love leads to the creation of the world, the teacher's love leads to the development of the student's knowledge and the alteration of his action. In both cases the flow must be reversed, and "spirit" returned to "spirit."

Poems of Devotion

This part consists of poems that were written for recitation at various points of the synagogue prayer service. Much of Ibn Gabirol's liturgical poetry (scholars assume he was employed as a *shaliah tzibbur*, a prayer leader) involved a major innovation in Hebrew religious verse. In these poems, the poet followed out a "classicizing" tendency that Sa'adiah Gaon had introduced into some of his own liturgical work. Breaking with the free meter and hyped-up, neologizing (and often rabbinic) diction of the traditional piyyut of the previous five hundred years, Ibn Gabirol introduced prosodic elements brought over from his secular poetry, such as a biblical purity of diction and an Arabic cleanness of form. At the same time, his new, clear synagogue poetry subtly wove the person of the poet, or at least a psalm-like "I," into this essentially communal verse. Finally, Ibn Gabirol introduced thematic changes into the service, as erotic, metaphysical, and contemplative topoi, also adapted from his secular work and from Arabic literature, made their way into his liturgical writing. The majority of these poems employ quantitative meters, but they often involve more elaborate rhyme schemes and strophic constructions than the verse of Part I. This selection represents many but by no means all of the liturgical genres and forms. A number of the poems included here are still sung or recited in synagogues around the world.

The poems in this section have been drawn from Yarden's two-volume edition of sacred poems, *Shirei Qodesh*: Volume I: New Year and the Day of Atonement—92 poems; Volume II: The Three Pilgrimage Festivals (Tabernacles, Passover, The Feast of Weeks) and miscellaneous verse—152 poems.

BEFORE MY BEING (126:L)

Schirmann says this poem's genre isn't known, but that it may be a *baqashah* (poem of petition), as the first line is repeated at the end of the poem. Yarden suggests that it may be a *reshut lenishmat*. (For an explanation of these terms, see note below to "I Look for You," "All the Creatures of Earth and Heaven," and "Three Things.") Scheindlin describes it as a poem about the creation of the human species, not just the individual person, and notes that its bitter ambiguity makes it "a song of experience; to read it as a song of innocence misses the point" (*Gazelle*, 209–13). Scheindlin also writes about the poem in "Contrasting Religious Experience in the Liturgical Poems of Ibn Gabirol and Judah Halevi," where he examines Ibn Gabirol's Neoplatonism and Halevi's transcendentalism. In Ibn Gabirol's religious scheme, notes Scheindlin, divinity is approached through contemplation and interiority—God is within human consciousness; in Halevi's poems God is distant and trust comes through obedience to religious law and its revelation. As in many of Ibn Gabirol's poems, examination of the microcosm of the "I" leads to contemplation of the macrocosm, and what appears to be a naive expression of religious faith is actually a complex formulation of much less comforting philosophical understanding. Ibn Gabirol's genius is such that the poem's "experience" contains the level of naive faith within it, without canceling that dimension of experience. It is all the more startling, then, to consider that the poem was possibly part of the liturgy.

Line 1: Cf. Jeremiah 1:5: "Before I formed thee in the belly I knew thee"; Psalms 119:41: "Let Thy mercies also come unto me, O Lord."

2: Cf. *Sefer Yetzirah* 2:5: "He created from utter chaos and made of the void existence." Ibn Gabirol uses this image at least five other times in his poems, including the famous instance of *Kingdom's Crown* (section IX). Scheindlin notes the ambiguity of the Hebrew syntax, maintained in the English here, which establishes the ironic reading of the poem: the line implies that God destroys existence—brought existence or being to nothing—and also created existence from nothingness. The soul was pure before its descent into the world of the body.

3–4: Cf. Psalms 139:15: "My frame was not hidden from Thee, when I was made in secret, and curiously wrought in the lowest parts of the earth"; Job 10:10: "Hast thou not poured me out as milk, and curdled me [made me solid] like cheese?"

5: Cf. Genesis 2:7: "He . . . breathed into his nostrils the breath of life." *Neshamah* in the biblical citation and the poem is both "breath" and "soul." Scheindlin (in Mirsky, *Piyyut in Tradition*, 72) quotes George Herbert on prayer: "God's breath in man returning to his birth."

6: Cf. Jonah 2:3: "Out of the belly of the netherworld cried I"; also Psalms 139:15 (lines 3–4 above). Following the *Targum* to the verse in Psalms, Yarden glosses: "out of the belly of my mother."

7: Cf. 2 Samuel 7:18: "Then David the king went in, and sat before the Lord; and he said: Who am I, O Lord, God, and what is my house, that Thou hast brought me thus far?"

8: Cf. Psalms 71:17: "O God, Thou has taught me from my youth."

9: Cf. The central prayer of the liturgy, the *Amidah*: "O favor us with knowledge, understanding, and discernment. Blessed art Thou, O Lord, gracious Giver of knowledge." The line literally reads: "Who taught me understanding and made me wondrous [more than other creatures]?"

9–10: Cf. Isaiah 64:7: "We are the clay and Thou our potter, and we all are the work of Thy hand"; Jeremiah 18:6: "O house of Israel, can not I do with you as this potter?"; Job 10:9: "Remember, I beseech Thee, that Thou has fashioned me as clay; and wilt thou bring me into dust again?"; Ezekiel 29:3: "I have made it for myself."

11–12: Cf. Psalms 32:5: "I acknowledge my sin unto Thee, and mine iniquity have I not hid. I said, I will make confession concerning my transgressions unto the Lord"; Genesis 3:13: "And the woman said: the serpent beguiled me and I did eat."

13: Cf. Job 27:11: "That which is with the Almighty will I not conceal." Scheindlin: "In Ibn Gabirol's allegorical interpretation of the Garden of Eden, the serpent represents the vegetative and the animal souls"—as opposed to the higher, rational soul.

13–14: See line 1, though now the "mercy" and act of God have taken on an ironic cast. Calling the confession of line 13 "not the humble expression of that feeling of being transparent before God ... [but] a taunt," Scheindlin notes the possible use in line 14 of the Hebrew *hesed*, "mercy" or "kindness," as a homonym, meaning "shame," from Leviticus 20:17: "If a man shall take his sister ... and see her nakedness, and she see his nakedness: it is a shameful thing (*hesed hu*)," i.e., I am a sinner; but you in your so-called kindness created me. See also Herbert's poem, "Judgement": "Thou shalt finde my faults are thine."

THREE THINGS (138:L)

A *reshut*. Acrostic: "Shelomoh." The *reshut*, literally, "introduction" or "permission," is a piyyut in which the *payytan*—as an individual—introduces a congregational prayer. Various prayers were preceded by *reshuyot*, including the *nishmat*, *qaddish*, *borehu*, *yotzer* and others. The *reshut* was one of the most important Andalusian innovations in the field of liturgical poetry. The Andalusian *reshut* tended to be lyrical and contemplative in its emphases, and Ibn Gabirol's *reshuyot* are particularly powerful and fine. The term always brings to mind for me Robert Duncan's "Opening of the Field" and its "place of first permission / everlasting omen of what is." (For more on the *reshut*, see Scheindlin's *Gazelle*, chapter 2.)

The acrostic signature of the poet was standard practice in much of the Hebrew liturgical poetry, in which the individual voice remained distinct but was also merged with the communal voice of the prayer. By weaving his name into the fabric of the verse, the poet was able, in a sense, to quietly copyright the work.

Scheindlin comments: "Of all of Ibn Gabirol's poems, this miniature masterpiece most clearly, succinctly and beautifully evokes the inward-looking character of his religious thought and experience" (*Gazelle*, 191–93). He notes the poem's progression from far-off sky to earth to mind, adding that "the author of the Psalms might very well have been inspired by sky and earth to praise God; but that the mind of man should also be a source of inspiration is a distinctively medieval contribution to religious thought." One might extend this observation to note that the progression inward, this time from the macrocosm into the microcosm implies of course the reverse motion as well, with the poet's meditation, or reflection, now containing all the world and leading with renewed complexity back out to its wonders. Also characteristic is the opposition of first person and second person throughout the poem—so that a poem in praise of God is in fact held intact compositionally by the (on the face of it odd) repetition of the first-person pronouns. The opening recalls Kant's comment: "There are two things that fill my soul with holy reverence and ever-growing wonder—the spectacle of the starry sky that virtually annihilates us as physical beings, and the moral law which raises us to infinite dignity as intelligent agents" (in *The Psalms*, Soncino, Psalm 19).

Line 3: Cf. Isaiah 26:8: "To Thy name and to Thy memorial is the desire of our soul"; Psalms 8:4, 10: "When I behold Thy heavens, the work of Thy fingers . . . How glorious is Thy name in all the earth." On the use of God's name, see note to "The Hour of Song," lines 3–4.

4: Cf. Psalms 19:2: "The heavens declare the glory of God, and the firmament showeth His handiwork"; Psalms 45:18: "I will make Thy name to be remembered"; Isaiah 8:2: "I will take unto Me faithful witnesses to record."

5–7: Cf. Isaiah 42:5: "He that spread forth the earth"; Job 38:4–5: "Where wast thou when I laid the foundations of the earth?. . . Who determined the measures thereof?. . . Or who stretched the line upon it?"

8: Cf. Psalms 34:2: "I will bless the Lord at all times"; Psalms 104:1: "Bless the Lord, O my soul." In lines 7–8 there is an elusive play on *adanai* ("foundations")—as in "the extender of my foundations" (line 7, literally)—which is juxtaposed with *adonai* ("my Lord"), the name of God (line 8).

9: Cf. Psalms 39:4; Psalms 5:2; Psalms 19:15: "Let the words of my mouth and the meditation of my heart be acceptable before Thee."

I LOOK FOR YOU (24:L)

A *reshut lenishmat* for the Day of Atonement, and one of the more famous poems in the liturgy, as it appears in many prayerbooks. Acrostic: "Shelomoh."

Lines 1–4: Cf. Psalms 62:7: "He only is my rock and my salvation, my high tower, I shall not be moved"; Psalms 5:4: "Hear my voice, O Lord, at day break, at day break I plead [order my prayer] before you, and wait" (NJPS). Line 4 might also read "my morning prayer and my evening prayer."

6: Literally, "afraid"—without "confused." Cf. Job 23:15: "Therefore I am affrighted of His Presence, when I consider Him, I am afraid of Him."

7–8: Cf. Lamentations 3:60; 1 Chronicles 28:9: "For the Lord . . . understandeth all the imaginations of the thoughts"; Jeremiah 20:12: "O Lord . . . that seest the reins and the heart"; Genesis 6:5: "And the Lord saw that the wickedness of man was great in the earth, and that every imagination of the thoughts of his heart was only evil continually."

9–10: Cf. Judges 8:3: "What was I able to do in comparison with you?" In the original this line runs over the hemistich caesura and breaks the symmetry of the verse—as though to mirror the thrust of the lines: try as they might, the heart and tongue aren't capable of composing praise fit for the Lord. The English doesn't reflect this specifically; instead, its clipped rhythms establish a sense of ongoing insufficiency, though the cadence soothes in its own right. Mirsky and Scheindlin point out that the source of the idea here is the Arabic maxim: *innamaa 'l-insaan / al-qalb wa-'l-lisaan* ("The being of man is the heart and tongue"). See also "Two Things Meet in Me" (13:L).

11–12: Cf. Job 6:11; Isaiah 26:5.

13–16: Cf. Psalms 69:31–32: "I will praise the name of God with a song, and will magnify Him with Thanksgiving. And it shall please the Lord better than a bullock that hath horns and hoofs"; Psalms 104:34: "Let my musing be sweet unto Him"; 2 Samuel 22:50: "Therefore I will give thanks unto Thee"; Job 27:2–4: "As God liveth, who hath taken away my right; . . . all the while my breath is in me, and the spirit of God is in my nostrils, surely my lips shall not speak unrighteousness." As is customary in this type of poem, the final line of the poem leads in to the powerful Sabbath-morning *nishmat* prayer, which *Pesahim* 118a refers to as "The Blessing of Song": "The breath of every living being shall bless Thy name, O Lord our Lord, and the spirit of all flesh shall ever glorify and extol Thee, O our King. . . . Were our mouths filled with song as the sea, our tongues with melody as the murmuring waves; could our lips utter praise as the spacious firmament; were our eyes glowing light as the sun and the moon; our hands spread forth as the eagles of heaven, and our feet, swift as the hinds, we would still be unable to thank and bless Thee sufficiently, O Lord our God, God of our fathers, for even one of the thousands, yea, infinite blessings which Thou hast bestowed upon our fathers and upon us" (*High Holiday Prayer Book*, 58–59).

FORGET YOUR GRIEF (87:L)

A *tokhehah* for the afternoon service on the Day of Atonement. Acrostic: "Shelomoh Hazak." This poem is found in the *Mahzor Vitry*, an important French prayerbook from the late eleventh century that was enlarged in successive editions. The *tokhehah* (exhortation) is a penitential poem addressed to one who has sinned. Death is often summoned in the course of the poem, as a reminder of what is to come. A poem of perspective. The irregular stanzas are in the original. The idea for a refrain is from R. Loewe.

Lines 1–4: Literally, "my longing (moaning) soul." Cf. Job 9:27: "If I say: 'I will forget my complaint, I will put off my sad countenance'"; Psalms 88:13: "Shall Thy wonders be known in the dark? And Thy righteousness in the land of forgetfulness?"; *Sefer Yetzirah* 4:13: "Seven earths are world, forgetfulness, wilderness, universe, land, valley." "Sorrows" in the English collapses the larger sense of the Hebrew "the distress of the land of forgetfulness."

5–8: Cf. Psalms 86:13: "Thou hast delivered my soul from the lowest netherworld"; Ecclesiastes 2:16: "For of the wise man, even as of the fool, there is no remembrance for ever; seeing that in the days to come all will long ago have been forgotten."

9–11: Cf. Psalms 114:7: "Tremble, thou, earth, at the presence of the Lord."

12–16: Cf. Psalms 42:6; Isaiah 47:12.

17–18: Cf. Job 7:1–2: "Are not [man's] days like the days of a hireling? As a servant that eagerly longeth for the shadow, and as a hireling that looketh for his wages"; Leviticus 19:13. The refrain reads literally: "The day you expect the enactment of your acquisition," implying the world to come. (For more on the philosophical background to the notion of acquisition in this poem, see Loewe, *Ibn Gabirol*, 92).

19–23: Cf. Ezekiel 7:27: "The king shall mourn and the prince shall be clothed with appallment."

24–27: Cf. Psalms 49:18: "For when he dieth he shall carry nothing away; his wealth shall not descend after him"; Ecclesiastes 5:14: "Naked shall he go back as he came, and shall take nothing for his labour, which he may carry away in his hand"; *Avot* 6:9: "In the hour of a man's death it is neither silver nor gold nor precious stones nor pearls which accompany him but Torah and good works only"; Ecclesiastes 12:7: "And the dust returneth to the earth as it was, and the spirit returneth unto God who gave it."

28–32: Cf. Psalms 11:1: "How say ye to my soul: 'Flee, thou! to your mountain, ye birds?'"; Proverbs 27:8: "As a bird that wandereth from her nest, so is a man that wandereth from his place"; refrain, see note to lines 17–18.

37–40: Cf. Isaiah 21:15: "And they fled away from . . . the bent bow"; Psalms 49:11: "For . . . wise men die, the fool and the brutish together perish, and leave their wealth to others."

41–47: The English departs some from the literal Hebrew of lines 41–42, which echoes 1 Samuel 15:9 and is itself uncertain (NJPS). It might mean either "cheap and worthless" (other commentary has "despised and corrupt/spoiled") or, in keeping with Ibn Gabirol's predilection for referring to his illness in his work, "dissolving and issuing [flowing out] as though from a wound" (cf. Leviticus 15:2: "When any man hath an issue out of his flesh . . ."). Also, Proverbs 11:4: "Riches profit not in the day of wrath."

48–52: Literally, "is picked by death." Cf. Jeremiah 49:9; Judges 9:27; 2 Kings 17:9; Job 31:4; Job 13:27.

53–58: The court—i.e., the court of the heavenly king. Cf. Psalms 116:7: "Return, O my soul, unto thy rest"; *Avot* 2:15 (20 in Herford): "R. Tarphon said:—The day is short and the work is great, and the labourers are sluggish, and the wages are high and the householder is urgent"; *Avot* 6:4: "This is the way of Torah: A morsel with salt shalt thou eat and water by measure shalt thou drink"; Proverbs 17:1: "Better is a dry morsel and quietness therewith, than a house full of feasting with strife."

59–65: Cf. Isaiah 50:11: "You shall lie down in sorrow"; Job 19:29: "Be ye afraid of the sword, for wrath bringeth the punishment of the sword, that ye may know there is a judgment."

67–71: Cf. Hosea 11:11: "They shall come trembling as a bird out of Egypt, and as a dove out of the land of Assyria"; Deuteronomy 24:14.

72–80: Cf. Deuteronomy 33:27: "The eternal God is a dwelling-place"; Proverbs 12:2: "A good man shall obtain favor of the Lord."

THE HOUR OF SONG (150:L)

A *reshut*. Acrostic: "Shelomoh." It isn't clear what liturgical element the poem introduces. Schirmann has suggested that it is a *reshut lenishmat*, Broyer that it may in fact be a *reshut l'baruch sh'amar* ("Blessed is He Who said . . ."). Mirsky notes that the poem has direct parallels in Bahya Ibn Paquda's *The Duties of the Heart*: see "On the Reliance Upon God Alone" and "On the True Love of God" (Ibn Paquda, 232, 426). Ibn Paquda is generally believed to have lived after Ibn Gabirol, though some scholars place him before the poet.

Lines 1–4: Cf. Psalms 31:2–6: "In thee, O Lord, have I taken refuge; let me never be ashamed; Deliver me in Thy righteousness. Incline Thine ear unto me, deliver me speedily; Be Thou to me a rock of refuge, even a fortress of defense, to save me. For Thou art my rock and my fortress. Therefore for Thy name's sake lead me and guide me. Bring me forth out of the net that they have hidden for me; For Thou art my stronghold. Into thy hand I commit my spirit." See also Ibn Paquda on "The Unity of God": "Since it is impossible for the mind to think of Him in any form and for the imagination to conceive of Him in any shape, we find the Scriptures attributing most of His praise and glorification to His Name. . . . Since all we can grasp are His existence and His Name, the books of the Law and of the Prophets mention this Name frequently, in connection with the sky and the earth, the world, and the winds" (Ibn Paquda, 138–39). See also Parnes, "On The Name" in *MiBen LaMa'arakhot*.

5–8: Literally, "there is no helper." Cf. Psalms 142:5: "Look on my right hand, and see, for there is no man that knoweth me"; Isaiah 63:5: "I looked and there was none to help"; Psalms 31:6, above (lines 1–4). "Loneness" is an epithet for the soul, as in Psalms 22:21.

9–12: Cf. Ecclesiastes 2:10: "And whatsoever mine eyes desired I kept not from them; I withheld not my heart from any joy; for my heart had joy of all my labor; and this was my portion from all my labor"; Psalms 142:6: "I have cried unto Thee, O Lord; I have said: 'Thou art my refuge, my portion in the land of the living'"; Ecclesiastes 2:21: "For there is a man whose labor is with wisdom, and with knowledge, and with skill; yet to a man that hath not labored therein shall he leave it for his portion."

13–16: "I'm immersed" for *eshgeh* is based on Yarden's note, which reads "I occupy myself," and also on Proverbs 5:19–20: "A lovely hind and a graceful doe, let her breasts satisfy thee at all times; with her love be thou ravished (*tishgeh*) always. Why then wilt thou, my son, be ravished with a strange woman?"

8: Cf. Job 35:10: "But none saith: 'Where is God my Maker, who giveth songs in the night.'" "Worship" and "work" in Hebrew are identical and from the same root: *'a-b-d.*

TWO THINGS MEET IN ME (13:L)

A *reshut lenishmat kol hai* for the New Year. Acrostic: "Shelomoh." Mirsky notes that the poem directly reflects the discussion of "heart and tongue" in Ibn Paquda's *Duties of the Heart*: "Finally, all service is reduced to the service of heart and tongue . . . *For this commandment which I command thee this day . . . is not in heaven . . . Neither is it beyond the sea . . . but the word is very nigh unto thee in the mouth and in thy heart, to do it*" (Ibn Paquda, 90). While the "two things" of the poem are clearly heart and tongue, there is also, however, a more complex weave of spirit and soul, sacrifice (service or the labor of the priest) and vision (the act of the prophet). All are inadequate to praise the speaker's God, and yet he must—or longs to—praise Him nonetheless. (See also "I Look for You," note to line 9.)

Line 1: Cf. Psalms 85:11: "Mercy and truth are met together."
3–4: Cf. Ruth 2:5; Genesis 18:2; Joshua 8:33.
5–8: Cf. Psalms 35:28: "And my tongue shall speak of Thy righteousness and of Thy praise all the day."
9–12: Cf. Psalms 119:141: "I am small and despised"; and Job 15:14–16: "What is man, that he should be clean? And he that is born of a woman, that he should be righteous? Behold, He putteth no trust in His holy ones; Yea, the heavens are not clean in His sight. How much less one that is abominable and impure, man who drinketh iniquity like water!"
13–17: Cf. Leviticus 5:7: "And if his means suffice him not for a lamb, then he shall bring his forfeit for that wherein he hath sinned, two turtle-doves, or two young pigeons." Also, *Menahot* 110a: "It is said of a large ox, *an offering made by fire of a sweet savour*, and of a small bird . . . and of a meal offering . . . to teach you that it is the same whether a man offers much or little, so long as he directs his heart to heaven . . . You do not sacrifice for My sake, but for your own sakes."
18–19: Cf. Psalms 104:34: "Let my prayer be pleasing to Him" (NJPS).
20–21: Literally, "like an offering by a visionary/dreamer [*hozeh*] or sprinkler [*mazeh*]" i.e., a prophet or a priest.

SMALL IN MY AWE (12:L)

A *reshut* for the New Year. Acrostic: "Shelomoh." These four lines are a freely rendered excerpt from a short poem whose conclusion reads, literally, "Lord who is the fullness of the world and knows no end, could one such as me praise you, and with what? The angels on high cannot contain your glory, how much less can I contain it; you have been gracious and increased your mercies and to you the soul will increase its thanksgiving." I have kept to the truncated free version, which I translated many years ago, as a thread to that early personal point of entry, and to emphasize the force of the image that opens the poem. There are many ways into the Hebrew poetry of the middle ages—this is one.

Lines 1–4: Cf. Proverbs 16:19: "Better it is to be of a lowly spirit with the humble, than to divide the spoil with the proud"; *Ta'anit* 16a: "R. Judah said, [they send before the ark one] . . . who is meek"; Ezekiel 17:6: "a spreading vine of low stature"; Psalms 22:7: "But I am a worm, and no man; a reproach of men, and despised of the people."

OPEN THE GATE (145:L)

A *reshut*. Acrostic: "Shelomoh." The congregation of Israel to God.

Lines 1–2: The poem begins with a reversal of the situation in the Song of Songs 5:2, where the woman waits in her room and hears her beloved: "Harken! my beloved knocketh: 'Open to me, my sister, my love . . .'" In this poem the terms are reversed and the feminine congregation of Israel is asking her lover, the Lord, to open the gate and come to help her. Scheindlin comments: "Its language derives neither from the Song of Songs nor from love poetry. . . . [The poem] is a complaint about Israel's suffering in exile written in the language of Rabbinic eschatology." Bialik-Ravnitzky comment: "The poet is knocking at the gates of heaven, of mercy."

3: Cf. Psalms 6:4: "My soul is sore affrighted"; Ezekiel 27:35: "And their kings are horribly afraid."

4: The poem departs from the Song of Songs' vocabulary and the sense of distress is intensified with references to "my mother's maid," in this case Hagar, Sarah's handmaid. Genesis 16:1–4 tells the story of Hagar and her child, Ishmael, whom she bore to Abraham. After Hagar conceived, "her mistress was despised in her eyes."

5–6: After Isaac was born to Sarah and Abraham, Sarah had her husband send Hagar and Ishmael away into the "wilderness of Beersheba." Cf. Genesis 21:15–17: "And the water in the bottle was spent, and she cast the child under one of the shrubs. And she went, and sat her down over against him . . . and

273

lifted up her voice, and wept. And God heard the voice of the lad." Also Ezekiel 31:10: "His heart is lifted up."

7–9: The allegorical vocabulary is extended here. "Midnight's blackness" is the exile from the Land of Israel; "wild ass" is a traditional epithet for Islam—Scripture having noted that Ishmael would be a "wild ass of a man" (Genesis 16:12); and Christianity is called a "wild boar" (Leviticus Rabbah 13:5, on Leviticus 11:7—"and the swine": "the swine, this is Edom"). Also Psalms 80:14: "The boar out of the wood doth ravage it." Scheindlin links the use of "middle" and "midnight" to Ibn Gabirol's (and others') attempts to calculate precisely the time of the redemption, noting the scriptural context in the Book of Daniel, which also alludes to a "specific date for the redemption."

10: Cf. Daniel 12:4: "But thou, O Daniel, shut up the words, and seal the book, even to the time of the end."

11: Cf. Jeremiah 45:3: "The Lord hath added sorrow to my pain."

12: Literally, "there is no one to understand for me—and I am ignorant" ("brutish"). Cf. Daniel 8:27: "I was appalled at the vision, but understood it not"; Psalms 142:5: "For there is no man that knoweth me"; Psalms 73:22: "I was brutish and ignorant; I was as a beast before Thee." The English "blind" departs somewhat from the Hebrew, which is like that of the Psalms: "brutish and ignorant." I've let the music bring the English in a slightly different direction, one that picks up on trapped aspects of Ibn Gabirol's character that are made explicit in other poems.

MY THOUGHTS ASKED ME (129:L)

A *reshut lenishmat*. Acrostic: "Shelomoh." *Mahzor Vitry*, 8 (in the section of poems at the back). Conspicuous prose parallels can be found in Ibn Paquda (chapters 3 and 10). See also, Mirsky, *From Duties . . .*, 288–89.

Lines 4–6: Cf. Psalms 42:3: "My soul thirsteth for God, for the living God . . . a prayer unto the God of my life"; Genesis 3:16: "Thy desire shall be to thy husband"; Psalms 63:2: "My soul thirsteth for Thee, my flesh longeth for Thee."

7–9: Cf. Isaiah 61:10: "I will greatly rejoice in the Lord, my soul shall be joyful in my God"; Psalms 16:5: "O Lord, the portion of mine inheritance and of my cup"; Psalms 77:4: "When I think thereon, O God, I must moan"; Psalms 55:3: "I am distraught in my complaint, and will moan." The translation of line 9 swerves some for its effect, though the visceral "disquiet" (as *ahim*, "I moan," is visceral) is very much in keeping with the tenor of Ibn Gabirol's religious longing and "unsatisfied" nature on the one hand, and the context of the biblical usage on the other.

11–12: Some editions (Schirmann, *Mahzor Vitry*) have "goodness" or "pleasure" instead of "song." Davidson and Yarden have "song." Cf. Nehemiah 8:6: "And Ezra blessed the Lord, the great God."

ANGELS AMASSING (28:L)

An *ofan* for the Day of Atonement. Acrostic: "Shelomoh." The *ofan* is a piyyut that is incorporated into the liturgy to accompany the prayer that blesses the "Creator of the holy ones . . . fashioner of ministering angels, whose ministering angels all stand in the heights of the universe and proclaim loudly and together with awe the words of the living God and King of the universe. . . . And the *ofanim* and holy creatures with a great noise raise themselves towards the seraphim. Facing them they give praise, saying: 'Blessed is the glory of the Lord from His place.'" The term literally means "wheels," as in Ezekiel's vision of the wheels within wheels; in the biblical verse cited, however, it means a kind of angel. The *ofanim* employ various and often complex strophic structures. Normally, says Schirmann, they describe the holiness of the angels and sometimes the world of creation. Formally the *ofan* relies on considerable (Hopkins-like) internal rhyme and rhythmic turbulence to mirror the rush and noise of the angels. The imagery of this particular poem (which served as a model for Ibn Gabirol's successors) is drawn from scriptural and aggadic descriptions of the chariot. The scriptural imagery comes from Ezekiel and Kings, the aggadic imagery derives from the liturgy ("To the blessed Lord they will offer pleasant things . . . and proclaim hymns and His praises"), *Pirkei Rabbi Eliezer* 4 and the Heikhalot hymns, *Sefer Yetzirah*, *Sifra Deuteronomy* 306, and *Tanhuma Buber* Exodus 115: "[The angels'] main purpose is to sing hymns in praise of God and to proclaim His sanctity." The following from *Pirkei Rabbi Eliezer* establishes the situation: "Four classes of minority angels minister and utter praise before the Holy One, blessed be He: the first camp (led by) Michael on His right, the second camp (led by) Gabriel on his left, the third camp (led by) Uriel before Him, and the fourth camp (led by) Raphael behind Him. And the Shekhinah of the Holy One, blessed be He, is in the center. He is sitting on a throne high and exalted. His throne is high and suspended above in the air. The appearance . . . is like the color of amber. And the adornment of the crown is on His head, and the ineffable Name is upon his forehead."

Lines 1–2: The English opening to a certain extent reflects the heavy alliterative effect of the Hebrew, which sounds like this: "*Shinannim sha'anannim kenitzotzim yilhavu / lahateihem ma'ateihem ke'ein qalal yitzhavu.*" *Shinannim* means "thousands" and is an epithet for "angels." It is drawn from Psalms 68:18: "The chariots of God are myriads, even thousands upon thousands." *Sha'anannim* (not directly translated here) is understood by most commentators to mean "tranquil" or "at ease" (as in Amos 6:1: "at ease in Zion"), implying a quiet before the recitation of the prayer cited in Isaiah. Others understand the line as implying "noise" such as the angels in the poem actually make. Cf. Ezekiel 3:12–13: "Then a spirit lifted me up, and I heard behind me the voice of a great rushing: . . . also the noise of the wings of the living creatures as they touched one another, and the noise of the wheels beside them, even the noise of a great rushing." Following Schirmann, I read it as a derivative of the root *sh-a-h* and the word *sha'on* (see *Sefer HaShorashim leRadaq*, 362–63 and Even Shoshan's *HaMilon HaHadash*—as in Isaiah 37:29: "For that thine *uproar* is come up into Mine ears"). Cf. *Exodus Rabbah* 29:2: "Twenty-two thousand (angels) came down with the Holy One Blessed Be He to Sinai, as it is said: [above, Psalms 68:18]." One might also read the angels as thoughts, and see the poem as a whole as the Vision of a Loud Mind. (See note to lines 7–11 below.)

2: Cf. Ezekiel 1:7: "And [the four living creatures] sparkled like the color of burnished brass."

3: Cf. Isaiah 6:1–2: "In the year that King Uzziah died I saw the Lord sitting upon a throne high and lifted up, and His train filled the temple. Above Him stood the seraphim"; also 1 Kings 22:19: "I saw the Lord sitting on His throne, and all the host of heaven standing by Him on His right hand and on His left."

4–5: Like the fourth and fifth lines of each stanza, these directly anticipate the important liturgical station that will follow the poem. Cf. *Sifra Nedava* 2:12: "Not even the immortal angels are able to see the glory of the Lord"; Isaiah 6:3: "And one called unto another and said: Holy, holy, holy, is the Lord of hosts; the whole earth is full of his glory."

6: Cf. Psalms 29:1: "Ascribe unto the Lord, O ye sons of might, ascribe unto the Lord glory and strength." The Targum reads "divisions of angels" for "sons of might"—*bnei elim*—which is one of the more common biblical terms for angels. Other terms for angels that appear in the poem include *serafim, erelim, hashmalim,* and *hayot.* The terms are elusive in the original, and in the poem usually only their associations are translated.

7–8: The Hebrew specifies the species of angels here: *erelim* and *hashmalim*. *Erelim* appear in Isaiah 33:7: "Valiant ones cry without" and in *Ketubot* 104b: "The angels [*erelim*] and the mortals have taken hold of the holy ark. The angels overpowered the mortals and the holy ark has been captured." Jastrow defines them literally as "messengers." *Hashmalim* is based on Ezekiel 1:4: "Behold . . . a great cloud, with a fire flashing up, so that a brightness was round about it . . . as the color of electrum" and *Hagigah* 13b: "What does [the word] *hashmal* mean?—Rab Judah said: Living creatures speaking fire." Also Ezekiel 1:14: "And the living creatures ran and returned as the appearance of a flash of lightning"—a phrasing that figures in *Sefer Yetzirah*, chapter 1, where it refers to the heart's (or mind's) activity and risks.

9: "The angels consist of fire and water, or according to another account, of four heavenly elements: mercy, strength, beauty, and dominion, corresponding to the four earthly elements: water, fire, earth, and air" (*Encyclopedia Judaica*, "Angels and Angelology"). Avraham Ibn Ezra recalls the intellectual aspect of the angels as well, in his biblical commentary to Genesis 28:12 (Jacob's ladder): "And R. Shelomoh the Spaniard [Ibn Gabirol] said that a ladder alludes to the upper soul, and the angels of god—wisdom's thought."

10: Cf. Isaiah 29:23: "They shall sanctify the Holy One of Jacob, and shall stand in awe of the God of Israel." Also the Sabbath Qedusha, see note to line 16 below.

14: Cf. Daniel 12:1: "Michael . . . the great prince."

16: Cf. Genesis 1:9: "Let the waters under the heaven be gathered together"; *Bahir* 11: "Michael the prince on the right of the Holy One Blessed Be He is water and hail"; The Sabbath Qedusha (Mussaf): "We will revere You and sanctify You according to the counsel of the holy seraphim . . . . His ministering angels ask one another, 'Where is the place of His glory?'"

17: "Partition" is the word used for the cover or curtain before the Holy Ark in the synagogue, *pargod*. Cf. *Pirkei Rabbi Eliezer* 4: "Seven angels created in the beginning serve Him before the veil which is called *pargod*."

19–23: The language of this stanza is drawn both from that of the Tent of Meeting (Exodus 40:22) and Gabriel's coming to overturn Sodom (*Baba Metzia* 86b and Genesis 18:16).

20–21: The word *serafim* derives from *saraf*, burned. Cf. *Bahir* 11b: "And Gabriel the prince on the left of the Holy One Blessed Be He is fire"; 2 Kings 2:11: "Behold, there appeared a chariot of fire and horses of fire, which parted them both asunder; and Elijah went up by a whirlwind into heaven." Cf. 2 Kings 18:17: "And the King of Assyria . . . sent . . . a great army unto Jerusalem."

26: Cf. Song of Songs 4:4: "builded with turrets" (NJPS: "to hold weapons")—i.e, Nuriel was a picture of strength and power.

27: Cf. Jeremiah 47:3: "At the noise of the stamping of the hoofs of his strong ones"; Job 26:11: "The pillars of heaven tremble"; Job 22:14: "He walketh in the circuit of heaven."

28: Cf. Exodus 3:14: "I am that I am"—the Lord's answer when Moses asks him what his name is. Literally, "I-am, the creator of the heavens and the netherworld."

31: Cf. Job 16:19: "Behold, My witness is in heaven, and he that testifieth of me is on high."

33: *Hagigah* 13b: "Sandalfon . . . stands behind the chariot and wreathes crowns for his Maker"; Job 31:36: "I would bind it unto me as a crown." Also *Sefer Yetzirah* 3:7: "He made the letter *alef* king over breath and bound a crown to it."

38: Cf. *Pirkei Rabbi Eliezer* 4: "And the creatures stand in fear and terror"; for "will set strong," literally, "their feet were straight" (Ezekiel 1:7).

41: In the Qedusha prayer the word "Holy" is repeated three times, as in the quote from Isaiah 6:3. "Holy" in Hebrew denotes separation.

ALL THE CREATURES OF EARTH AND HEAVEN (211:L)

Double acrostic: "Shelomoh." A *baqashah* (supplication, petition), i.e., a sub-genre of the *selihot*, or penitential poems. Schirmann notes two types of *baqashot*. The first is a long, meditative poem composed in the rhymed prose called (in Arabic) *saj'a*. This is the form of Ibn Gabirol's *Kingdom's Crown* and that of Sa'adiah Gaon's two magisterial *baqashot* and the great *baqashah* of Bahya Ibn Paquda. The second type of *baqashah* is, like the poem at hand, a mid-length metered poem, mono-rhymed or strophic.

This poem is the first piyyut in the Italian prayerbook (*Mahzor Roma*), sung immediately after the biblical *"Shirat HaYam"* (The Song of the Sea). In several other editions it is placed with the *baqashot*, to be sung before the liturgy proper (after *Adon 'Olam*). S. D. Luzzatto notes that the refrain is in dispute, as earlier versions of the poem in other prayerbooks do not contain it. Bialik-Ravnitzky note the reliance on the language of the *Sefer Yetzirah*.

Lines 1–3: Cf. Zechariah 14:9 and the end of the prayer *Adon 'Olam* (Lord of the World): "And the Lord shall be king over all the earth; in that day shall the Lord be One and His name one."

4: Cf. *Sefer Yetzirah* 1:1: "With thirty-two hidden paths of wisdom engraved Yah, the Lord of hosts . . .," that is, the twenty-two letters of the alphabet and the ten *sefirot*.

5–7: Literally, "They tell of your greatness to all who fathom their mystery." Cf. Psalms 145:6: "I will tell of thy greatness"; the *Alenu* prayer: "For the kingdom is yours and you will reign for all eternity"; *Sefer Yetzirah* 1:6 (Long Version): "The unique Master, God faithful King, dominates [the ten Sefirot of Nothingness] from His Holy dwelling until the eternity of eternities."

12: Bialik-Ravnitzky read: "The hearts of men in observing the created world find that all being but that of the Lord undergoes variation and can be counted and weighed (measured)"; Mirsky, Yarden, and others read "repetition" or "renewal" for "variation." Cf. Ezra 8:34: "The whole by number and by weight."

14: Cf. Ecclesiastes 12:11: "The words of the wise are as goads . . . they are given from one shepherd."

18–21: Cf. Ecclesiastes 3:11: "He hath set the world in their heart, yet so that man cannot find out the work that God hath done from the beginning even to the end"; *Sefer Yetzirah* (Long Version) 6:3: "Three Fathers and their progeny, seven subduers and their host, twelve diagonal boundaries. As proof of this,

trusted witnesses, are the Universe, the Year, and the Soul"; Genesis 28:14:
"Thou shalt spread abroad to the west and to the east, to the north, and to the
south"; Psalms 89:38: "[It] shall be steadfast as the witness in the sky"; Exodus
17:12: "The one on the one side, and the other on the other side."

25–28: 1 Chronicles 29:14: "All things come of Thee"; Genesis 30:20: "God hath
endowed me (*zavadni*) with a good dowry"—Bialik reads "emanates in ema-
nation" for *nizvad zavod*, Yarden "is given"; Psalms 102:27: "They shall perish
but Thou shalt endure"—see also *Kingdom's Crown* I; 1 Samuel 6:5: "Ye shall
give glory unto the God of Israel"; Malachi 2:10: "Have we not all one father?"
Lines 25 and 26 contain precisely the same progression of terms as lines 8 and
9 in the sixth poem of R. Hai Gaon in *Yediot HaMakhon* vol. 3.

HE DWELLS FOREVER (6:L)

A *mustajaab l'malkhiyot*. Triple acrostic: "Shelomoh HaQatan Bar Yehuda." *Mus-
tajaab* is an Arabic term meaning "response." Like the *baqashah*, it is an un-
metered choral kind of *selihah* (penitential poem). It opens with a biblical verse,
and the end of each strophe then rhymes with that verse or even ends with the
same word. This poem is recited during the New Year service in the Sephardic
liturgy, as part of the additional prayers dealing with the Kingdom of God. It
picks up on the line from Psalms 145:13: "Thy kingdom is a kingdom for all
ages" (or in the NJPS: "Your kingship is kingship for eternity"—literally "of all
worlds"), then weaves together numerous motifs drawn directly from the *Sefer
Yetzirah*.

Lines 1–5: Cf. Isaiah 57:15: "For thus saith the High and Lofty One that inhab-
iteth eternity, whose name is holy: I dwell in the high and holy place"; *Sefer
Yetzirah* 1:1: "High and exalted, dwelling in eternity"; *Sefer Yetzirah* (long ver-
sion) 6:1: "The living El Shaddai, high and exalted, dwelling in eternity"; Isaiah
2:11: "And the Lord alone shall be exalted"; Psalms 148:13; Ecclesiastes 4:8:
"There is one that is alone, and he hath not a second"; *Sefer Yetzirah* 1:5: "The
Creator is One. He has no second"; *Pirkei Rabbi Eliezer* 3: "From what place
were the heavens created? From the light of the Holy One, blessed be His
garment"; *Sefer Yetzirah* 1:1: "He created His universe with three books" (*se-
farim*), or three words, with the s-f-r root: *sefer, sefar, sippur*—text, number,
telling or story.

6–10: "Against them inscribed ten without end . . . five against five—literally,
"are aligned" or "in agreement." Moshe Idel argues that this refers to the
Qabbalistic notion of the existence of ten additional, supernal *sefirot* above the
standard ten—an existence acknowledged by all the important Qabbalis-
tic schools of the thirteenth century. Idel traces the tradition to various

pre-Qabbalistic texts, including this poem (Idel, *HaSefirot Sheme'al*, 278). Cf. *Pirkei Rabbi Eliezer* 3: "The Holy One, blessed be He, consulted the Torah . . . to create the world"; *Genesis Rabbah* 1:1: "*Amon:* pedagogue . . . So the Holy One, blessed be He, looked in the Torah and created the world"; Genesis 31:30: "Thou sore longest for thy father's house"; *Sefer Yetzirah* 1:1–2: "The ten *sefirot* [spheres] of Nothingness . . . their measure is ten which have no end . . . ten like the number of ten fingers, five opposite five."

11–15: Cf. *Sefer Yetzirah* 1:5: "Know, think, and depict that the Master is unitary and the Creator is One, and he has no second, and before one what does one count"; *Sefer Yetzirah* 6:1: above lines 1–5.

16–20: "Caught in a siege"—cf. *Sefer Yetzirah* 1:5: "Their end is embedded in their beginning and their beginning in their end"; also, *Sefer Yetzirah* 1:5, lines 11–15 above; *Sefer Yetzirah* 6:3: "A proof of this, trustful witnesses."

21–25: Cf. *Sefer Yetzirah* 2:1: "Twenty foundation letters"; *Sefer Yetzirah* 3:3: "Fire is above and water is below, and breath [wind] is the decree dividing between them"; *Sefer Yetzirah* 5:3: "Twelve elementals . . . with them He formed twelve constellations [of the zodiac] in the universe."

26–30: Cf. *Sefer Yetzirah* 2:5: "From Chaos He formed substance, and He made that which was not into that which is. He carved great stones [pillars] out of air that cannot be grasped"; *Sefer Yetzirah* 1:12: "Chaos is an azure line that surrounds all the world; Void consists of the spongy rocks that are established in the abyss, between which water emanates."

31–35: Cf. *Sefer Yetzirah* 1:14: "He selected three letters from among the Elementals, and fixed them in His great Name, YHVH; with them He sealed the six directions"; *Sefer Yetzirah* 1:13: "[Sefirah] four is fire from water. With it he engraved and carved the throne of Glory, *serafim, ofanim*, and the holy *hayyot* [creatures] and the ministering angels"; Genesis 1:14: "let [the lights be] for signs, and for seasons, and for days and years."

36–40: Cf. *Sefer HaRazim* 7:29: "He hung the world like a cluster of grapes"; *Genesis Rabbah* 68:9: "The Holy One, blessed be He, is the place of the world and the world is not his place"; Isaiah 26:4: "For the Lord is God, an everlasting rock."

41–45: "Life beyond time"—literally, "eternal life." Cf. *Sefer Yetzirah* 1:9: "Ten *sefirot* of Nothingness, one is the spirit of the living God, His throne is established of old [eternally]"; Psalms 93:2: "Thy throne is established of old"; Psalms 145:11: "They shall speak of the glory of Thy kingdom"; 1 Chronicles 29:12: "Thou rulest over all"; Genesis 1:2: "The spirit of God hovered over the face of the waters."

46–50: Cf. Psalms 113:4: "The Lord is high above all nations."

51–55: Cf. The Prayer for the New Moon: "Who with his word creates the heavens, and their hosts with the breath of his mouth"; Psalms 33:6: "By the word of the Lord were the heavens made; and all the host of them by the breath of his mouth"; *Sefer Yetzirah* 6:1: "Exalted (*nasa*) ... because he supports (*nosei*) and sustains the entire universe [world]"; Isaiah 46:4: "I have made, and I will bear, Yea, I will carry, and will deliver"; Isaiah 40:28: "Hast thou not known ... the everlasting God, the Lord, the Creator of the ends of the earth, fainteth not, neither is weary?"; Job 5:13: "He taketh the wise in their own craftiness."

56–60: Cf. Job 26:7: "He ... hangeth the earth over nothing"; Job 28:11: "And the thing that is hid bringeth he forth to light."

61–65: Job 11:10: "And if He pass by, and shut up, or gather in"; 1 Samuel 2:7: "The Lord maketh poor and maketh rich ... [He] bringeth low and also lifteth up"; Job 16:12: "He hath taken me by the neck and dashed me to pieces"; Isaiah 2:12–14: "For the Lord of hosts hath a day upon all that is proud and lofty ... upon all the high mountains."

66–70: Cf. Proverbs 30:8; Ezekiel 34:26: "I will cause the shower to come down in its season."

71–75: Cf. 1 Samuel 2:6: "The Lord killeth, and maketh alive"; Psalms 17:14; Ezekiel 37:8: "And I beheld and, lo, there were sinews upon them, and flesh came up, and skin covered them above; but there was no breath in them"; Job 10:11: "Thou hast clothed me with skin and flesh, and knit me together with bones and sinews."

76–80: Cf. Genesis 2:7: "He ... breathed into his nostrils the breath of life"; Genesis 3:19: "In the sweat of thy face shalt thou eat bread, till thou return unto the ground"; the *Nishmat* prayer: "Thou arouseth those who sleep and awakeneth men from their slumber"; Daniel 12:2: "And many of them that sleep in the dust of the earth shall awake, some to everlasting life, and some to reproaches and everlasting abhorrence."

AND SO IT CAME TO NOTHING (81:L)

A piyyut for the Additional Prayers of the Day of Atonement. An alphabetical acrostic is embedded in the Hebrew, with "Shelomoh" following. Like "The Mountain of Sion is Barren," this poem recalls earlier (c. fifth century C.E.) piyyutim such as Yosse Ben Yosse's *"Ain lanu kohen gadol lekhapeir be'adeinu"* (We have no high priest to atone for us), as it contrasts the ritual glories of the past with the ruins of the exilic present. The list that follows in lines 5–20 is drawn from a combination of scriptural and talmudic sources. On occasion I depart from the order and literal meaning in the interest of sound and comprehension in English.

Lines 1–4: Cf. Isaiah 64:10: "Our holy and our beautiful house, where our fathers praised Thee, is burned with fire; and all our pleasant things are laid waste."

5–6: Cf. *Yoma* 2a: "What is *Birah*? Rabbah b. Bar Hana in the name of R. Johanan said: There was a place on the Temple mount called Birah, Resh Lakish said: The whole sanctuary is called *Birah*, as it is written: "And to build the *Birah* [palace] for which I have made provision [1 Chronicles 29:19]"; *Middot* 5:3–4: "Six offices were in the courtyard [of the Temple] . . . the office made of hewn stone, there the great Sanhedrin of Israel was in session"; *Sanhedrin* 94b: "That wicked man [Sennacherib] said: First will I destroy [His] nether abode [the Temple on earth], and then the upper."

7–8: Cf. *Tamid* 3:5: "The shambles was located at the north of the altar, and on it were eight short pillars, and square blocks of cedar wood were on them. And iron hooks were set into them . . . on which they would suspend [the slaughtered beasts]"; Leviticus 9:19: "And the fat of the ox, and of the ram . . . that which covereth the inwards, and the kidneys, and the lobe of the liver."

9–10: 1 Kings 7:32: "And the axletrees of the wheels were in one base"; *Yoma* 3:3: "Five acts of immersion . . . does the high priest carry out on that day"; Leviticus 16:15–17: "Then shall he kill the goat of the sin-offering, that is for the people . . . when he goeth in to make atonement in the holy place . . . for himself, and for his household, and for all the assembly of Israel."

11–12: Cf. Leviticus 23:37: "an offering made by fire unto the Lord, a burnt-offering, and a meal-offering, a sacrifice, and drink-offerings"; Leviticus 24:5–6: "And thou shalt take fine flour, and bake twelve cakes . . . And thou shalt set them in two rows, six in a row, upon the pure table before the Lord"; Exodus 40:22–23: "And he put the table in the tent of meeting, . . . and he set a row of bread in order upon it before the Lord."

13–14: Cf. *Yoma* 5:4: "He slaughtered [the goat] . . . and he sprinkled some [of its blood] . . . like one who cracks a whip"; Leviticus 16:12: "And he shall take a censer full of coals of fire from off the altar before the Lord, and his hands full of sweet incense beaten small, and bring it within the veil."

15–16: Cf. Leviticus 4:11–12: "The skin of the bullock, and all its flesh . . . shall he carry forth without the camp unto a clean place, where the ashes are poured out"; *Yoma* 7:5: "The high priest serves in eight garments: tunic . . ."; Exodus 28:2: "And thou shalt make holy garments for Aaron . . . for splendor and for beauty."

17–18: Cf. Leviticus 16:10, 21, where the ritual sending of the scapegoat into the wilderness is discussed. The scapegoat is chosen by lot, Aaron confesses over the goat the iniquities of the people, and a man is appointed to lead it into the wilderness—"And the goat shall bear upon him all their iniquities unto a land which is cut off." *Yoma* 6:3 says that a priest was sent out with the goat to make sure that it didn't return to a settled area; 6:6–8 mentions the later practice of hurling the scapegoat from a cliff. The Hebrew refers to "Azazel"—whose precise meaning is uncertain, but which seems to imply a goat-demon of sorts, a ruler of the wilderness, into whose realm the scapegoat was sent (Levine, *Leviticus, JPS Torah Commentary*, 102–3).

HAVEN'T I HIDDEN YOUR NAME (135:L)

A *reshut*. Acrostic: "Shelomoh."

Lines 1–4: Cf. Psalms 63:2–7: "O God, Thou art my God, earnestly will I seek Thee; my soul thirsteth for Thee ... So will I bless Thee as long as I live; In Thy name will I lift up my hands"; Psalms 55:17–18: "As for me I will call upon God; and the Lord will save me. Evening, and morning, and at noonday, will I complain, and moan, and He hath heard my voice." Reuven Tsur (*Studies*, 24–33) has a fine analysis of the poem's paradoxes and its effective use of convention and ornament to deepen the representation of the experiential aspect of the poem. Here, for example, the rhyme in Hebrew calls for "my door" rather than just "door," and the image is made more complex, and initially confusing, because of that: The speaker moans/longs for the Lord, not like any beggar come to any door, but like one come to the speaker's door. So that the speaker is, as it were, begging to himself. In other words, the speaker is like a beggar before the Lord, and like a lord before the beggar at his door. He seeks admission to his own reflection, wherein God is somehow contained (lines 5–6; see also the note to "Three Things"). Similar paradoxes are set out in the following lines, and the seemingly conventional poem of praise becomes a powerful poem of experience.

5–6: Cf. 1 Kings 8:27: "Behold, heaven and the heaven of heavens cannot contain Thee; how much less this house that I have builded." Scheindlin notes the presence of the pun on *ve'ulam*, a homonym which means "and yet" in the poem and "a temple" in the allusion to the verse from 1 Kings. The paradox evident here, as Scheindlin makes clear, is the gist of the poem, and it resembles both the rabbinical saying, "The world is not His place, but rather He is the place of the world," and the Sufi tradition attributed to Muhammad according to which God said, "My earth and My heaven contain me not, but the heart of my faithful servant containeth Me."

7–8: Cf. Psalms 119:11: "Thy word I have laid up in my heart that I might not sin against Thee"; Job 10:13: "Yet these things thou didst hide in thy heart; I know that this is with thee"; Job 27:3: "All the while my breath is in me, and the spirit of God is in my nostrils"; Jeremiah 20:9: "And if I say: 'I will not make mention of Him, nor speak any more in His name,' then there is in my heart as it were a burning fire shut up in my bones, and I weary myself to hold it in, but cannot"; Psalms 17:3: "Thou hast tested me, and Thou findest not that I had a thought which should not pass my mouth." The notion of the desire to praise overflowing the boundary of the poet's lips Scheindlin likens to the flow of water in the ruler's fountain in "The Palace Garden" and of course to the metaphor of the divine fountain in *The Fountain of Life*.

LORD WHO LISTENS (93:L)

A *reshut* for the *qaddish* of the first day of Sukkot, the Festival of Booths. Acrostic: "Shelomoh."

Lines 1–2: Cf. Psalms 22:25: "For He hath not despised nor abhorred the lowliness of the poor; neither hath He hid His face from him"; Psalms 34:7: "This poor man cried, and the Lord heard"; Psalms 13:2: "How long wilt thou hide thy face from me?"; Psalms 10:1: "Why standest thou afar off, O Lord? Why hidest Thou Thyself in times of trouble?"

3–4: Literally, "calling day and night." Cf. Psalms 102:1; Psalms 61:3; Psalms 57:8; Psalms 112:7–8; Psalms 86:12–13.

5–6: Cf. Psalms 28:7: "In him hath my heart trusted"; Psalms 5:3: "Hearken unto the voice of my cry, my King, and my God; for unto Thee do I pray"; Genesis 41:15: "I have dreamed a dream, and there is none that can interpret it."

7–8: Cf. Psalms 27:4: "One thing have I asked of the Lord, that will I seek after: That I may dwell in the house of the Lord all the days of my life, to behold the graciousness of the Lord, and to visit early in His Temple"; Psalms 61:2: "Hear my cry, O God; attend unto my prayer"; Psalms 86:6: "Give ear, O Lord, unto my prayer; and attend unto the voice of my supplication"; *Shabbat* 19:5: "An infant is circumcised on the eighth, ninth, tenth, eleventh or twelfth days [after birth], never sooner [less], never later [more]."

I'VE MADE YOU MY REFUGE (M. Y. 14, 109)

This poem, a *reshut*, was recently discovered by Sigi Ben-Ari among the texts and scraps that comprise the Cairo Genizah collection. She discusses it in an article in *Mehqerei Yerushalayim beSifrut Ivrit*, Vol. 14, where she offers the interpretation that the poem deals with Ibn Gabirol's fear that the Muses, as it were, the "daughters of song," have deserted him at the start of a poem. Moshe Ibn Ezra, in his book of poetics, comments on the phenomenon as well: "As for the poet, his fortune shifts, and his muse [literally: 'the daughter of his song'] sometimes attends to him and sometimes rebels. . . . When his heart turns away, the poem starts to stray. Therefore one of them said: 'When the pain starts, there's no poem [song] in the heart.' And one of the best poets has stated: 'I am considered by people to be a great poet, but it sometimes happens to me that it's easier to pull out one of my molars than to write a single couplet [line]'" (155, Halkin).

Acrostic: "Shelomoh." Superscription: By Shelomoh HaQatan, May He Rest in Peace.

Line 1: Cf. Psalms 73:28: "I have made the Lord God my refuge, that I may tell of all Thy works."

2: Cf. 1 Samuel 2:7: "The Lord maketh poor, and maketh rich."

3: Literally, "I rose to declare your oneness with the first few words of the poem." In the Hebrew-Andalusian poetics, the first half of the distich in a given line, or *bayit*, is called the *delet* (door). The slight awkwardness in the symmetry of the lines and their off rhymes (poor/lord/store/sure) seeks to account for a similar difficulty in the Hebrew, which Ben-Ari suggests was due to the poet's difficulty in composition.

5: Cf. Psalms 31:20: "Oh how abundant is Thy goodness, which Thou hast laid up for them that fear Thee."

8–9: Literally, "What is my sin to you?"

10–11: Cf. Ecclesiastes 12:4: "And one shall start up at the voice of a bird, and all the daughters of music [song] shall be brought low." Standard rabbinical interpretations of this biblical passage say that it is describing the effects of aging on a person. In this vein Avraham Ibn Ezra comments as follows on the same verse from Ecclesiastes: "*And all the daughters of song shall be brought low*—this is the throat, which once gave song, though now its voice is bowed low." Ben-Ari, however, interprets the lines metaphorically—with the "daughters" of song here being the muses, or inspiration. She goes on to argue that in fact this is the only reasonable interpretation of the poem.

14: The final line of the poem is missing. Ben-Ari points out that the final line would likely provide the link to the poem's place in the liturgy.

LIPS FOR BULLOCKS (82:L)

For the Day of Atonement. Acrostic: "Shelomoh."

Lines 1–2: Cf. Lamentations 5:18: "the mountain of Sion which is desolate, the foxes walk upon it"; Daniel 9:16: "Because for our sins, and for the iniquities of our fathers, Jerusalem and Thy people are become a reproach to all that are round about us."

3–4: Cf. Leviticus 16:17: "And there shall be no man in the tent of meeting when he goeth in to make atonement."

5–6: Cf. Hosea 14:3: "Take with you words, and return unto the Lord, saying unto Him: 'Forgive all iniquity, and accept that which is good; so we will render for bullocks the offering of our lips.'" Also Psalms 68:31. (See note to "I Take Great Pleasure," line 9.)

7–8: Cf. 1 Kings 8:30: "Hear Thou in heaven Thy dwelling place"; Exodus 15:17: "The place, O Lord, which Thou hast made to dwell in"; Isaiah 64:10: "Our holy and our beautiful house . . . laid waste"; Isaiah 60:7: "I will glorify My glorious house."

9–10: Cf. Leviticus 16:13: "that the cloud of the incense may cover the ark-cover."

13: Literally, "like the hand of an appointed man." Cf. Leviticus 16:21–22 below (line 22) for full citation.

14: Cf. Micah 7:19: "He will again have compassion upon us; He will subdue our iniquities."

15–16: Cf. Ezekiel 32:2: "And Thou didst . . . trouble the waters with Thy feet, and foul their rivers"; Psalms 86:5: "For Thou, O Lord, art good and ready to pardon."

17–18: Cf. 2 Samuel 19:18 and Ibn Janaah for *titzlah*—to rush in, or cross over, cleave or break through. Also Exodus 30:35: "Thou shalt make of it incense . . . seasoned with salt [expertly blended—NJPS]."

19–20: Cf. Job 36:18: "Neither let the greatness of the ransom turn thee aside."

22: See note to "And So It Came to Nothing," line 17. Cf. Leviticus 16:21–22: "And Aaron shall lay both his hands upon the head of the live goat, and confess over him all the iniquities of the children of Israel, and all their transgressions, even all their sins; and he shall put them upon the head of the goat, and shall send him away by the hand of an appointed man into the wilderness. And the goat shall bear upon him all their iniquities unto a land which is cut off"; *Yoma* 6:6: "He then pushed it over backwards, and it rolled down the ravine, and it did not reach halfway down the mountain before it broke into pieces."

23: Cf. Isaiah 49:8: "In an acceptable time have I answered thee"; Psalms 22:25: "For He hath not despised nor abhorred the lowliness of the poor."

I TAKE GREAT PLEASURE (149:L)

A *reshut*. Acrostic: "Shelomoh HaQatan."

Lines 1–4: Cf. Isaiah 33:5: "The Lord is exalted for He dwelleth on high"; Deuteronomy 26:15: "Look forth from thy Holy habitation, from heaven"; Isaiah 35:10: "The ransomed of the Lord shall return . . . They shall obtain gladness and joy, and sorrow and sighing shall flee away"; Psalms 62:12: "Strength belongeth unto God; also unto Thee, O Lord, belongeth mercy."

5–8: Cf. 1 Kings 8:27: "Behold, heaven and the heaven of heavens cannot contain Thee; how much less this house that I have builded"; Psalms 68:36: "He giveth strength and power unto the people"; Daniel 10:17: "For how can this servant of my lord talk with this my lord?"; Deuteronomy 1:9–12: "I am not able to bear you myself alone"; also Deuteronomy 14:24; Psalms 119:34; Proverbs 8:35; *Avot* 2:4: "Do His will as if it were thy will that He may do thy will as if it were His will; annul thy will before His will."

9–12: Cf. Hosea 14:3; Psalms 69:31–32: "I will praise the Name of God with a song . . . and it shall please the Lord better than a bullock that hath horns and hoofs"; Numbers 5:15: "A meal-offering of memorial, bringing iniquity to remembrance"; Habakkuk 1:13: "Thou that art of eyes too pure to behold evil"; Psalms 25:18: "See mine affliction and my travail"; Psalms 43:3: "O send out Thy light and Thy truth."

13–16: Cf. *Midrash Tehillim* 19:17: "Lord, You are great, and my sins are great, it befits the Lord of greatness to forgive great sins"; *Siddur Rav Sa'adiah Gaon*, 408: "Our sins are exceedingly great, and greater still are Thy mercies"; Abu Nuwas (quoted in Yarden): "O Lord, if my sins have been great, I know that your mercies are greater still"; Exodus 34:7; Numbers 4:19; Psalms 31:6: "Into Thy hand I commit my spirit."

SEND YOUR SPIRIT (107:L)

A *mehayyeh* for Passover, the Prayer for Dewfall. Acrostic: "Shelomoh." A *mehayyeh* (one that brings back to life) is a piyyut based on the second blessing of *Amidah* prayer: "Blessed art Thou, O Lord, who callest the dead to life everlasting." The play on corpse/crops is not in the original, but extends from the poem's motifs of inversion, and is representative of the poet's technical and thematic inclinations.

Lines 1–2: Cf. Psalms 104:30: "Thou sendest forth thy spirit"; Nehemiah 9:20: "Though gavest also Thy good spirit to instruct them, and withheldest not Thy manna from their mouth and gavest them water for their thirst."

3–4: *Eretz hatzvi* ("the land of desire," or "the land of glory") in the original is an epithet for the Land of Israel, as in 2 Samuel 1:19: "Thy beauty [glory], O Israel, upon thy high places is slain." The word *tzvi* here means, literally, "that which is desired"—from the Arabic *saba*, to desire, aspire, feel sensual desire for—and contains an overtone of a person's desire for the *tzvi* (gazelle, or fawn), or the young man of so many wine poems. Cf. Jeremiah 3:19: "A pleasant land, the goodliest heritage of the nations."

5: Cf. Hosea 14:9: "From me is thy fruit found."

6: Cf. Psalms 145:9: "The Lord is good to all."

7–8: Cf. Psalms 85:7: "Wilt Thou not quicken us again."

YOU LIE IN MY PALACE ON COUCHES OF GOLD (131:L)

A *reshut*. Acrostic: "Shelomoh." The congregation of Israel is speaking to God, and the erotic imagery is allegorical. In a thorough and persuasive article on the erotic/allegorical controversy in Shmuel HaNagid's poetry, Matti Huss has outlined the characteristic indications of erotic verse in this context: 1) the relationship involved is clearly erotic; 2) it is not formalized in the sense that it involves engagement or marriage; 3) it is based on an inversion of patriarchal hierarchies (the woman is in control); 4) the man is the partner who initiates the relationship; 5) the relationship is "disharmonic," and consummation is ruled out; 6) the male voice is dominant; 7) the poem is either in the classical (mono-rhymed) style or a *muwashshah* (strophic poem). In allegorical verse, on the other hand: 1) the relationship is erotic; 2) the relationship is formalized in the manner of engagement or marriage; 3) the female partner is the one who takes the initiative (though she is *not* in control); 4) the relationship is driven by a promise on the part of the male partner that the relationship will be consummated at some future point and become harmonious; 5) the voice of the woman is dominant, or at least of equal status to that of the male; 6) the literal erotic level of the poem is either impossible or illogical; 7) the poem might be classical, strophic, or quasi-strophic, metered or unmetered. Not all the criteria, it should be noted, need be found in a given poem.

Raymond Scheindlin observes that this is one of the more obscure poems on redemption by Ibn Gabirol (there are thirteen in all), and he suggests that the text might be corrupt. In any event, in its ambiguous current form, it appears that *knesset Yisrael* (the congregation of Israel—grammatically feminine) is asking a complacent God (who is resting, as the allusion would have it, between the cherubim of the ark) to prepare her bed for the *admoni*, the "ruddy one"—an expression that alludes to 1 Samuel 16:12 and implies the "anointed one" or the Messiah. In the second stanza God is addressed as the lover, not the go-between. Finally, the logistics of the poem are somewhat confusing, as God is, at the beginning of the poem, inside the palace but inactive, but at the end of the poem the congregation of Israel calls him to enter the palace. (Another possibility is that the address shifts to the "ruddy one," the Messiah, whom the poet longs for, calling him "my fine gazelle.") The final call to the lover to drink at dawn, Scheindlin notes, "echoes countless Arabic and Hebrew wine poems" (*The Gazelle*, 93–107).

Line 1: Cf. 1 Samuel 4:4: "The Lord of hosts, who sitteth upon the cherubim"; Exodus 25:18: "And thou shalt make two cherubim of gold"; Amos 6:4: "[Ye] ... that lie upon beds of ivory, and stretch themselves upon their couches"; Esther 1:6: "The couches were of gold and silver."

3: Cf. 1 Samuel 16:10–12: "And Samuel said unto Jesse: 'Send and fetch [David] ...' And he sent, and brought him. Now he was ruddy, and withal of beautiful eyes, and goodly to look upon." The Hebrew uses the characteristic "ruddy," which would be awkward in the English; I've shifted the allusion to the next term of the *shibbutz*. Cf. also Song of Songs 5:10: "My beloved is white and ruddy"—which the Targum explains as: "Then the ecclesia of Israel began to speak about the praise of the Lord of the World, saying, 'It is God I desire to worship, for by day He wears a robe white as snow ... and His face is radiant as fire from the greatness of his wisdom'" (trans. Scheindlin).

4: Cf. Song of Songs 2:9: "My beloved is like a gazelle."

5: Cf. Psalms 44:24: "Awake, why sleepest Thou, O Lord?"

6: Cf. Isaiah 13:2: "Set ye up an ensign upon the high mountain." The Hebrew specifies Mount Hermon and (or) Senir, from which the Land of Israel can be seen.

7: Cf. Numbers 16:26: "Depart, I pray you, from the tents of these wicked men"; Genesis 16:12: "And he [Ishmael] shall be a wild ass of a man."

8: Cf. Proverbs 5:19: "A lovely hind and a graceful doe, let her breasts satisfy thee at all times."

9: Cf. Song of Songs 6:3: "I am my beloved's and my beloved is mine."

10–12: "Chambers" is actually "palace" in the original, the same word that appears in line 1. Cf. Song of Songs 8:2: "I would lead thee, and bring thee into my mother's house, that thou might instruct me; I would cause thee to drink of spiced wine, of the juice of my pomegranate."

Kingdom's Crown (22:L and Zeidman Edition)

Kingdom's Crown is essentially a contemplative poem of petition, or *baqashah*, though its hybrid composition renders it in many ways unique in Hebrew literature. While it was most likely intended for personal use—as a private meditation—and not for the synagogue, its powerful religious emphases and great popularity have led to its incorporation into the rite for the Day of Atonement, on which it is uttered quietly by individual worshippers. (See Elbogen, 259, and Fleischer in Schirmann, *History*, 333. Current practice varies from community to community; Fleischer notes that the poem was included in the prayerbooks of nearly all communities, Ashkenaz, Sepharad, North Africa, Romania, Corfu, and so on.) Each canto of the poem closes with a biblical quotation, often with a twist that shifts the meaning of the phrase or alters its polarity. (For more on the poem and its prosody, see Introduction, "Kingdom's Crown.")

Traditionally, the poem has been divided into three sections, or "movements"—in keeping with the musical analogy developed below—though the original contains no such division: section I serves as a prologue to the poem as a whole and opens with an address to the Creator (cantos I–IX); section II is a detailed (Ptolemaic) cosmology (cantos X–XXXII); and section III is a percussive confession of human failings that returns the speaker/reader to God (cantos XXXIII–XL). For all its ingenious use of biblical quotation and diverse sources including the Talmud, midrash, and early Hebrew liturgical verse from Palestine and Babylonia, the bulk of the poem is universal in its vision. According to Ratzhaby, the two principal sources of Muslim influence on the work were *The Epistles of the Brethren of Purity* and the writings of the Saragossan circle of Muslim poets of Ibn Gabirol's time and earlier. Key Jewish influences are Sa'adiah Gaon's poems of petition and the *selihot* (penitential poems) of the payytanic tradition.

My rendering of the poem takes its cue from the graphic arrangement of Y. A. Zeidman's definitive, and out-of-print, 1950 edition. Thorough annotation apart, Zeidman's great innovation was to set the poem out in lines that highlight the rhyme and syntactical (and hence rhythmic) movement of the cantos. This foregrounds the symphonic nature of the work, something that the standard and prayer-book editions obscure, and brings the reader back to the music of the poem—Basil Bunting's "patterns of sound drawn on a background of time." The poem's prosody, which has generally been ignored by previous translators, is addressed by D. Stewart in "*Saj'a* in the Qur'an: Prosody and Structure," where, among other things, the author calls into question the standard translation of this Arabic term as "rhymed prose." Stewart concludes that *saj'a* involves "a complex interplay of accentual meter, rhyme, and morphological pattern," and he agrees with the Egyptian poet Ahmad Shawqi's declaration that "*saj'a* is Arabic's second poetry" (*Saj'a*, 134).

Cross-references to Ibn Gabirol's philosophical works will be somewhat curtailed here in the interest of space. (The elaboration in the notes to the initial cantos of the first and second sections will give the reader a sense of the saturated nature of the poem as a whole.) Readers interested in further background detail should turn to the articles by Loewe and Ratzhaby, and to Schlanger's book on Ibn Gabirol's philosophy.

◆

MOTTO

Lines 1–2: Cf. Job 22:2: "Can a man be profitable unto God? Or can he that is wise be profitable unto Him?"; Job 34:9: "It profiteth a man nothing that he should be in accord with God"; *Pirkei Avot* 2:2: "For the merit of their fathers is their support."

5–6: Literally, "I've set it over [at the head of] all my hymns, and called it *Kingdom's Crown*," [or "the crown of the kingdom"]—where the poet enfolds the name of his poem and implies that it is a crown to the Living God's kingdom, i.e., a means of acknowledging and celebrating God's sovereignty. Other translations of the title *Keter Malkhut* are *The Kingly Crown* (Bernard Lewis), *The Kingdom's Crown*, *The Crown of Kingdom* (Lenowitz), *Kingship's Crown*, *The Royal Crown* (Loewe and others), and *A Crown for the King* (Slavitt). Each stresses one of the several connotations carried by the Hebrew. With *Kingdom's Crown* I have tried to emphasize the overall and abiding sense of majesty-in-creation—God's, but also the poet's—while maintaining the abstract aspects of the register and its esoteric implications. One possible source for the Hebrew title is the Book of Esther, 2:17: "He set the royal crown upon her head"; another possible source is *Pirkei R. Eliezer* XXIII, where the story of Noah and the flood is told; the context there suits that of Ibn Gabirol's poem: "All the animals are in the ark for twelve months, and Noah would stand there and pray before the Lord, saying: Lord of Creation, take me out of this prison, for my soul is weary of the smell of lions and bears and tigers. And the righteous on earth will crown you with the crown of [the] Kingdom [or "sovereignty"] for your having delivered me from this prison, as it is said, 'Bring my soul out of prison, that I may give thanks unto Thy name; the righteous shall crown themselves because of me [or 'glorify . . . in me'].'" (Psalms 142:8).

PART ONE (PROLOGUE)

Shelomoh Pines comments: "Gabirol gives poetic expression to the philosophical thought of *The Fountain of Life* in the first part of his poem *Keter Malkhut*. . . . Although the conceptual framework of *Keter Malkhut* is not identical in every detail to that of *The Fountain*, the differences are in many cases only of phrasing or emphasis." (*EJ*, 7, 243)

CANTO I: **Line 1:** Psalms 139:14: "Wonderful are thy works, and that my soul knoweth right well."

2–5: 1 Chronicles 29:11–12: "Thine, O Lord, is the greatness, and the power, and the glory, and the victory, and the majesty. . . . Thine is the kingdom, O Lord, and thou art exalted as head above all. Both riches and honor come of Thee, and Thou rulest over all." The translation of *netzah* has been problematic over the course of biblical and medieval translations. The term in Chronicles implies "triumph," and is translated with that word, or with "victory." In 1 Samuel 15:29: *Netzah Yisrael* is "The Glory of Israel." Later on the term comes to mean "eternity." I have followed the medieval commentator, Radaq, in his *Book of Roots*, where he says it implies "authority and might [or glory]."

6–7: See, "All the Creatures of Earth and Heaven," lines 1–2. Cf. Psalms 102:27: "They shall perish but Thou shalt endure."

8–9: Literally, "within whose counsel our ideas cannot stand"—cf. Jeremiah 23:18: "For who hath stood in the counsel of the Lord?" Jellinek suggests that "strength" (*gevurah*) is the Qabbalistic term, one of the *sefirot*, and that "the wise" of line 13 are Qabbalists (see Davidson, *Selected Religious Poems of Ibn Gabirol*, 174); and Klausner notes that the opening section of the poem mentions all ten of the Qabbalistic *sefirot*, from the highest, *keter*, to the lowest, *malkhut*. Gershom Scholem points out, however, that Jellinek and Klausner are reading against the historical grain, as the names of the *sefirot* were developed in the thirteenth century (see introduction under "Q" and Scholem, 162–3).

11–12: Cf. Habakkuk 3:4: "Rays hath He at His side; and there is the hiding of His power"; Proverbs 25:2: "It is the glory of God to conceal a thing." Zeidman points out that *sod* and *yesod*, literally "mystery/secret" and "foundation," here stand for "form" and "matter," key terms in Ibn Gabirol's philosophical scheme (see Zeidman, 8–9, and *Fountain of Life*, e.g., V:41). Falaqera uses *yesod* for "matter": "For there are only three [things] in being: matter-[*yesod*]-and-form, the first substance [God], and Will, which is the intermediary between the extremes" (Falaqera selections, I:3).

13: I.e., the four letters of the Name of God. Cf. *Kiddushin* 71a for the rabbis on Exodus 3:15, where a change of vocalization in "This is my name "forever" (*l'olam*) changes "forever" into "to be kept silent [secret]" (*l'alem*), and *Exodus Rabbah* 3:9. The knowledge of how to pronounce the four letters no longer resides with the wise.

14: Cf. Job 26:7: "He hangeth the earth over nothing."

15: Cf. Job 28:11: "The thing that is hid bringeth he forth to light."

16–18: "Your creatures." Cf. Psalms 31:20: "How abundant is thy goodness, which thou hast laid up [concealed] for them that fear thee."

19–21: Cf. Psalms 102:27–8: "They shall perish, but Thou shalt endure"; Isaiah 6:1: "sitting upon a throne high and lifted up." See Section II, canto XXIV for the location of the throne in the tenth sphere.

24–25: The translation follows Zeidman's gloss, especially "light's reflection." Cf. Lamentations 4:20: "Under his shadow we shall live"; *Fountain of Life* V:41: "And the impression of form in matter, when it reaches it from the Will, is like the return of the form of the one who gazes into a mirror at his reflection there." Literally, "the hidden dwelling in the secret heavenly place."

26–30: This world and the world-to-come. Cf. *Pirkei Avot* 2:21: "He used to say: The work is not upon thee to finish, nor art thou free to desist from it. . . . Faithful is the master of thy work who will pay thee the wages of thy toil. And know that the giving of the reward to the righteous is in the time to come." Also *The Epistles of the Brethren Purity* I:383: "And they have said in the books of wisdom: This world is a bridge. Cross over it into the world-to-come [the Hereafter] . . . For this world is a house of action, the one to come a house of reward."

31: Cf. Exodus 2:2: "And when she saw him that he was a goodly child, she hid him"—of Moses, though here the words refer to God and the reward to come. See also *Hagigah* 12a, which glosses the verse from Genesis, "And God saw the Light, that it was good"—this being the primary light that could be seen from "one end of the world to the other," but which, after witnessing the corrupt generation of the flood and the dispersion, God hid and reserved for the righteous.

CANTO II: Lines 1–3: Cf. Deuteronomy 6:4: "The Lord is One." Also the Sara-gossan Arabic poet and judge, Abu 'Amar Ahmed Bin 'Issa al-Albiri, a contem-porary of Ibn Gabirol: "You, oh Creator, in your greatness have created dura-tion, not in the time of duration's time. / You bring about all and without cease, so that my Lord remains without place. / It is you whom words of lofty description raise; / his loftiness is lifted beyond what the eye can discern." There is an illuminating discussion of the notion of "oneness" implied in the medieval use of the expression "God is one" in Wilensky (206–7), where the author stresses that "one" here does not indicate the first in a series, but rather the Absolute One that is the basis of all numbers but "is not itself a member of any numerical series." She finds this Neoplatonic notion in the *Fountain of Life* as well. See note to "He Dwells Forever," lines 11–15 (p. 280).

4–6: Cf. Exodus 16:15: "For they knew not what it was."

7–10: Cf. Deuteronomy 13:1: "Thou shalt not add there to, or diminish from it."

12: "Formed" for *qanui* follows Zeidman and Genesis 14:19. Others read "owned."

15–18: Cf. Psalms 39:2: "I said: I will take heed to my ways, that I sin not with my tongue." The translation of "my speech" follows Zeidman, meaning, "my meditation" or "my thinking."

21: Cf. Ecclesiastes 4:10: "Woe to him that is alone when he falleth"—where the poet once again changes the meaning (and reading) of the biblical inlay. The translation follows Zeidman's reading. An alternative translation might read: "How could the One ever fall?"

CANTO III: Lines 1–4: Cf. Job 42:5–6: "I have heard of Thee by the hearing of the ear; but now my eye seeth Thee; wherefore I abhor my words, and repent"; also al-Albiri, note to Canto II, lines 1–3.

8–10: Cf. *Bereshit Rabbah* 68:3 (to Genesis 28:11): "He is the place of the world and the world is not His place"; Sa'adiah Gaon: "Apropos of [the category of] *place*, I say that it is inconceivable for several reasons that the Creator should have need for occupying any place whatsoever.... As regards ... *time*, it is inconceivable that the concept of time could be applied to the Creator be-cause of the fact that He is Himself the Creator of all time." (*The Book of Belief and Opinion*, 124).

11–13: Cf. Ecclesiastes 7:24: "That which is is far off, and exceeding deep; who can find it out?"

CANTO IV: Line 1: Cf. Joshua 3:10: "The living God is among you."

8–9: Cf. Psalms 144:4: "Man is like unto a breath"; *Pirkei Avot* 3:1: "Know ... where you are going— to a place of dust and worms and maggots."

13: Cf. Genesis 3:22: "And now, ... take also of the tree of life, and eat, and live for ever."

CANTO V: Line 3: Literally, "and every advantage a disadvantage [or 'lack']"—i.e., every excellence negligible beside the excellence of God.

5: The word "chariot" (*merkavah*) might also be read as "idea," according to Zeidman, "throne of glory" according to Yarden, or the verbal noun "composition," according to Halper, from the root r-k-b.

7: Cf. Nehemiah 9:5: "Blessed be Thy glorious Name, that is exalted above all blessing and praise."

CANTO VI: Lines 1–4: Cf. Deuteronomy 3:24: "What God is there in heaven or on earth, that can do according to Thy works, and according to . . . Thy mighty acts?"

8–11: Cf. Deuteronomy 33:26: "There is none like God, riding through the heavens to help you, Through the skies in his majesty" (NJPS). Also *Yoma* 69b. The Andalusian Ibn 'Abd Rabbah (d. Córdoba c. 940) writes: "Praise be to God for his tolerance in the wake of his knowing [of our sin], and his forgiveness in the wake of his ability [to punish]" (*Al-'Iqd Al-Fariid*, in Ratzhaby, 57).

12–14: Cf. Psalms 145:9: "The Lord is good to all; and His tender mercies are over all His works"; Genesis 6:4: "The same were the mighty men that were of old"—in the poem, literally, "these [the mercies] are the strength everlasting."

CANTO VII: Line 1: Cf. Psalms 36:10: "For with Thee is the fountain of life; in Thy light do we see light."

2–5: Cf. Isaiah 59:2: "But your iniquities have separated between you and your God, and your sins have hid His face from you"; Lamentations 3:44: "Thou hast covered thyself with a cloud, so that no prayer can pass through."

6–8: The reading follows Zeidman; other Hebrew editions read: "will be revealed in the upper world of beauty." Cf. Genesis 22:14. Also *Ta'anit* 31a: "Ulla Bira'ah said in the name of R. Eliezer: In the days to come the Holy One, blessed be He, will hold a chorus for the righteous and He will sit in their midst in the Garden of Eden and every one of them will point with his finger towards Him, as it is said [Isaiah 25:9], 'Lo, this is our God, For whom we waited.'"

9–12: Cf. Isaiah 60:19: "The Lord shall be unto thee an everlasting light"; Numbers 23:13: "Thou shalt see but the utmost part of them, and shalt not see them all."

CANTO VIII: Lines 1–3: Cf. Deuteronomy 10:17: "For the Lord your God He is God of gods, and Lord of lords, the great God, the mighty and the awful."

4–7: Cf. Isaiah 43:10, 12 and 44:8: "Ye are my witnesses"; *Siddur Sa'adiah Gaon* (48, line 18): "All is your witness."

13–17: Cf. Psalms 9:16: "The nations are sunk down in the pit that they made;

in the net which they hid is their own foot taken"; Isaiah 24:18: "It shall come to pass that he who fleeth from the noise of the terror shall fall into the pit"; Psalms 55:24: "into the nethermost pit"—or "the pit of destruction" (Koren translation).

18–19: Cf. Psalms 107:30: "He led them unto their desired haven"; Isaiah 49:4: "I have labored in vain."

20–24: Cf. Isaiah 57:2: "He entereth into peace, they rest in their beds, each one that walketh in his uprightness"; 1 Samuel 6:12: "And they . . . turned not aside to the right hand or to the left"; Esther 6:4: "Now Haman was come into the outer court of the King's house."

32–33: The translation expands on the Hebrew image somewhat to account for the overtones of the Hebrew and its sound.

34–35: Cf. Ecclesiastes 3:20: "All go unto one place."

CANTO IX: This entire section reverberates against the "autobiography of wisdom" as it is set forth in Proverbs 8, especially 22–31: "The Lord made me as the beginning of His way, the first of His works of old . . ."

Lines 1–4: Cf. Proverbs 16:22: "Understanding is a fountain of life unto him that hath it"; Jeremiah 10:14: "Every man is proved to be brutish, without knowledge," and again, Psalms 36:10, which also explicitly mentions the "fountain of life" that gives the poet's major philosophical work its title.

7: Cf. Proverbs 8:30: "Then I was by him as a nursling."

8–10: Cf. Isaiah 40:14: "with whom took he counsel, and who instructed him, and taught him in the paths of right, and taught him knowledge, and made him to know the way of discernment."

11–13: Pines calls these and the following lines "among the most remarkable" of the poem. Cf. *Genesis Rabbah* 1:2, on "artist": "I was an instrument of the artistry of the Holy One, blessed be He"; Zeidman adds: "like a workman and artist [or artisan] with whose help the Holy One, blessed be He, created the world." See note to lines 20–22.

14–15: Cf. *Sefer Yetzirah* 2:6: "He formed substance out of chaos, and made nonexistence into existence." Davidson notes: "According to Empedocles, vision was occasioned by particles continually flying off the surface of bodies which met with others proceeding from the eye" (*Selected Religious Poems of Ibn Gabirol*, 178). And Dante: "Both that which never dies and that which dies / are only the reflected light of that / Idea which our Sire, with Love, begets: / . . . From there, from act to act, light then descends / down to the last potentialities, / where it engenders nothing / but brief contingent things . . . and thus, beneath / Idea's stamp, light shines through more or less. . . . / For . . . Nature always works defectively—she passes on that light much like an artist / who knows his craft but has a hand that trembles." (*Paradiso* XIII:52, trans. A. Mandelbaum).

16–19: Cf. *The Epistles of the Brethren of Purity*, Part I, Letter 8: "And know, my brother! Every flesh-and-blood artist has need of six things in order to complete his work ... Primary matter, place, time, tool, vessel and movement. ...; whereas the exalted Lord has no need of any of these, all of which are his creations and works." (Zeidman, 23); Proverbs 9:1: "Wisdom has builded her house; she has hewn out her seven pillars"; *Sefer Yetzirah* 1:12: "Fire from water, with it He engraved and carved the throne of glory. ...*"; Malachi 3:3: "He shall sit as a refiner and purifier of silver."

20–22: In the Hebrew the second-person anaphora is broken and the subject changes to the third person, standing either for the metaphorical "artist [artisan] or worker" of line 13, or, in the gendered Hebrew, for God's desire or will (lines 12)—*voluntas* in the Latin *Fountain of Life*, and *hefetz* in the Hebrew at this point in the poem. Emanating from God, this desire works like an artist, or artisan, to fashion the world. In the subsequent lines the pronouns are all third-person in the original; in line 24 the agency is extended to third-person feminine "hand of desire."

These lines have drawn extensive commentary for their relevance to the study of early Qabbalah. In particular, see Pines, "*Veqara el ha'ayin veniqb'a*," Scholem, "*'Iqvotav shel Gabirol baqabbalah*," and Liebes (in the notes to "I Love You" and his article cited there). Pines argues that these lines were most likely influenced by the Muslim philosopher Ibn Sinna's (Avicenna, 980–1037) commentary to the Quran, Sura *al-Falaq* (The Rising Day). Idel points out (cited in Pines) that there is another close parallel in Qabbalistic literature, namely, in *Sefer HaYihud*, which speaks of the *sefirah keter* ("crown") as follows: "It is called a ... light that is made like a crack changing from matter to matter until it splits and in that splitting the powers of all the *sefirot* are drawn from it" (Pines, "*Veqara*," 339). Liebes, who says that Pines's claim is interesting but open to criticism, proposes a more provocative and compelling interpretation—one that resonates with much of what comes through in poems such as "The Palace Garden," namely, that the image contains residues of an early myth, deriving perhaps from Persian Manicheism and Greek gnosticism. The line, he offers, holds a conscious (or semi-conscious) echo of the Orphic creation myth of the egg and the god Phanes, who shines out of the egg as it cracks. Going even further, though with considerable reservation, he notes the similarity between the Greek word *oion* (egg) and the Hebrew word *'ayin* (nothing, or nothingness). The latter, he says, is a nothingness of plenitude. In Aristophanes' *The Birds*, he notes, "the cosmic egg is called *hypenemion oion*, namely, 'an egg carried by the wind', or 'a wind egg'" (Liebes, *Studies*, 82–83). Cf. also Genesis 1:3–4: "And God said: 'Let there be light,' and there was light. ... And God divided the light from the darkness. And God called the light Day"; Isaiah 58:8: "Then shall thy light break forth as the morning"; Proverbs 3:20: "By his knowledge the depths were broken up"; Genesis 31:25:

"Now Jacob had pitched his tent in the mountain"; Psalms 136:6: "to him that spread forth the earth above the waters."

The interruption of section I's anaphora—"You are the . . ."—by "He called" signals the transition to section II of the poem, the cosmology.

23–26: The imagery here is taken from the description of the wilderness sanctuary in Exodus. Cf. Exodus 36:17: "And he made fifty loops on the edge of the curtain that was outmost in the first set"—where "set" is understood by Zeidman as referring to the system of the spheres, which section II of the poem will map. In the dramatic deployment here, God's desire or will, literally "the power [of his/its hand]" (Ibn Gabirol identifies God's will as "the power of unification") reaches from the highest "innermost chamber" of the tenth sphere (canto XXIV) to the "outermost edge" of the lower creation, with earth at its center. Cf. also Isaiah 44:24: "Thus says the Lord, thy redeemer, and he that formed thee from the womb; I am the Lord that maketh all things; that stretchest the heavens alone"; Isaiah 40:12: "Who has . . . meted out heaven with the span."

PART TWO (COSMOLOGY)

Readers of *Kingdom's Crown* have long had a certain prejudice against this section of the poem. As noted in the introduction, the rabbis of the middle ages were concerned about its confusion of science and religion; twentieth-century guides to teachers have suggested that students would be more interested in the emotionalism of sections I and III, and that the detail of section II called for something of an acquired taste. It seems to me that the opposite is true: the musical and physical detail of section II establishes a palpable sense of grandeur and kingdom, without which the effect of the prologue and confession would be considerably reduced. The cosmology, as I see it, contains some of the most powerful and sublime sections of the poem.

CANTO X: Line 1: The second section of the poem begins at the center of the Ptolemaic universe, with the sublunary sphere—the globe of earth and water surrounded by air and fire. The poem then begins its ascent up through the ten spheres of the moon, Mercury, Venus, the sun, Mars, Jupiter, Saturn, the fixed stars (the zodiac), the all-encompassing (diurnal) sphere, and then the sphere of intelligence (the source of angels). Above this tenth sphere is the "place of the souls of the righteous after death," universal matter, the Throne of Glory, and the "Effulgence of Divine Glory: the Source of Soul" (see Loewe, *Ibn Gabirol*, 114). Cf. Psalms 106:2: "Who can express the mighty acts of the Lord?"

2: Zeidman notes that the notion of the earth as a sphere appears in the Jerusalem Talmud (*Avodah Zarah*: 3:1): "It is said: The earth is made like a ball . . .

R. Yonah said: Alexander of Macedon, when he asked to ascend on high and ascended on high, rose until he saw the earth as a ball and the seas as a bowl"; the full term "ball of earth," he notes, was renewed in Hebrew by Ibn Gabirol. Prior to that it appears of course in Pythagoras, and the Muslim cosmographers drew on earlier Greek sources. (Umberto Eco has an entertaining discussion of the question of the earth's shape in "The Force of Falsity," *Serendipities*, 4–6.) *The Epistles of the Brethren of Purity* I:162: "The parts of the water were lighter than the parts of the land and the water stood over the land. And since the parts of the wind were lighter than the water the wind was set over the water."

3: Earth and water are the first two of the four primary elements, which figure prominently in Ibn Gabirol's early ethical treatise, *The Improvement of the Moral Qualities*. Cf. *The Epistles* I:116: "The elements are four, namely: fire, wind, water, and earth."

4: Wind is the third element. In an effort to establish a sense of motion and dimension, and to maintain the musical flow of the poem, I have varied the English for *galgal* throughout—here "wheel," but a few lines later "circuit," and, more often, "sphere."

5: Cf. Ecclesiastes 1:6: "The wind goeth toward the south, and turneth about unto the north; It turneth about continually in its circuit, and the wind returneth again to its circuits."

10: Cf. Ibn Gabirol, *The Fountain of Life* I:5, 5: "The universal essence . . . is not unified however . . . it is reduced to two principles . . . the universal matter and universal form."

11: Cf. Hosea 2:2: "And the children of Judah . . . shall appoint themselves one head, and shall go up out of the land." The *shibbutz* again employs the biblical phrase in a different context entirely.

13: Cf. Genesis 2:10: "And a river went out of Eden to water the garden; and from thence it was parted, and became four heads." Avraham Ibn Ezra's commentary (in M. Friedlander's *Essays on the Writings of Abraham Ibn Ezra*, 40) reads as follows: "And now I will reveal to you by allusion the secret of the garden and the rivers. . . . And I have not found this matter discussed by any of the sages except R. Solomon Ibn Gabirol, who was a great sage and saw into the matters of the soul's mystery. . . . And the 'river'—is like a mother (which is to say, the universal natural common matter) to all bodies; and the 'four heads' [fonts]—are the roots— [the elements of fire, wind, water, dust]." In the standard editions of his commentary Ibn Ezra writes: "And he who understands this mystery will understand how the river diverges."

Canto XI: Lines 1–4: Cf. Genesis 1:16: "And God made the two great lights."
5–6: Cf. 1 Samuel 6:9: "If it goeth by the way of its own border" (a direct quote in the Hebrew, with the order of the words changed). Ibn Gabirol's figures,

taken no doubt from the astronomical literature available to him, most likely the *Epistles* (see Loewe, "Treatment of Sources" and Ratzhaby, "*Shirat Keter Malkhut*"), are sometimes remarkably accurate. Scholars have compared them with the related contemporary literature, and R. Loewe (*Ibn Gabirol*, 115) presents a table showing how the figures for the volume of the planets compare with Ptolemy's calculations and a recent computation. Here, for instance, Ibn Gabirol says the moon is 1/39th the size of the earth (.0256); Ptolemy has it at 1/40th (.025), and a recent computation at .02. A second table shows the periodicity of the heavenly bodies: Ibn Gabirol states that it takes the moon 29.5 days to circle the earth, whereas recent computations for the synodic period show the correct figure to be 29.53 days. *The Epistles* (II:33) have the same wording, literally: "The moon is a part of nine-and-thirty parts of the earth."

9–12: Cf. *The Epistles* (I:141): "The moon bears testimony to the affairs of the world and the condition of its inhabitants according to increase and lack, change and destruction."

13: Cf. Psalms 145:10–12: "All Thy works shall praise Thee, O Lord . . . to make known to the sons of men . . . mighty acts, and the glory of the majesty of [Thy] kingdom."

CANTO XII: Lines 1–4: Cf. Psalms 104:19: "who appointedst the moon for seasons."

5: Cf. Genesis 1:16: "the lesser light to rule the night."

10–14: A description of an eclipse. The "dragon"—*teli* in Hebrew—is a legendary snake-like creature that occasionally rises up and tries to swallow the sun or the moon, thereby causing an eclipse. Sa'adiah Gaon notes in the introduction to his *Book of Belief* (26): "It has likewise been reported about certain uneducated people of our own nation that they labor under the illusion that something resembling a whale swallows the moon, as a result of which it becomes eclipsed." The term "the line of *teli*," however, appeared in medieval books of astronomy. *Sefer Yetzirah* 6:1 also mentions *teli*; see Kaplan, 234 for extensive discussion of the term. Also *Bahir* 106.

15–19: Cf. Joshua 4:24: "that all the peoples of the earth may know the hand of the Lord, that it is mighty"; Psalms 75:8: "For God is judge; He putteth down one, and lifteth up another"; 2 Samuel 1:10: "I was sure that he could not live after . . . he was fallen."

28–30: Cf. Deuteronomy 4:19: "The sun and the moon and the stars, even all the host of heaven."

31–34: Cf. Ecclesiastes 5:7: "For one higher than the high watcheth, and there are higher than they." Also, *Leviticus Rabbah* 31:9, on worship of the sun.

35: Cf. Isaiah 41:20: "That they may see, and know, and consider, and understand . . . that the hand of the Lord hath done this."

42–43: Cf. 1 Kings 15:13: "And also Maacah his mother he removed from being queen, because she had made an abominable image for an Asherah; and Asa cut down her [abominable] image."

CANTO XIII: Lines 1–6: Cf. Psalms 71:15: "My mouth shall tell of Thy righteousness." Bialik-Ravnitzky and Yarden read "one twenty-two thousandth."

7–13: Cf. *Shabbat* 156a and b for talmudic explanations of the planets' influences on character. Also Habakkuk 1:3: "there is strife, and contention ariseth."

16: Proverbs 1:4: "to give prudence to the simple, to the young man knowledge and discretion."

CANTO XIV: Line 5: Cf. Isaiah 61:10: "as a bride adorneth herself with her jewels."

9: Cf. *Baraita de Shmuel HaQatan* 9: "Venus is appointed over charm and grace and love, and over passion and desire and fruitfulness and over increase of humankind and beasts, and over the fruit of the land and the fruit of the tree"; *Ketubah* 8a: "Blessed art Thou, O Lord, . . . who hast created joy and gladness, bridegroom and bride, rejoicing and song, mirth and delight."

15–16: Cf. Deuteronomy 33:14: "precious things of the fruits of the sun . . . and the precious things of the yield of the moon."

CANTO XV: Lines 8–16: Cf. Psalms 144:10: "O God . . . who givest salvation unto kings"; Daniel 11:21: "upon whom had not been conferred the majesty of the kingdom"; Proverbs 20:2: "The terror of a king"; 1 Kings 20:18: "Whether they are come out for peace . . . or whether they are come out for war"; Daniel 2:21: "He removeth kings, and setteth up kings"; 1 Samuel 2:7: "He bringeth low and also lifteth up."

17–20: Cf. Nehemiah 9:6: "And the host of heaven worshippeth Thee"; Proverbs 8:2: "Where the paths meet, she standeth."

21: Cf. Esther 2:14: "In the evening she went, and on the morrow she returned."

CANTO XVI: Lines 1–4: This canto is still about the sun. Cf. Genesis 1:14: "And let [the lights in the firmament] be for signs, and for seasons, and for days, and years."

4–8: Cf. Genesis 1:12: "And the earth brought forth tree bearing fruit, wherein is the seed thereof"; Job 38:31: "Canst thou bind the chains of the Pleiades, or loose the bands of Orion?"; *Genesis Rabbah* 10:6: "R. Simon said: There is not a single herb that does not have a constellation in heaven which strikes it and says, 'Grow,' . . . R. Hanina b. Papa and R. Simon said: Pleiades binds the fruit and Orion draws it out between knot and knot, as it is written, *'Canst thou lead forth the constellations in season?'* (Job 38:32); R. Tanhum b. R. Hiyya and R. Simon said: The constellation which ripens the fruits."

24: Cf. Psalms 78:4: "His strength, and His wondrous works that He hath done."

26: Cf. Daniel 1:4: "youths . . . skilful in knowledge and discerning in thought, and such as had the ability to stand in the king's palace."

28: Cf. Genesis 24:10: "All goodly things of his master's in his hand." Ratzhaby notes the Arabic proverb from which the line might derive: "The power of the servant [derives] from the power of his lord."

CANTO XVII: In the Hebrew here the sun is grammatically feminine, the moon masculine. The genders are reversed in the English. Loewe comments that the dynamic described is drawn from the Muslim *Epistles:* "The intellect, with the permission of Allah, gives life to the sun and moon as representing respectively the first and male and second and female principles which, by their union, generate all things—a concept to which Gabirol is obviously alluding." ("Sources," 184).

Lines 1–5: "stars above"—the remaining heavenly bodies, Mars, Jupiter, and Saturn. "Stars . . . below"—already named. The sun occupies a middle position in the planetary system. "Spot of whiteness beneath it," i.e., beneath the sun. The Hebrew for this is obscure, *baheret,* cf. Leviticus 13:23: "But if the bright spot stay in its place, and be not spread, it is the scar of the boil (*baheret*) . . ." (*Pentateuch and Rashi's Commentary, Leviticus*)— where leprosy is being discussed. NJPS translates it as "discoloration." "Beneath it" could also be "in its place."

11: Cf. Exodus 25:37: "Thou shalt make the lamps thereof seven, and they shall light the lamp thereof."

20: Literally, "for a day and a half-hour and a few moments."

21–22: Cf. Psalms 19:6: "As a bridegroom coming out from his chamber."

CANTO XVIII: **Lines 8–15:** Cf. Jeremiah 20:11: "The Lord is with me as a mighty warrior"; Nahum 2:4: "The shield of his mighty men is made red"; Deuteronomy 32:24: "the devouring of the fiery bolt"; *Baraita de Shmuel HaQatan* 9: "Mars is appointed over the blood and the sword and evil and contention and struggle, and convulsions and wounds and battle and hatred and jealousy and enmity and competition and blows and . . . fire and broken down walls."

18: Cf. Proverbs 1:16: "For their feet run to evil, and they make haste to shed blood."

CANTO XIX: **Line 4:** Cf. Isaiah 1:21: "It was full of judgment; righteousness [*tzedeq*—Hebrew for Jupiter as well] lodged in it" (Koren translation).

7: *Bereshit Rabbah* 10:4: "There is a planet that completes its orbit in twelve years and this is Jupiter."

10: Cf. *Shabbat* 156a: "He who is born under Jupiter [*tzedeq*] will be a right-doing man [*tzadqan*] . . . . right doing in good deeds."

13: Cf. Psalms 46:10: "He maketh wars to cease unto the end of the earth."

14: Cf. 2 Kings 22:5: "let them deliver it unto the hand of the workmen that have the oversight of the house of the Lord, . . . to repair the breaches of the house."

15: Cf. Psalms 9:9: "He will judge the world in righteousness."

CANTO XX: Line 7: *Genesis Rabbah* 10:4: "And there is a planet that completes its circuit in thirty years and this is Saturn."

8–11: Cf. *Baraita de Shmuel HaQatan* 9: "Saturn is appointed over poverty and misery and illness and destruction."

13: Cf. Isaiah 28:21: "That He may do His work, strange is His work, and bring to pass His act, strange is His act."

CANTO XXI: Line 5: Cf. Exodus 28:8: "the skilfully woven band, which is upon it"—which describes the High Priest's ephod. The twelve constellations were also known as the "band [belt] of the zodiac." Zeidman points out that the allusion to the High Priest's garments is significant, noting Avraham Ibn Ezra's commentary to the verse from Exodus: "No one will understand this mystery [secret] who has not studied *Sefer HaMiddot*. And the mystery [secret] of the divine artistry."

7: Cf. 1 Kings 7:24: "Cast when it [the molten sea] was cast . . ."

12: The word for the zodiac, *mazzalot*, appears only once in the Bible (2 Kings 23:5), where it means "constellations"—from the Akkadian *mazaltu*, "the standing of the stars." The related word in Phoenician and Aramaic means "star of destiny" or "fortune."

15: Literally, "and sets them above them [above the creatures below]."

17: Cf. Isaiah 40:26: "Lift up your eyes on high, and see: who hath created these? He that bringeth out their host by number, He calleth them all by name."

18: Cf. Numbers 4:19: "Aaron and his sons shall go in, and appoint them every one to his service and to his burden."

CANTO XXII: Line 6: Cf. Ezekiel 1:10: "As for the likeness of their faces, they had the face of a man."

3: See Canto XXI, line 12, note.

8: Cf. Numbers 27:20: "And thou shalt put of thy honor [authority—NJPS] upon him."

9: Cf. Leviticus 21:3: "and for his sister, a virgin, that is near unto him."

12–15: Cf. Genesis 21:20: "And God was with the lad [Ishmael], and he grew . . . and became an archer"; Jeremiah 51:30: "Their might hath failed."

19: Cf. Jonah 2:1: "Now the Lord prepared a great fish."

20–22: Cf. Genesis 25:16: "These are . . . twelve princes according to their nations."

CANTO XXIII: Line 1: Psalms 44:22: "Would not God search this out? For He knows the secrets [hidden things] of the heart"; Job 28:11: "The thing that is hid bringeth he forth to light"; Job 11:6: "that He should tell thee the secrets of wisdom."

7–8: The power of the ninth sphere is such that it reverses what should have been the natural movement of the other spheres—west to east. See notes to "The Garden," lines 21–22.

14: Cf. Isaiah 41:12: "They . . . shall be as nothing, as a thing of nought."

17: Cf. Isaiah 40:17: "All the nations are as nothing before Him; They are accounted by Him as things of nought, and vanity."

CANTO XXIV: Line 4: Cf. 1 Kings 6:17: "The house, that is, the Temple, before [the Sanctuary]"—where the Hebrew for Temple is *heikhal*, and might also be translated "palace" or "chamber."

5: Cf. Leviticus 27:32: "The tenth shall be holy to the Lord."

9: Cf. Habakkuk 3:4: "Rays hath He at His side; And there is the hiding of His power."

10–13: Cf. Song of Songs 3:9-10: "King Solomon made himself a palanquin of the wood of Lebanon. He made the pillars thereof of silver, the top thereof of gold"; "his throne" (*matzavto*) or "base" has a variant reading, *misbato*, "couch" or "table"—Song of Songs 1:12: "while the king sat at his table."

15–16: Cf. Genesis 4:7: "unto thee is its desire."

CANTO XXV: Lines 1: Cf. Psalms 92:6: "O Lord! Thy thoughts are very deep."
2: The circle of mind doesn't participate in the rotation of the other spheres.

3–4: "Spirits on high" are angels: Ibn Ezra on Exodus 3:15: "Know that there are three worlds: . . . the lower word . . . and the intermediary world . . . and the upper world which is the world of the holy angels . . . and the soul of humankind." Zeidman notes: both souls and angels were created from the glow of the circle of mind.

5–8: This stanza collapses the Hebrew somewhat. Cf. Genesis 3:24: "A flaming sword which turned every way."

9–10: Cf. Exodus 35:35: "to work all manner of workmanship"—which tells of Bezalel and Oholiab, who built the Sanctuary. Cf. also Ezekiel 1:12 and the "likeness of the living creatures": "Whither the spirit was to go, they went."

11–14: Cf. *Fountain of Life* V:4: "The soul resembles clear glass"; Ezekiel 1:1ff. on the "living creatures," especially 1:22: "And over the heads of the living creatures there was the likeness of a firmament like the color of the terrible ice"; also *Pirkei Rabbi Eliezer* 4.

15–19: Cf. Ecclesiastes 8:10: "They . . . went away from the holy place"; *Genesis Rabbah* 31:27. See also "Angels Amassing" for similar imagery and source material on the angelic camps. Cf. also Numbers 2:2: "every man with his own standard"; Psalms 45:2: "the pen of a ready writer."

23: Cf. *Berakhot* 10a: "the soul sees but is not itself seen."

24–25: The terms for the angels are from Psalms 78:48, Isaiah 6:6, Proverbs 26:18, Psalms 68:5, and *Yalqut Shim'oni*, Daniel 4:32. Cf. *Pirkei Rabbi Eliezer* 4: "The angels are created on the second day, when they are sent (as messengers) by His word they are changed into winds, and when they minister before Him they are changed into fire, as it is said, 'Who makest winds Thy messengers, the flaming fire Thy ministers'" (Psalms 104:14).

28: Cf. Ezekiel 1:14: "the living creatures . . . as the appearance of a flash of lighting."

29–46: Cf. Daniel 7:10: "A fiery stream issued and came forth from before him; Thousand thousands ministered unto him"; Lamentations 2:19: "Arise, cry out in the night, at the beginning of the watches"; Psalms 65:7, 1 Chronicles 29:13: "We thank Thee and praise Thy glorious name"; the prayer service for the Day of Atonement, prior to the confession: "We are Thy servants, and Thou our Master"; also Psalms 100:3; Isaiah 64:7: "But now, O Lord, Thou art our Father; we are the clay, and Thou our potter, and we all are the work of Thy hand."

CANTO XXVI: Lines 3–6: On the "Throne of Glory" see *Pesahim* 54a: "Seven things were created before the world was created, and these are they: The Torah, repentance, the Garden of Eden, Gehenna, the Throne of Glory, the Temple, and the name of the Messiah. . . . The Throne of Glory and the Temple, for it is written, 'Thou throne of glory, on high from the beginning, Thou place of our Sanctuary' (Jeremiah 27:12)"; also notes to Canto XXIV.

9: Cf. Exodus 34:3: "And no man shall come up with thee [. . . onto the mount]."

CANTO XXVII: Lines 1–3: *Shabbat* 152b: "R. Eliezer said: The souls of the righteous are hidden under the Throne of Glory."

4–6: Cf. 1 Samuel 25:29: "The soul of my lord shall be bound in the bundle of life with the Lord."

7–9: Cf. Isaiah 40:30–31: "Even the youths shall faint and be weary . . . But they that wait for the Lord shall renew their strength"; Job 3:17: "There . . . the weary are at rest"; *Genesis Rabbah* 9:7; Esther 9:16. The verse involves a play on Genesis 9:19: "The sons of Noah"; *noah* also means "rest" in Esther 9:16.

11: Cf. *Berakhot* 17a on the pleasures of the world-to-come, below (line 16).

14: Cf. Exodus 38:8: "The mirrors of the serving women."

16–20: Descriptions of the world-to-come and its pleasures abound in rabbinical literature. See, for an elaborate example, *Yalqut Shim'oni* to Genesis (in Zeidman). A more concise description is found in *Berakhot* 17a: "In the future world there is no eating nor drinking nor propagation nor business nor jealousy nor hatred nor competition, but the righteous sit with their crowns on their heads feasting on the brightness of the divine presence, as it says, *And they beheld God, and did eat and drink* (Exodus 24:11)." Also *HaMelekh ve Ha-Nazir*, chapter 35, on the pleasures of the "world of intelligence and mind, which have absolutely nothing in common with any other kind of pleasure."

21–24: Cf. Numbers 13:27: "A land [that] . . . . floweth with milk and honey; and this is the fruit of it."

Canto XXVIII: Lines 5–6: *Hagigah* 12b: "'*Araboth* is that in which there are Right and Judgment and Righteousness; the treasures of life and the heavens of peace and the heavens of blessing, the souls of the righteous and the spirits and the souls which are yet to be born."

7–8: Cf. Isaiah 59:20: "them that turn from transgression."

9–10: Cf. Isaiah 30:33: "The breath of the Lord, like a stream of brimstone"; Ezekiel 38:22: "And I will cause . . . an overflowing shower, and great hailstones, fire, and brimstone"; Hosea 6:6–7: "For I desire mercy, and not sacrifice, and the knowledge of God rather than burnt offerings. But they . . . have transgressed the covenant"; *Yalqut Shim'oni*, Ecclesiastes, 976: "He created the Garden of Eden [beside] Gehinnom so that one could be saved from the other, and what is the space between them? R. Hanina said: A wall the width of a hand-breadth."

11–13: Cf. Proverbs 22:14: "The mouth of a strange woman is a deep pit: he that is abhorred of the Lord shall fall therein."

14–19: Cf. Zechariah 14:6; Job 24:19: "Drought and heat consume the snow waters; so doth the nether-world those that have sinned"; Deuteronomy 4:11: "And the mountain burned with fire unto the heart of heaven, with darkness, cloud, and thick darkness"; Genesis 15:17; *Hagigah* 12b.

20–23: Cf. Habakkuk 1:12: "O Lord, Thou hast ordained them for judgment, and Thou, O Rock, hast established them for correction"; Job 37:12: "They are turned round about by His guidance . . . Whether it be for correction, or for His earth, or for mercy, that He cause it to come."

Canto XXIX: Lines 1–5: Ezekiel 28:7: "They shall defile thy brightness"; Ezekiel 28:17: "thou hast corrupted thy wisdom by reason of thy brightness"; Isaiah 51:1: "Look unto the rock whence ye were hewn, and the hole of the pit whence ye were digged."

6–10: Cf. Numbers 11:17: "And I will take of the spirit which is upon thee."

11–14: Cf. Psalms 29:7: "The voice of the Lord heweth out flames of fire"; Isaiah 30:33: "The breath of the Lord . . . doth kindle it"; Genesis 2:15: "to dress it and to keep it [the Garden of Eden]"; Exodus 3:2: "The bush burned with fire, and the bush was not consumed."

15–16: See note to canto IX, line 14; Exodus 19:18: "Now mount Sinai was altogether on smoke, because the Lord descended upon it in fire."

Canto XXX: Lines 1–5: Cf. Isaiah 10:22: "Destruction is decreed" (NJPS).

8–10: Cf. Psalms 89:49: "What man . . . shall not see death?"; *The Fountain of Life* V:43: "What is the fruit that we will achieve in this study? Release from death and attachment [devotion] to the source [fountain] of life."

11: Cf. Proverbs 12:2: "A good man shall obtain favor of the Lord."

12: Cf. Proverbs 31:25: "She laugheth at the time [end] to come."

14: Cf. Isaiah 54:8: "In a little wrath I hid My face."

15: Cf. Leviticus 13:46: "He is unclean; he shall dwell alone; without the camp."

16–18: Cf. Leviticus 12:4: "She shall touch no hallowed thing, nor come into the sanctuary, until the days of her purification be fulfilled."

Canto XXXI: Lines 4–5: Cf. Proverbs 15:24: "The path of life goeth upward for the wise that he may depart from the nether world beneath"; Jonah 4:6: "to deliver him from his evil."

6–7: Cf. Job 33:6: "I also am formed out of the clay"; Genesis 2:7: "Then the Lord God formed man of the dust of the ground, and breathed into his nostrils the breath of life."

8: Cf. Numbers 11:17 (above, canto 29, note to lines 6–10).

11–12: Literally, "you've shut him [man]." Likewise in the following two lines, where the translation continues the first-person plural.

13–14: Cf. Exodus 25:11: "Within and without shalt thou overlay it," where Ibn Gabirol plays on *titzapenu* ("thou shalt overlay it"), taking it to mean "thou shalt see it" (also *titzapenu*) in addition to the play on "within" (the body/the home) and "without."

Canto XXXII: Line 6: Cf. Psalms 51:17: "O Lord, open Thou my lips, and my mouth shall declare Thy praise."

7–8: Cf. Psalms 71:18: "Until I have declared Thy strength unto the next generation."

9: Cf. Psalms 116:16: "I am Thy servant, the son of Thy handmaid."

11: Or, "for a very little while . . ."

12–14: Cf. Job 26:14: "Lo, these are but the outskirts of His ways"; Psalms 139:17: "How great is the sum of [Thy thoughts]"; Proverbs 4:22: "For they are life unto those that find them."

21: Cf. 2 Samuel 7:27: "Therefore hath Thy servant taken heart to pray this prayer unto Thee."

23–24: Cf. Job 11:6: "Know therefore that God exacteth of thee less than thine iniquity deserveth."

25–27: 1 Samuel 29:4: "For wherewith should this fellow reconcile himself unto his lord? Should it not be with the heads of these men [leaders]?" i.e., he can appease his Lord only with his "finest praises" (line 23). The English mirrors the figure of the Hebrew, in which the construct form is used in line 23 for "finest praises" [literally, "heads of the praises"] and then repeated in part in line 27 with only the first part of the compound, i.e., "finest" ["heads of"].

PART THREE (CONFESSION)

CANTO XXXIII: Having ascended as high as one might ascend and mapped the cosmos, the poem now picks up where the final cantos of Part II left off, with the link between God, man, and man's conduct in the world. This topic was raised in the context of potential service in the previous cantos; here the poet takes stock and finds himself wanting. A long confession begins, initially with a furious weave of biblical quotations (much, but not all, of which is traced below); it is both personal and, in keeping with the nature of the confession from the liturgy for the Day of Atonement, universal throughout. Read against the backdrop of the poetry that appears in this volume, however, it is not hard to identify the powerfully individual accents of this final sequence.

Lines 1–4: Cf. Ezra 9:6: "O my God, I am ashamed and blush to lift up my face to Thee"; Jeremiah 22:22. Also *Berakhot* 17a: "Raba on concluding his prayer added the following: My God, before I was formed I was not worthy [to be formed] and now that I have been formed I am as if I had not been formed. I am dust in my lifetime, all the more in my death. Behold, I am before Thee like a vessel full of shame and confusion."

12–13: Cf. Job 7:5: "My flesh is clothed with worms, and clods of dust"; Genesis 2:7.

14: Cf. Habakkuk 2:19: "Woe unto him that says to the wood: 'Awake!', to the dumb stone: 'Arise!'"

15: Cf. Psalms 144:4: "Man is like unto a breath; his days are as a shadow that passeth away."

16: Cf. Psalms 78:39: "a wind that passeth away, and cometh not again."

17: Cf. Psalms 140:4: "Viper's venom is under their lips."

18: Cf. Jeremiah 17:9: "The heart is deceitful above all things"; Jeremiah 9:25: "But all the house of Israel are uncircumcised in the heart."

19: Cf. Proverbs 19:19: "A man of great wrath."

20–22: Cf. Proverbs 6:18: "A heart that devises wicked thoughts"; Psalms 101:5: "Whoso is haughty of eye and proud of heart, him will I not suffer"; Proverbs 14:12; Isaiah 6:5; Proverbs 28:18: "He that is perverse in his ways."

23–26: Cf. *Yoma* 87b: "What are we, and what is our life"; Isaiah 40:17; Deuteronomy 31:27: "how much more after my death."

27: Cf. *Pirkei Avot* 3:1: "Know whence thou camest, and wither thou art going, and before whom thou art destined to give account and reckoning."

28–29: Cf. Esther 4:16: "I will go in unto the king, which is not according to the law"; *Ta'anit* 7b: "Any man who is insolent stumbles in the end."

30–33: Cf. Ezekiel 6:9: "I have been anguished . . . with their eyes, which are gone astray after their idols"; Ezekiel 22:24: "A land that is not cleansed."

34–35: Cf. *Pirkei Avot* 1:13: "A name that is widespread loses its fame; one who does not add [to his knowledge] causes [it] to cease." The English departs some from the literal meaning in order to incorporate the acoustic effect of the line: *"yoseef v'lo yasoof."*

CANTO XXXIV: Lines 1–2: Cf. Ezra 9:6: "Our iniquities are increased over our head"; Jeremiah 5:6; *Yoma* 87b: "R. Judah said: Our iniquities are too many to count, and our sins too numerous to be counted."

3–7: Cf. *Horayoth* 10a; Psalms 65:8: "who stillest the roaring of the seas, the roaring of their waves, and the tumult of the peoples"; 1 Kings 8:34: "Then hear Thou in heaven and forgive the sin of Thy people."

8–9: An alphabetical confession begins here, again, along the lines of the confession from the liturgy: *"ashamnu, bagadnu, gazalnu"* ("We have trespassed, we have dealt treacherously, we have robbed").

14: Cf. Psalms 119:69: "The proud have forged a lie."

16: Cf. Deuteronomy 21:18: "a stubborn and rebellious son."

21: The English collapses the Hebrew, which reads, literally: "I have disobeyed your commandments and strayed, and yet Thou art just in all that is come upon us; for Thou hast dealt truly, but we have done wickedly"—which incorporates a quotation from Nehemiah 9:33, with a change of person from the scriptural plural to the poet's singular.

CANTO XXXV: Lines 1–2: Cf. Genesis 4:6: "And the Lord said unto Cain: 'Why art thou wroth? and why is thy countenance fallen?'"

3–4: Cf. 1 Samuel 24:18: "And [Saul] said to David: 'Thou art more righteous than I; for thou hast rendered unto me good, whereas I have rendered unto thee evil.'"

10: Cf. Genesis 2:7: "And [the Lord God] . . . breathed into his nostrils the breath of life."

13–16: Cf. Psalms 103:13: "Like as a father hath compassion upon his children, so hath the Lord compassion upon them that fear them"; Numbers 11:12: "Carry them in thy bosom, as a nursing father carrieth the sucking child"; Psalms 22:10: "For Thou art He that took me out of the womb; Thou madest me trust when I was upon my mother's breasts"; Psalms 16:11: "In Thy presence is fulness of joy, in Thy right hand bliss for evermore."

18–19: Cf. 2 Chronicles 34:31: "And the king stood in his place"; Hosea 11:3: "And I, I taught Ephraim to walk, taking them by their arms."

20–23: Cf. Proverbs 1:2: "To know wisdom and instruction"; Proverbs 1:27: "When trouble and distress come upon you"; Psalms 81:8: "Thou didst call in trouble, and I rescued thee"; Isaiah 26:20: "Hide thyself for a little moment, until the indignation be overpast"; Isaiah 49:2: "In the shadow of His hand hath He hid me; . . . In His quiver hath He concealed me."

24–27: Cf. *Megillah* 13b: "The Holy One, blessed be He, does not smite Israel when He has created for them a healing beforehand."

28–30: Cf. Psalms 116:6: "The Lord preserveth the simple; I was brought low and He saved me"; Psalms 3:8: "For Thou hast smitten all mine enemies upon the cheek, Thou hast broken the teeth of the wicked"; the *nishmat* prayer: "Thou . . . hast rescued us from dire and lingering illness."

31–36: Cf. Ezekiel 14:21: "How much more when I send my four sore judgments against Jerusalem, the sword, and the famine, and the evil beasts, and the pestilence, to cut off from it man and beast"; the *nishmat* prayer: "During famine Thou didst feed us, and didst sustain us in plenty; from the sword Thou saved us."

37–38: Cf. Deuteronomy 8:5: "As a man chasteneth his son, so the Lord thy God chasteneth thee"; Jonah 2:3: "I called out of mine affliction."

39–41: Cf. 1 Samuel 26:21: "Because my life was precious in thine eyes this day"; the *Amidah* prayer: "Hear our voice: Do not, our King, turn us before You empty away."

42–44: Cf. *Haftorah* prayer: "Blessed art Thou . . . who hast chosen the Torah . . . and the prophets of truth and righteousness."

47–48: Cf. Psalms 74:18: "Remember this . . . how a base people have blasphemed Thy Name"; 2 Chronicles 36:16: "But they mocked the messengers of God, and despised his words."

50–51: Cf. Leviticus 13:23, and canto XVII, note to line 5, though the use of *baheret* (macula, bright spot) here is different. Gertner notes that its use resembles that of "whiteness" in Matthew XXIII:27, which has "hypocrites . . . like white-washed tombs, which outwardly appear beautiful, but within they are full of dead men's bones and all uncleanness"; and in the midrash, where the whiteness of plagues symbolizes heresy. He also notes that the Syriac Version of Scripture has a form of the same root—*shabhar*—for "boasting hypocrisy."

52: Cf. *Berakhot* 17a (note to canto XXXIII, lines 1–4).

53–54: Cf. Leviticus 11:33: "And every earthen vessel, whereinto any of them falleth, whatsoever is in it shall be unclean."

Canto XXXVI: Lines 1–3: Cf. Genesis 32:11: "I am not worthy of all the mercies, and of all the truth, which Thou hast shown unto Thy servant."

10–11: Gabirol seems to be identifying the *yetzer ha-ra'* (evil inclination, or impulse) with Satan (literally, the obstructer), as in *Baba Batra* 16a: "A tanna taught: Satan comes down to earth and seduces, then ascends to heaven and awakens wrath; permission is granted to him and he takes away the soul. . . . Resh Lakish said: Satan, the evil prompter, and the Angel of Death are all one." Cf. Zechariah 3:1: "And he showed me Joshua the high priest standing before the angel of the Lord, and Satan standing at his right hand to accuse him"; Job 9:18: "He that . . . would not suffer me to take my breath, but fill me with bitterness." Gertner (185) has extended discussion of this passage: he cites Matthew 4:3: "And the tempter came to him" and *Genesis Rabbah* 22:6 (on Genesis 4:5–6), which has extensive commentary on the strategies used by *yetzer ha-ra'*, which is equated with "the enemy." *Kiddushin* 30b: "Our rabbis taught: The Evil Desire is hard [to bear], since even his Creator called him evil. . . . R. Isaac said: Man's Evil Desire renews itself daily against him . . . . And R. Simeon b. Levi said: Man's Evil Desire gathers strength against him daily and seeks to slay him. . . and were not the Holy One, blessed be He, to help him [man], he would not be able to prevail against him." Gertner argues for a translation that personifies evil as the "cruel tempter," but this seems to me to conjure an image of a red devil holding a pitchfork. The force of temptation is powerful enough.

12–15: Cf. Job 41:5: "Who shall come within his double bridle?"; Jonah 1:13: "Nevertheless the men rowed hard to bring it to the land; but they could not."

16: Cf. Psalms 33:10: "He maketh the thoughts of the peoples to be of no effect"; Numbers 30:3: "He shall not break his word"; Deuteronomy 23:24: "That which is gone out of thy lips thou shalt observe and do."

17–18: Cf. Proverbs 6:18; Psalms 36:4: "The words of his mouth are iniquity and deceit"; Psalms 120:7: "I am all peace; but when I speak, they are for war."

19–20: Cf. Psalms 110:1: "Sit thou at My right hand, until I make thine enemies thy footstool"; 1 Kings 2:5: "And put the blood of war upon his girdle that was about his loins."

25–26: Cf. Genesis 32:9: "If Esau come to the one camp and smite it, then the other camp which is left shall escape."

31: Zeidman reads "the enemy"—as in Jeremiah 15:8: "I cause anguish [or "alarm" or "the enemy"] and terrors to fall upon her suddenly"; Schirmann reads "the city", as in 2 Samuel 18:3: "Now it is better that thou be ready to succour us out of the city."

33: Cf. Numbers 22:6: "Peradventure I shall prevail, that we might smite them, and that I may drive them out of the land."

Canto XXXVII: Lines 3–5: Cf. Psalms 51:11: "Hide Thy face from my sins, blot out all mine iniquities"; Psalms 102:25: "I say: 'O my God, take me not away in the midst of my days.'"

8: Literally, "my equipment," i.e., my penance.

10–13: Cf. Ecclesiastes 5:14–16; Jeremiah 20:18: "Wherefore came I forth out of the womb to see labor and sorrow, that my days should be consumed in shame?"

16–18: Cf. Jeremiah 10:24: "O Lord, correct me, but in measure; not in thine anger, lest thou diminish me."

20: Cf. Psalms 8:5: "What is man, that thou art mindful of him? and the son of man, that thou thinkest of him?"; Psalms 144:3–4: "Lord, what is man, that Thou takest knowledge of him? . . . Man is like unto a breath"; Proverb 21:6: "The getting of treasures by a lying tongue is a vapor driven to and fro."

21–24: Cf. Job 28:25: "When He maketh a weight for the wind."

25–26: Cf. Isaiah 53:4–7: "We did esteem him stricken, smitten of God, and afflicted. . . . He was oppressed."

27–29: Cf. Psalms 1:4: "The wicked . . . are like the chaff which the wind driveth away"; Isaiah 41:2: "His sword maketh them as the dust, His bow as the driven stubble"; 2 Kings 19:26: "They were as the grass of the field . . . as corn blasted."

30: Cf. Ecclesiastes 3:15: "Only God can find the fleeting moment" (Koren translation). JPS: "God seeketh that which is pursued."

31–34: Cf. Numbers 12:12: "When he cometh out of his mother's womb"; Exodus 16:20: "And it [the manna] bred worms."

35–38: Cf. Psalms 1:4: "Not so the wicked; but they are like the chaff which the wind driveth away"; Proverbs 28:21: "For a man will transgress for a piece of bread." Also Jaahiz, *Kitaab al-Bayaan wa al- Tabyiin:* "If he's hungry experience weakens him, if he's content he makes light of favor."

41–43: Cf. 2 Samuel 2:18: "And Asahel was as light of foot as one of the roes that are in the field"; Job 34:37: "And he multiplies words against God"; Psalms 18:20: "And He brought me forth also unto a large place."

44–45: Cf. Psalms 147:13: "For He hath made strong the bars of thy gates"; Jeremiah 9:20: "For death is come up into our windows, it is entered into our palaces."

46–52: Cf. Judges 16:9: "Now she had liers-in-wait abiding in the inner chamber"; Ecclesiastes 2:2: "I said of laughter: 'It is mad'; and of mirth: 'what doth it accomplish?'"; Ecclesiastes 9:12: "For man also knoweth not his time." Also *A Thousand and One Nights:* "Death in ambush awaits you; ready, therefore, your steps for the day of resurrection"; Horace: "But fear and dangers haunt the Lord/into all places: and black care/Behind him rides, or, if on board/A ship, 'tis his companion there." (*Odes* III: 1, trans. R. Fanshawe)

52–55: Cf. Jeremiah 23:17: "And . . . every one that walketh in the stubbornness of his own heart"; Judges 13:25: "And the spirit of the Lord began to move [Samson]"; *Genesis Rabbah* 9: "Were it not for the evil inclination man would not build a house and marry a woman and raise children and conduct business."

58: Cf. Ezekiel 1:13: "And it flashed up and down among the living creatures."

59–62: Cf. Job 31:25: "If I rejoiced because my wealth was great, and because my hand had gotten much"; Job 15:21: "In prosperity the destroyer shall come upon him"; Job 27:19: "He openeth his eyes, and his wealth is not."

67–70: 1 Samuel 26:10: "The Lord shall smite him; or his day shall come to die; or he shall go down into battle, and be swept away"; Job 20:24: "If he flee from the iron weapon, the bow of brass shall strike him through."

71–72: Psalms 124:4–5: "Then the waters had overwhelmed us"; Deuteronomy 28:59: "sore sickness, and of long continuance."

74–75: Cf. Job 7:20: "So that I am a burden unto myself"; Job 20:14: "It is the gall of asps within him."

77–78: Cf. 2 Kings 2:23: "There came forth little children out of the city, and mocked him"; Isaiah 3:4: "And babes shall rule over them."

79–80: Cf. Isaiah 1:14: "They are a burden unto me."

82: I.e., the graveyard. Cf. *Berakhot* 18b.

85–87: Cf. Lamentations 4:5: "They that were brought up in scarlet embrace dunghills"; Ezekiel 26:16: "Then all the princes of the sea shall . . . lay away their robes, and strip off their richly woven garments; . . . they shall sit upon the ground"; Job 7:21: "For now shall I lie down in the dust"; Genesis 3:19: "Dust thou art and unto dust thou shalt return."

91–95: Cf. *Pirkei Avot* 2:20: "The day is short and the work is great and the laborers are sluggish and the wages are high and the householder is urgent"; Exodus 5:13: "And the taskmasters were urgent."

100: Cf. Deuteronomy 8:16: "To do thee good at thy latter end."

101: Cf. Psalms 103:10: "He hath not dealt with us after our sins, nor requited us according to our iniquities."

103: The last word of the line—*hemdah*—is in some dispute: in the old JPS translation, 2 Chronicles 21:20, it appears as: "And he departed *joyless.*" Zeidman understands: "and he departed against his will." NJPS implies "without praise," based on the Septuagint and the Arabic parallel, the verb *hamada,* to praise.

Canto XXXVIII: Lines 1–3: Cf. Genesis 4:13: "Cain said to the Lord: 'My punishment is greater than I can bear,'"; Joshua 7:9: "And what wilt Thou do for Thy great name?"

6–7: Cf. Job 13:15: "Though He slay me, yet will I trust in Him; but I will argue my ways before Him."

8–9: Cf. Psalms 139:7–12: "Whither shall I go from Thy spirit? Or whither shall I flee from Thy presence? If I ascend up into heaven, Thou art there: If I make my bed in the nether-world, behold, Thou art there." Ratzhaby notes several parallels in Arabic literature, most directly the Muslim prayer to be recited, like the Hebrew *Shema,* before sleep: "O Lord, in your will I will take shelter from your anger; in your forgiveness—from your punishment; I will take shelter in Thee from Thee" (in al-Ghazzali's *On the Duties of Brotherhood*); and again the Saragossan Abu 'Amr al-Albiri: "He who lured from God, fleeing from God to God." See also Yitzhaq Ibn Mar Sha'ul's famous *baqashah*, which would have been known to Ibn Gabirol: "Lord, do not judge me according to my sins / and do not gauge my wage by my deeds." Scheindlin notes another parallel and likely source of influence in Abu Nuwas's ascetic Baghdadi rival, the late eighth/early ninth century poet Abu-l-'Atahiya (in whose work Goldziher finds Buddhist elements): "My God, do not punish me, for I acknowledge that which I have done."

10: Cf. Psalms 19:7: "His going forth is from the end of the heaven, and his circuit unto the ends of it; and there is nothing hid from the heat thereof"; Psalms 121:5: "The Lord is thy shade"; Isaiah 51:16.

11–14: Cf. 1 Samuel 15:27; Genesis 32:27: "And he said: 'I will not let thee go, except thou bless me.'"

15: Cf. Job 10:9: "Remember . . . that Thou hast fashioned me as clay."

17–19: Cf. Jeremiah 21:14: "I will punish you according to the fruit of your doings"; Isaiah 3:10.

20–23: Literally, "until I've prepared my provision," as in XXXVII, line 6–8. Cf. Isaiah 48:9: "For My name's sake, I will defer Mine anger"; Proverbs 19:11; Genesis 47:29: "And the time drew near that Israel must die."

24–27: Cf. Exodus 12:33: "And the Egyptians were urgent upon the people, to send them out of the land in haste . . . their kneading-troughs being bound up in their clothes upon their shoulders"; *Berakhot* 17a: "Sovereign of the Universe, it is known full well to Thee that our will is to perform Thy will, and what prevents us? The yeast in the dough and the subjection to foreign powers"—"in the dough" here, it is noted, means "in desire, the evil inclination," which causes ferment in the heart.

28–32: Cf. Sa'adiah's second *baqashah* (*Siddur Sa'adiah*, 75): "See my impoverishment (*'onyii*), and not my iniquity (*'avoni*) . . . and see my labors (*'amali*) and not my deceit (*ma'ali*) . . . May my troubles be ransom to my sins, and my distress be set against my transgression"; Lamentations 3:19: "Remember my affliction and mine anguish, the wormwood and the gall"; 1 Kings 20:29: "And they encamped one over against the other."

33–40: Cf. Genesis 4:16: "And Cain went out from the presence of the Lord, and dwelt in the Land of Nod"; Psalms 119:75: "I know, O Lord, that Thy judgements are righteous, and that in faithfulness Thou hast afflicted me"; Deuteronomy 8:16: "Who fed thee in the wilderness with manna, which thy fathers knew not, that He might afflict thee, and that He might prove thee, to do thee good at the latter end?"

41–44: Cf. Jeremiah 31:20: "Therefore My heart yearneth for him, I will surely have compassion upon him, saith the Lord"; Lamentations 4:11: "The Lord hath accomplished His fury, He hath poured out His fierce anger'"; Psalms

103:10: "He hast not ... requited us according to our iniquities"; 2 Samuel 24:16: "The Lord ... said to the angel that destroyed the people: 'It is enough.'"

45–48: Cf. Job 10:5–6: "Are Thy days as the days of a man ... that Thou inquirest after mine iniquity, and searchest after my sin?"; Job 7:12: "Am I a sea or a sea monster [dragon], that Thou settest a watch over me?" Literally, "an antelope" or "bison"—for "bull" (Deuteronomy 14:5 and Isaiah 51:20).

49–53: Cf. Leviticus 26:39: "And they that are left of you shall pine away in their iniquity in your enemies' lands"; Zechariah 14:12; Proverbs 23:5: "Wilt thou set thine eyes upon it? It is gone."

54–55: Cf. Deuteronomy 5:21–22: "We have seen this day that God doth speak with man, and he liveth. Now therefore why should we die? for this great fire will consume us."

56–62: Cf. Jeremiah 24:6: "And I will set Mine eyes upon them for good"; Joshua 8:22: "And they smote them, so that they let none remain or escape"; Exodus 10:5: "And they shall eat the residue of that which is escaped, which remaineth unto you from the hail."

63–64: Cf. Joel 1:4: "That which the locust hath left"; Deuteronomy 28:38: "The locust shall consume it"; *Genesis Rabbah* 24:5: "R. Judah said: It was fitting that the Torah should have been given through Adam. Whence does this follow? The Holy One, blessed be He, said: 'He is the creation of My hands.'"

65–66: Cf. Job 35:3: "Thou inquirest: 'What advantage will it be to Thee?'"

67: Cf. Psalms 128:2: "When thou eatest the labor of thy hands."

CANTO XXXIX: **Lines 1–4:** Cf. Malachi 3:7: "Return unto Me, and I will return unto you"; the Morning Liturgy: "Cause us to return, O our father, unto Thy Law; draw us near ... unto Thy service, and bring us back in perfect repentance unto Thy presence."

5–6: Cf. Psalms 10:17: "Lord, Thou hast heard the desire of the humble: Thou wilt direct their heart, Thou wilt cause Thine ear to attend."

7–8: Cf. *Berakhot* 17a (and the end of the *Amidah* prayer): "Open my heart to Thy Law, and let my soul pursue Thy commandments."

9–10: Cf. the liturgy for the Day of Atonement, at the opening of the ark: "Ordain for us good decrees of salvation and comfort and annul all severe decrees concerning us."

11–12f.: Cf. the morning liturgy: "O lead us not into the power of ... temptation, and into the power of scorn.... Deliver me this day from mishap."

13–15: Cf. Psalms 57:2: "Be gracious unto me, O God, ... for in Thee hath my soul taken refuge; Yea, in the shadow of Thy wings will I take refuge."

16: Cf. Exodus 4:12: "Now therefore go, and I will be with thy mouth"; Psalms 19:15: "Let the words of my mouth and the meditation of my heart be acceptable before Thee."

17–18: Cf. Psalms 39:2: "I said: 'I will take heed to my ways, that I sin not with my tongue; I will keep a curb upon my mouth.'"

19–26: Cf. Psalms 106:4–5: "Remember me, O Lord, when Thou favorest Thy people"; the liturgy: "Cause Thy face to shine upon Thy sanctuary that is desolate."

27–30: Cf. Psalms 102:15: "For Thy servants take pleasure in her stones, and love her dust"; Isaiah 61:4: "And they shall build the old wastes, they shall raise up the former desolations."

CANTO XL: **Line 4:** Cf. The liturgy for the Day of Atonement, *Avinu Malkeinu*: "Our father, Our King, be gracious unto us and answer us, though we have no worthy deeds."

5–10: Cf. Nehemiah 5:13: "Even thus be he shaken out, and emptied"; Isaiah 24:1: "Behold the Lord maketh the earth empty"; Hosea 10:1: "Israel is a ravaged vine; how should he bring forth fruit to himself?" (NJPS); Esther 8:5: "If . . . the thing seem right before the king"; 1 Kings 8:38: "What prayer and supplication soever be made by any men."

14f.: Cf. The liturgy for the Day of Atonement—"May it be Thy will . . . again in Thine abundant compassion to have mercy upon us and upon Thy Sanctuary."

17: Cf. Genesis 45:10: "And thou shalt be near unto me."

18: Zeidman reads: "Remember me in the council of peace."

19–20: Cf. Psalms 4:7: "Lord, lift Thou up the light of Thy countenance upon us"; Numbers 6:25–26 and the liturgical Blessing of the Priests: "The Lord make His face [to] shine upon thee, and be gracious unto thee: the Lord lift up His countenance upon thee and give thee peace."

21–22: Cf. Psalms 103:10: "He hath not dealt with us after our sins, nor requited us according to our iniquities"; Psalms 39:9: "Make me not the reproach of the base."

23–24: Cf. Psalms 102:25: "O my God, Take me not away in the midst of my days"; Psalms 27:9: "Hide not Thy face from me."

25–26: Cf. Psalms 51:4: "Wash me thoroughly from mine iniquity, and cleanse me from my sin"; Psalms 51:13: "Cast me not away from Thy presence."

27–28: Cf. Psalms 71:20: "Thou . . . wilt quicken me again"; Psalms 73:24: "Thou wilt guide me with Thy counsel, and afterward receive me with glory"; NJPS has "and led me toward honor," noting that the Hebrew is uncertain.

29–33: Cf. Genesis 15:15: "Thou shalt go to thy fathers in peace"; Hosea 11:7: "And though they call them upwards, none at all will lift himself up."

34–36: Cf. Psalms 17:14: "From men of the world, whose portion is in this life."

37–39: Cf. Job 33:30: "that he may be enlightened with the light of the living"; Psalms 89:16: "They walk, O Lord, in the light of Thy countenance"; Psalms 71:20: "Thou . . . wilt . . . bring me up again from the depths of the earth."

40–42: Cf. Isaiah 12:1: "And in that day thou shalt say: 'I will give thanks unto Thee, O Lord; for Thou wast angry with me, Thine anger is turned away, and Thou comfortest me.'"

43–45: Cf. Psalms 62:13: "Also unto Thee, O Lord, belongeth mercy; for Thou renderest to every man according to his work."

46–47: The morning liturgy for Shabbat and Festivals, *U'vemaqhalot*: "For this is the duty of all creatures towards Thee, O Lord . . . . to give thanks unto Thee, to laud, adore, and praise Thee."

48–55: Cf. The morning liturgy for Shabbat and Festivals, *Shokhen ʻad*: "It is befitting for the upright to praise Him . . ." etc. These lines follow the outline of the prayer.

56–57: Cf. Psalms 86:8: "For there is none like unto Thee among the gods, O Lord; and there are no works like Thine."

58–61: Cf. The end of the *Amidah* prayer and Psalm 19:15: "Let the words of my mouth and the meditation of my heart be acceptable before Thee, O Lord, my Rock, and my Redeemer."

BIBLIOGRAPHY

✦

Poetry by Ibn Gabirol in Hebrew

Ben Ari, S. "Two New Poems of Solomon Ibn Gabirol" [Hebrew]. *Mehqerei Yerushalayim be Sifrut Ivrit* 14 (1993): 107–113.

Bialik, Hayim Nahman, Ravnitzky. Y. H., ed. *Shirei Shelomoh ben Yehudah ibn Gabirol*. 7 vols. Tel Aviv: Dvir, 1924–32.

Brody, Hayim, Schirmann, Jefim, and Ben David, Israel, eds. *Shelomoh ibn Gabirol: Shirei HaHol*. Jerusalem: Schocken Institute, 1975.

Fleischer, E. "Addenda to the Corpus of Classical Spanish-Hebrew Poetry" [Hebrew]. *Mehqerei Yerushalayim be Sifrut Ivrit* 14 (1993): 31–68.

Schirmann, Y., ed. *Ibn Gabirol: Shirim Nivharim*. Jerusalem–Tel Aviv: Schocken, 1967.

Yarden, Dov, ed. *Shirei HaQodesh le-Ribbi Shelomoh ibn Gabirol im Perush*. 2 vols. Jerusalem: Dov Yarden, 1971–73.

———. *Shirei HaHol le-Ribbi Shelomoh ibn Gabirol im Perush*. 2 vols. Jerusalem: Dov Yarden, 1975–76.

Zeidman, Y., ed. *Keter Malkhut*. Jerusalem: Mossad HaRav Kook, 1950.

Prose by Ibn Gabirol

Bar-On, Noah, ed. *R. Shelomoh ben Gabirol: Sefer Tiqqun Middoth HaNefesh*. Tel Aviv: Mahbarot LeSifrut, 1951.

Blaubstein, Jacob, ed. and trans. *Sefer Meqor Hayyim Le R. Shelomoh ben Gabirol*. Jerusalem: Mahbarot LeSifrut, 1926.

Cohen, A., ed. and trans. *Solomon Ibn Gabirol's Choice of Pearls*. New York: Bloch, 1925.

Habermann, A. M., ed. *Sefer Mivhar HaPeninim*. Jerusalem: Sifriyat HaPo'alim, 1947.

Wise, Stephen, ed. and trans. *The Improvement of the Moral Qualities*. [Arabic original and English translation], New York: Columbia University Press, 1901.

Other Translations of the Poetry in English

Carmi, T., ed. *The Penguin Book of Hebrew Verse*. New York: Penguin, 1981.

Davidson, I., ed. and Zangwill, I., trans. *Selected Religious Poems of Solomon Ibn Gabirol*. Philadelphia: Jewish Publication Society, 1923.

Davis, N. *Songs of Exile by Hebrew Poets*. Philadelphia: The Jewish Publication Society, 1901.

De Lange, Nicholas. "Solomon Ibn Gabirol: Four Poems." *The Tel Aviv Review* 1 (1988): 59–66.

Goldstein, David. *The Jewish Poets of Spain*. Harmondsworth: Penguin, 1965.

Lazarus, Emma. *The Poems of Emma Lazarus*, Vol. 2, *Jewish Poems: Translations*. Boston and New York: Houghton Mifflin, and Co., 1899.

Lenowitz, Harris. "The Crown of Kingdom." In *A Big Jewish Book*, ed. J. Rothenberg. Garden City: Anchor/Doubleday, 1978.

———. "The Crown of the Kingdom." *Montemora* 5, New York, 1979: 218–29.

Levi, David. In *The Forms of Prayer for the Day of Atonement, According to the Customs of the Spanish and Portugese Jews*. Vol. 3. London, 1790.

Lewis, Bernard. *The Kingly Crown*. London: Vallentine-Mitchell, 1961.

Loewe, Raphael. In *Ibn Gabirol*. New York: Grove Weidenfeld, 1989.

———. In *The Rylands Haggadah*. Tel Aviv: Steimatzky, 1988.

Lucas, A. *The Jewish Year*. London: Macmillan, 1898.

Mandelbaum, Allen. "Cedars of Lebanon, Seven Secular Poems." *Commentary* 11, 2 (1951): 181–83.

Rakosi, Carl. *Collected Poems of Carl Rakosi*. Orono: National Poetry Foundation/University of Maine, 1986.

Scheindlin, Raymond. *The Gazelle: Medieval Hebrew Poems on God, Israel, and the Soul*. Philadelphia: Jewish Publication Society, 1991.

———. *Wine, Women, & Death: Medieval Hebrew Poems on the Good Life*. Philadelphia: Jewish Publication Society, 1986.

Slavitt, David. *A Crown for the King*. London: Oxford University Press, 1998.

Other Sources

BIBLICAL

The Holy Scriptures, According to the Masoretic Text. Philadelphia: Jewish Publication Society, 1917/1955.

Tanakh, the Holy Scriptures: The New JPS Translation. Philadelphia: Jewish Publication Society, 1985.

The Holy Scriptures. Jerusalem: Koren Publishers, 1980.

RABBINICAL LITERATURE
(listed in English translation when possible)

Babylonian Talmud. Ed. I. Epstein. London: Soncino Press, 1990.

Beit Midrash. Ed. A. Jellinek. Jerusalem: Wahrmann Books, 1967.

High Holiday Prayerbook. Ed. M. Silverman. Hartford: Prayer Book Press. 1951.

Midrash Rabbah. Ed. A. Myrkin. Yavneh, 1986.

Miqra'ot Gedolot. Jerusalem: Pa'er Offset Edition, 1972.

The Mishnah, a New Translation. Trans. Jacob Neusner. New Haven: Yale University Press, 1988.

Pentateuch with Targum Onkelos, Haftaroth and Rashi's Commentary. Trans. M. Rosenbaum and A. M. Silbermann. Jerusalem: Silbermann/Feldheim, 1973.

Pirkei Avot: The Ethics of the Talmud: Sayings of the Fathers. Trans. R. Travers Herford. New York: Schocken Books, 1945/1962.

Pirkei Rabbi Eliezer. Jerusalem: Eshkol, 1983.

Sabbath and Festival Prayer Book. Ed. Morris Silverman. Rabbinical Assembly of America, 1946/1954.

Sefer Yetzirah: The Book of Creation. Trans. A. Kaplan. York Beach: Weiser, 1990/1997.

Siddur Rav Sa'adia Gaon. Ed. I. Davidson, S. Assaf, B. I. Yoel. Jerusalem: Mekitzei Nirdamim/Reuven Maas, 1985.

Additional Bibliography
(books cited and background reading)

Adams, H. *The Education of Henry Adams.* Boston: Houghton Mifflin, 1918.

Adonis. *An Introduction to Arab Poetics.* Trans. C. Cobham. Austin: University of Texas Press, 1990.

Ajami, M. *The Alchemy of Glory: The Dialectic of Truthfulness and Untruthfulness in Medieval Arabic Literary Criticism.* Washington D.C.: Three Continents, 1988.

————. *The Neckveins of Winter: The Controversy Over Natural and Artificial Poetry in Medieval Arabic Literary Criticism.* Leiden: Brill, 1984.

Alcalay, A. *After Jews and Arabs.* Minneapolis: University of Minnesota Press, 1993.

Arberry, A. J., trans. *The Spiritual Physick of Rhazes.* London: John Murray, 1950.

Ashtiany, J., and T. M. Johnstone, J. D. Latham, R. B. Serjeant, and G. Rex Smith. *'Abbasid Belles-Lettres.* Cambridge: Cambridge University Press, 1992.

Ashtor, E. *The Jews of Moslem Spain.* 3 vols. Philadelphia: Jewish Publication Society, 1973.

Bargebuhr, F. P. *The Alhambra: A Cycle of Studies on the Eleventh Century in Moorish Spain.* Berlin: Walter de Gruyter & Co., 1968.

————. "Ibn Gabirol's Poem Beginning Ahavtikha." *The Review of Religion* 15 (1950): 5–18.

Barnestone, Willis. *The Other Bible.* San Francisco: Harper & Row, 1984.

Bar Yosef, Avraham. *Poems from the Middle Ages* [Hebrew]. Hotsa'ah LeOr, 1993.

Berger, Harry, Jr. *Green World and Second World.* Berkeley: University of California Press, 1988.

Boswell, J. *Christianity, Social Tolerance, and Homosexuality*. Chicago: University of Chicago Press, 1980.

Brann, Ross. *The Compunctious Poet*. Baltimore: Johns Hopkins University Press, 1991.

————. *Languages of Power in Islamic Spain*. Bethesda: CDL Press, 1997.

Bregman, D. "Tsenefat Hur: A Motif in the Secular Poetry of Solomon Ibn Gabirol" [Hebrew]. *Mehqerei Yerushalayim* 10–11 (1988): 445–467.

Brenan, Gerald. *The Face of Spain*. London: The Turnstile Press, 1950.

Breuer, Z. *The Liturgical Poetry of Ibn Gabirol* [Hebrew]. Jerusalem: Magnes, 1993.

Cantarino, V. "Ibn Gabirol's Metaphysic of Light." *Studia Islamica* 26 (1967): 49:71.

Charlesworth, J. *The Old Testament Pseudepigrapha*. 2 vols. New York: Doubleday, 1983.

Cohen, M. *Under Crescent and Cross*. Princeton: Princeton University Press, 1994.

Cole, P., trans. and ed. *Selected Poems of Shmuel HaNagid*. Princeton: Princeton University Press, 1996.

Coomaraswamy, A. K. *Traditional Art and Symbolism*. Princeton: Princeton University Press, 1977.

Darwish, M. Interview in *Haderim* 12 [Hebrew]. Tel Aviv (1996): 172–98.

De Silva, C. *Alhambra: Arena of Assassins*. London: Diamond Books, 1994.

Dickie, J. "The Hispano-Arab Garden: Its Philosophy and Function." *Bulletin of the School of Oriental and African Studies* 31 (1968): 237–48.

Dronke, P. *Medieval Latin and the Rise of European Love-Lyric*. Oxford: Oxford University Press, 1968 (second edition).

Eco, Umberto. *Serendipities: Language and Lunacy*. New York: Columbia University Press, 1998.

Elbogen, I. M. *The Development of the Hebrew Liturgy* [Hebrew]. Trans. Y. Amir. Tel Aviv: Dvir, 1972.

Elitzur, Shulamit. "Epigrams and Riddles" [Hebrew]. *'Alon leMoreh LeSifrut* (1997): 20–34.

————. "The Bee that Recites the Shema" [Hebrew]. *Leshonenu La'am* 39, 7/8 (1989): 40–44.

Fleischer, E. *Liturgical Poetry in the Middle Ages* [Hebrew]. Jerusalem: Keter, 1975.

————. *The Yotser: Its Emergence and Development* [Hebrew]. Jerusalem: Magnes Press, 1984.

————. "Thoughts on the Character of Spanish-Hebrew Poetry" [Hebrew]. *Pe'amim* 2 (1979): 15–21.

————. "The Culture and Poetry of the Jews of Spain in Light of the Genizah" [Hebrew]. *Pe'amim* 41 (1990): 5–21.

————. "On Dunash Ben Labrat, His Wife, and His Son" [Hebrew]. *Mehqerei Yerushalayim* 5 (1984): 189–202.

————. "Early Hebrew Poetry in Spain" [Hebrew]. *Asufot* 2 (1988): 227–69.

Friedlander, M. *Essays on the Writing of Abraham Ibn Ezra*. Vol. 4. London: Trubner [no date].

Gertner, M. "On Translating Medieval Hebrew Poetry." *Journal of the Royal Asiatic Society* 3/4 (1962).

Ginzberg, L. *Legends of the Jews*. 7 vols. Philadelphia: Jewish Publication Society, 1909/1967.

Glinert, L. "Hebrew." In *Encyclopedia of Jewish Thought*. New York: Free Press, 1987.

Goitein, S. *Jews and Arabs: Their Contacts through the Ages*. New York: Schocken, 1955.

————. *Mediterranean Society*. 5 Vols. Berkeley: University of California Press, 1967–88.

Goodenough, E. R. *Jewish Symbols in the Greco-Roman Period*. Princeton: Princeton University Press, 1953, 1988.

Grabar, Oleg. *The Alhambra*. Sebastopol: Solipsist Press, 1978, 1992.

————. *The Formation of Islamic Art*. New Haven: Yale University Press, 1973, 1987.

————. *The Mediation of Ornament*. Princeton: Princeton University Press, 1992.

Greenberg, M. "Job." In *The Literary Guide to the Bible*. Ed. R. Alter, F. Kermode. Cambridge, MA: Harvard University Press, 1987.

Grunebaum, G. E. von. "The Aesthetic Foundation of Arabic Literature." *Comparative Literature* 4, 4 (1952): 323–40.

————. "The Response to Nature in Arabic Poetry." *Journal of Near Eastern Studies* 4 (1945): 137–51.

Halevi, Yehudah. *The Book of the Kuzari*. Trans. H. Slonimsky. New York: Schocken, 1964.

————. *On the Sea*. Trans. Gabriel Levin. Jerusalem: Ibis Editions, 1998.

Halkin, A. S. "The Medieval Jewish Attitude Toward Hebrew." In *Biblical and Other Studies*. Ed. A. A. Altman. Cambridge, MA: Harvard University Press, 1962.

Halper, B. "The Scansion of Mediaeval Hebrew Poetry." *Jewish Quarterly Review* NS 4 (1913–14): 153–224.

Hamori, Andras. *On the Art of Medieval Arabic Poetry*. Princeton: Princeton University Press, 1974.

————. "On Paranomasia in Abu Tammam's Style." *JSS* 12 (1967): 83–90.

Heine, Heinrich. *The Complete Poems of Heinrich Heine*. Trans. Hal Draper. Boston: Suhrkamp/Insel, 1982.

Horace. *Horace in English*. Ed. D. Carne-Ross and K. Haynes. London: Penguin, 1996.

————. *The Odes and Epodes of Horace*. Trans. Joseph Clancy. Chicago: University of Chicago Press, 1960.

Huss, Matti. "Literal and Allegorical Reading: The Erotic Poems of Shmuel Ha-Nagid" [Hebrew]. *Mehqerei Yerushalayim* 15 (1995).

————. "On Haim Schirmann's History of Hebrew Poetry in Muslim Spain" [Hebrew]. *Mada'ei HaYahadut* 36 (1995): 231–43.

————. Review of *Me'il Tashbets*, by Israel Levin. *Pe'amim* 64 (1995): 141–48.

Ibn Ezra, Moshe. *Kitab al-Muhaadara wal-Mudhaakara* [Arabic/Hebrew]. Ed. and trans. A. S. Halkin. Jerusalem: Mekitzei Nirdamim, 1975.

Ibn Janaah. *Sefer HaShorashim*. Berlin: MeKitsei Nirdamim, 1896.

Idel, Moshe. "The Sefirot Above the Sefirot" [Hebrew]. *Tarbiz* 58 (1982): 239–80.

————. *Golem*. Albany: State University of New York Press, 1990.

Imamuddin, S. M. *Muslim Spain*. Leiden: Brill, 1965.

Itzhaki, M. *Towards the Garden Beds: Hebrew Garden Poems in Medieval Spain* [Hebrew]. Tel Aviv: Notza ve'Keset, 1988.

Jastrow, M. *A Dictionary of the Targumim, the Talmud Babli and Yerushalmi, and the Midrashic Literature*. 1903.

Jayyusi, S., ed. *The Legacy of Muslim Spain*. 2 vols. Leiden: Brill, 1994.

Jonas, H. *The Gnostic Religion*. Boston: Beacon Press, 1958, 1991.

Katz, Sarah. *Openwork, Intaglios, and Filigrees: Studies and Research on Shlomo Ibn Gabirol* [Hebrew]. Jerusalem: Mossad HaRav Kook, 1992.

Klar, B. "Poetry and Life." In *Studies and Essays* [Hebrew]. Tel Aviv: Mahbarot LeSifrut, 1954.

Klausner, Y. "R. Shelomo ben Gabirol" [Hebrew]. Introduction to *Meqor Hayyim*, trans. Blaubstein. Jerusalem: Philosophical Library, 1926.

Kozodoy, N. "Reading Medieval Hebrew Love Poetry." *AJS Review* 2 (1977): 111–29.

Levin, I. *The Embroidered Coat: Genres of Hebrew Secular Poetry in Spain* [Hebrew]. 3 Vols. Tel Aviv: HaKibbutz Hameuchad, 1995.

————. "Neoplatonic Mystical Tendencies in Ibn Gabirol's Poetry" [Hebrew]. *B'Orah Mad'a*. Ed. Zvi Malachi. Lod: Haberman Institute, 1986.

————. "On Plagiarism and Originality in the Hebrew Poetry in Spain in the Middle Ages" [Hebrew]. In *Peles*. Ed. N. Guvrin. Tel Aviv: University of Tel Aviv Press, 1980.

Levine, B. A. *Leviticus: JPS Torah Commentary*. Philadelphia: Jewish Publication Society, 1989.

Lewis, B. *The Jews of Islam*. Princeton: Princeton University Press, 1984.

Liebes, Y. "The Book of Creation in R. Shelomoh Ibn Gabirol and a Commentary on His Poem 'I Love You'" [Hebrew]. *The Proceedings of the Second International Congress on the History of Jewish Mysticism*, 1987: 73–123.

————. *Studies in Jewish Myth and Jewish Messianism*. Albany: State University of New York Press, 1993.

Loewe, R. *Ibn Gabirol*. New York: Grove Weidenfeld, 1989.

————. "R. Ibn Gabirol's 'Shinannim Sha'anannim'" [Hebrew]. In *Exile and Dias-*

pora. Ed. A. Grossman, M. Mirsky, and Y. Kaplan. Jerusalem: Ben Tsvi Institute, 1988.

————. "Ibn Gabirol's Treatment of Sources in the Keter Malkhut." In *Studies in Jewish Religion and Intellectual History*. Ed. S. Stein and R. Loewe. University: University of Alabama Press, 1979.

Lorca, Federico García. *Deep Song and Other Prose*. Trans. Christopher Maurer. New York: New Directions, 1980.

Loy, M. *The Lost Lunar Baedeker*. New York: Farrar, Straus, & Giroux, 1996.

Al-Ma'arri, Abu'l-'Ala'. *The Quatrains of Abu'l-'Ala*. Trans. Ameen Rihani. New York: Doubleday, Page, & Co., 1903.

————. "The Meditations of Al-Ma'arri." In R. Nicholson's *Studies in Islamic Poetry*. Cambridge: Cambridge University Press, 1921.

Mack M. *Alexander Pope: A Life*. New Haven: Yale University Press, 1985.

Malachi, Z., ed. *Studies on Shelomoh Ibn Gabirol* [Hebrew]. Tel Aviv: Tel Aviv University Press, 1985.

Massignon, L. *Testimonies and Reflections: Essays*. Trans. Herbert Mason. South Bend: Notre Dame University Press, 1989.

Meisami, Julie. *Medieval Persian Court Poetry*. Princeton: Princeton University Press, 1987.

Menocal, María Rosa. *The Arabic Role in Medieval Literary History: A Forgotten Heritage*. Philadelphia: University of Pennsylvania Press, 1987.

————. *Shards of Love*. Durham and London: Duke University Press, 1994.

Mirksy, A. *The Beginnings of the Piyyut* [Hebrew]. Jerusalem: Iyyunim, 1966.

————. *From Duties of the Heart to Songs of the Heart: Jewish Philosophy and Ethics and Their Influence on Hebrew Poetry in Medieval Spain* [Hebrew]. Jerusalem: Magnes, 1992.

Murray, S., and W. Roscoe, eds. *Islamic Homosexualities: Culture, History and Literature*. New York: New York University Press, 1997.

Nasr, S. H. *An Introduction to Islamic Cosmological Doctrines*. Albany: State University of New York Press, 1993.

Nicholson, R. A. *Studies in Islamic Poetry*. Cambridge: Cambridge University Press, 1921.

Nykl, A. R. *Hispano-Arabic Poetry and Its Relations with the Old Provencal Troubadours*. Baltimore: J. H. Furst, 1946.

Pagis, D. *Change and Tradition in Secular Hebrew Poetry: Spain and Italy*. [Hebrew]. Jerusalem: Keter, 1976.

————. *Hebrew Poetry of the Middle Ages and the Renaissance*. Berkeley: University of California Press, 1974.

————. *Secular Poetry and Poetic Theory: Moses Ibn Ezra and His Contemporaries*. Jerusalem: Mossad Bialik, 1970.

————. *Poetry Aptly Explained: Studies and Essays on Medieval Hebrew Poetry* [Hebrew]. Ed. E. Fleischer. Jerusalem: Magnes, 1993.

Parnes, A. "Ecstatic Experience in the Life of R. Shelomoh Ibn Gabirol" and "The Divine Name in the Liturgical Poetry of R. Ibn Gabirol." In *MiBen LaMa'arakhot* [Hebrew]. Tel Aviv: Mahbarot LeSifrut, 1950.

Pellat, C. *The Life and Works of Jahiz: Translations of Selected Texts*. Berkeley: University of California Press, 1969.

Pines, S. "He Called to Nothing Which Split: On *Keter Malkhut*" [Hebrew]. *Tarbiz* 50 (1980): 339–47.

————. "Did Ibn Gabirol Slander the Nation?" *Tarbiz* 34 (1964–65): 372–78.

————. "Ibn Gabirol." In *Encyclopedia of Philosophy*. Vol. 4. New York: MacMillan: 265–66.

Plato. *The Collected Dialogues of Plato*. Ed. Edith Hamilton and Huntington Cairns. Princeton: Princeton University Press, 1961.

Price, A. W. *Love and Friendship in Plato and Aristotle*. Oxford: Clarendon, 1989.

Ratzhaby, Y. "The Confession in *Keter Malkhut*" [Hebrew]. *Orlogin* 12 (1956): 247–55.

————. "*Keter Malkhut* in Light of Arabic Literature" [Hebrew]. *Biqoret U'farshanut* 2–3 (1972): 47–60.

————. "Night Visions in the Poetry of HaNagid and Ibn Gabirol." *Tarbiz* 47 (1977–78): 56–90.

————. "Flowers in Our Spanish Poetry" [Hebrew]. In *B'Orah Mad'a*. Ed. Z. Malachi. Lod: Haberman Institute, 1985.

————. *Selected Poems from the Spanish Golden Age: Edited with an Introduction and Commentary*. Tel Aviv: Am Oved, 1994.

Robinson, J. *The Nag Hammadi Library*. San Francisco: Harper & Row, 1981.

Rosenthal, F., ed. *The Classical Heritage in Islam*. London: Routledge, 1975.

Roth, N. "Sacred and Secular in the Poetry of Ibn Gabirol." *Hebrew Studies* 20–21 (1979–80): 75–79.

————. "'Deal Gently with the Young Man': Love of Boys in Medieval Hebrew Poetry of Spain." *Speculum* 57 (1982): 20–51.

————. "The Care and Feeding of Gazelles: Medieval Arabic and Hebrew Love Poetry." In *Poetics of Love in the Middle Ages*. Ed. M. Lazar and N. Lacy. Fairfax: George Mason Unversity Press, 1989.

Saadia Gaon. *The Book of Beliefs and Opinions*. Trans. from the Arabic and the Hebrew by Samuel Rosenblatt. New Haven: Yale University Press, 1948, 1976.

————. *HaEgron*. Ed. N. Allony. Jerusalem: Academy of the Hebrew Language, 1969.

Said, Edward. *Orientalism*. New York: Pantheon, 1978.

Sammons, J. *Heinrich Heine: A Modern Biography*. Manchester: Carcanet, 1979.

Scheindlin, Raymond P. "Contrasting Religious Experience in the Liturgical poems of Ibn Gabirol and Judah Halevi." *Prooftexts* 13, 2 (1993): 141–62.

————. "Ibn Gabirol's Religious Poetry and Sufi Poetry." *Sefarad* 54, no. 1 (1994): 109–41.

————. "Poet and Patron: Ibn Gabirol's Poem of the Palace and Its Gardens." *Prooftexts* 16, 1 (1996): 31–47.

————. "The Hebrew Qasida in Spain." In *Qasida Poetry in Islamic Asia and Africa*. Ed. S. Sperl and C. Shackle. Leiden: Brill, 1996.

Schimmel, A. *Calligraphy and Islamic Culture*. New York: New York University Press, 1984.

Schirmann, J. *Hebrew Poems from Spain and Provence* [Hebrew]. 4 vols. Tel Aviv–Jerusalem: Dvir-Mossad Bialik, 1954/59.

————. "The Ephebe in Medieval Hebrew Poetry." *Sefarad* 15 (1955): 55–68.

————. "Shelomoh Ibn Gabirol and R. Yonah Ibn Janaah" [Hebrew]. In *Sefer Hanokh Yalon*. Ed. S. Lieberman, S. Abramson, E. Y. Kutscher, and S. Esh. Jerusalem: Kiryat Sepher, 1963.

————. *Studies in the History of Hebrew Poetry and Drama*. Vol. 1 [Hebrew]. Jerusalem: Mossad Bialik, 1979.

————. *History of Hebrew Poetry in Muslim Spain* [Hebrew]. 2 vols. Ed. Ezra Fleischer. Jerusalem: Magnes, 1995.

Schlanger, Y. *The Philosophy of Shelomoh Ibn Gabirol* [Hebrew]. Jerusalem: Magnes, 1979.

Scholem, G., "Traces of Ibn Gabirol in Kabbalah" [Hebrew]. *Me'assef Sofrei Eretz-Yisrael* (1940): 159–178.

Schopenhauer, A. *Religion and Other Essays*. Trans. T. B. Saunders. London: Swan Sonnenschein, 1890.

Sells, M. *Desert Tracings: Six Classic Arabian Odes*. Middletown: Wesleyan University Press, 1989.

Septimus, D. "He'arot leDivrei Hazal beShirat Sefarad." *Tarbiz* 53 (1984): 607–14.

Simhoni, Y. N. "R. Shlomo Ibn Gabirol" [Hebrew]. *Hatequfah* 10, 12, 17 (1921–23): 143–223, 149–88, 248–94.

Sperl, S. *Mannerism in Arabic Poetry*. Cambridge: Cambridge University Press, 1981.

————. "Islamic Kingship and Arabic Panegyric in the Early Ninth Century." *Journal of Arabic Literature* 8 (1977): 20–35.

Stetkevych, J. *Zephyrs of Najd: The Poetics of Nostalgia in the Classical Arabic Nasib*. Chicago: University of Chicago Press, 1993.

————. "The Arabic Lyrical Phenomenon in Context." *Journal of Arabic Literature* 6 (1975): 57–77.

————. "Arabic Poetry and Assorted Poetics." In M. Kerr, ed. *Islamic Studies: A Tradition and Its Problems*. Malibu: Undena Publications, 1980.

Stetkevych, S. *Abu Tammaam and the Poetics of the Abbasid Age*. Leiden: Brill, 1991.

Stewart, D. "Saj' in the Qur'an: Prosody and Structure." *Journal of Arabic Literature* 21 (1991).

Stillman, N. *The Jews of Arab Lands*. Philadelphia: Jewish Publication Society, 1979.

Tsur, R. *Studies in Medieval Hebrew Poetry*. Tel Aviv: Daga, [no date].

Al-Udhari, A. and G.B.H. Wightman. *Birds Through an Alabaster Ceiling: Three Abbasid Poets, Ibn Al-Ahnaf, Ibn Al-Mu'tazz, and Al-Ma'ari*. Harmondsworth: Penguin, 1981.

Van Gelder, G. J. "The Abstracted Self in Arabic Poetry." *Journal of Arabic Literature* 14 (1983–84): 22–30.

Waley, Arthur. *Madly Singing in the Mountains*. Ed. Ivan Morris. New York: Harper, 1972.

Walzer, R. "Arabic Transmission of Greek Thought to Medieval Europe." *Bulletin of the John Rylands Library* 29 (1945–46): 160–83.

Wasserstein, D. *The Rise and Fall of the Party-Kings: Politics and Society in Islamic Spain, 1002–1086*. Princeton: Princeton University Press, 1985.

———. "The Language Situation in Al-Andalus." In *Studies in the Muwashshah and the Kharja*. Ed. A. Jones and R. Hitchcock. Oxford: Ithaca Press, 1991.

Wasserstrom, S. *Between Muslim and Jew*. Princeton: Princeton University Press, 1995.

Weiss, J. "Court Culture and Court Poetry" [Hebrew]. *Proceedings of World Congress of Jewish Studies* 1 (1952): 396–403.

Wijnhoven, J. "The Mysticism of Ibn Gabirol." *Journal of Religion* 45 (1965): 137–52.

Wilenksy, S. O. Heller. "Isaac Ibn Latif: Philosopher or Kabbalist?" In *Jewish Medieval and Renaissance Studies*. Ed. A. Altmann. Cambridge, MA: Harvard University Press, 1967.

Wolfson, E. *Through a Speculum That Shines*. Princeton: Princeton University Press, 1994.

Wright, J. W., and E. Rowson. *Homoeroticism in Classical Arabic Literature*. New York: Columbia University Press, 1997.

Yahalom, Y. *Poetic Language in the Early Piyyut* [Hebrew]. Jerusalem: Magnes, 1985.

———. "Scripture and Spirituality in Hebrew-Spanish Liturgical Poetry." Unpublished talk delivered at a conference on "Scripture and Liturgy," Harvard University (1997).

Yellin, D. *The Poetics of the Spanish-Hebrew Poetry* [Hebrew]. Jerusalem: Magnes, 1978.

———. "A Manuscript's Wanderings" [Hebrew]. *Moznayim* 11 (1931): 11–12.

Yosse Ben Yosse. *Piyyutei Yosse Ben Yosse* [Hebrew]. Ed. A. Mirksy. Jerusalem: Mossad Bialik, 1977.

Zemah, E. *KeShoresh Etz*. Tel Aviv: Sifriyat Po'alim, 1973.

The Lockert Library of Poetry in Translation